HOUSING IN THE MARGINS

IJURR-SUSC Published Titles

HOUSING IN THE MARGINS

Negotiating Urban Formalities in Berlin's Allotment Gardens

HANNA HILBRANDT

This edition first published 2021
© 2021 John Wiley & Sons Ltd.

Registered Office(s)
John Wiley & Sons, Inc., 111 River Street, Hoboken, NJ 07030, USA
John Wiley & Sons Ltd, The Atrium, Southern Gate, Chichester, West Sussex, PO19 8SQ, UK

Editorial Office
9600 Garsington Road, Oxford, OX4 2DQ, UK

For details of our global editorial offices, customer services, and more information about Wiley products visit us at www.wiley.com.

Wiley also publishes its books in a variety of electronic formats and by print-on-demand. Some content that appears in standard print versions of this book may not be available in other formats.

Library of Congress Cataloging-in-Publication Data
Names: Hilbrandt, Hanna, 1982- author. | John Wiley & Sons, Ltd.,
   publisher.
Title: Housing in the margins : negotiating urban formalities in Berlin's
   allotment gardens / Hanna Hilbrandt.
Description: Hoboken, NJ : John Wiley & Sons, Inc., 2021. | Includes
   bibliographical references and index.
Identifiers: LCCN 2020047032 (print) | LCCN 2020047033 (ebook) | ISBN
   9781119540915 (hardback) | ISBN 9781119540939 (paperback) | ISBN
   9781119540960 (pdf) | ISBN 9781119540908 (epub) | ISBN 9781119540946
   (ebook)
Subjects: LCSH: Land use--Germany--Berlin. | Housing--Germany--Berlin. |
   Housing policy--Germany--Berlin. | Allotment gardens--Germany--Berlin.
Classification: LCC HD660.B47 H55 2021 (print) | LCC HD660.B47 (ebook) |
   DDC 363.50943/155--dc23
LC record available at https://lccn.loc.gov/2020047032
LC ebook record available at https://lccn.loc.gov/2020047033

Cover image: Michael Berger
Cover design by Wiley

Set in 11/13pt Adobe Garamond Pro by Integra Software Services Pvt. Ltd, Pondicherry, India
Printed and bound by CPI Group (UK) Ltd, Croydon, CR0 4YY

C093287_250321

Contents

List of Illustrations

Series Editors' Preface

IJURR Studies in Urban and Social Change Book Series

The IJURR Studies in Urban and Social Change Book Series shares IJURR's commitments to critical, global, and politically relevant analyses of our urban worlds. Books in this series bring forward innovative theoretical approaches and present rigorous empirical work, deepening understandings of urbanization processes, but also advancing critical insights in support of political action and change. The Book Series Editors appreciate the theoretically eclectic nature of the field of urban studies. It is a strength that we embrace and encourage. The Editors are particularly interested in the following issues:

- Comparative urbanism
- Diversity, difference and neighborhood change
- Environmental sustainability
- Financialization and gentrification
- Governance and politics
- International migration
- Inequalities
- Urban and environmental movements

The series is explicitly interdisciplinary; the Editors judge books by their contribution to the field of critical urban studies rather than according to disciplinary origin. We are committed to publishing studies with themes and formats that reflect the many different voices and practices in the field of urban studies. Proposals may be submitted to Editor in Chief, Walter Nicholls (wnicholl@uci.edu), and further information about the series can be found at www.ijurr.org.

Walter Nicholls
Manuel Aalbers
Talja Blokland
Dorothee Brantz
Patrick Le Galès
Jenny Robinson

Acknowledgements

This book project has accompanied me for almost a decade. Many people, places, and institutions have shaped this journey and have to be thanked. I shall start by acknowledging the many respondents who were generous enough to open the doors into their lives and take time to answer my questions. I hope this book lives up to the ethical challenge this trust has posed.

Housing in the Margins started as my PhD thesis and the biggest thanks go to Allan Cochrane, John Allen, and Clive Barnett, who supervised this project and made the work on it a truly enjoyable experience. Allan Cochrane provided me with profound advice. I would also like to thank him for his incessant encouragement and belief in my work. Now that I myself am supervising PhD students, I am immensely grateful for being able to look back on such a valuable experience. John Allen's thought-provoking commentary inspired me to think more precisely about my claims, and his ideas shaped my postdoctoral life probably more than he knows. Clive Barnett's stimulating critiques always opened up new perspectives. My thanks extend to the Open University for providing me with financial, organizational, and intellectual support. At the OpenSpace Research Centre, I encountered great seminars, the opportunity to discuss my ideas, and fantastic companions who shared information, lunches, train rides to Milton Keynes, and after-work hours. In particular, Darren Umney listened and made me laugh, often via email, throughout three years of postgraduate research. At University College London, I was able to participate in the Stadtkolloquium group, where I would particularly like to thank Tauri Tuvikene and Susana Nevez Alves for joint conversations and first publishing experiences.

During my first fieldwork period in Berlin, I was welcomed as an associate fellow at the Center for Metropolitan Studies, and I would like to thank its staff and PhD fellows for their generous support. I developed much of my thinking by participating in its graduate school. The critical advice and companionship at the Center have been extremely valuable. Thanks also goes to the NYLON research network for two years of inspiring debate and special thanks to Christine Hentschel, whose shared enthusiasm for urban studies and tango made academia a much richer experience. At the Leibniz Institute for Research on Society and Space (IRS), where I spent my first postdoctoral period, I would particularly like to thank Matthias Bernt for sharing his detailed insights on urban development in Berlin.

I want to use this opportunity to thank Monika Grubbauer at the HafenCity University Hamburg, who made further empirical research and the development of my PhD into a book possible in the first place. To be sure, she always had my back, especially by creating time for me in which I could write. Perhaps more importantly, I could not have been luckier to find such fruitful and formative exchange. I would also like to thank Karin Wildner for her visionary mentorship throughout my postdoctoral years in Hamburg.

Many friends supported me throughout this project, in particular, Hilke Berger, Maya Ifland, Steffanie Hofrichter, Nihad El-Kayed, Hannah Schilling, and Josefine Fokdal. Some deserve special mention: Coco Wolf Gediehn was a wonderful companion in the hunt for an allotment plot; Jenny Jungehülsing listened to my endless worries and ideas about the thesis; Francesca Weber-Newth shared in the ups and downs of my life between Germany, the UK, and many conferences, putting immense efforts into reading various drafts, and becoming a dear friend on this intellectual journey. Thanks also go to Michael Berger for contributing the book's cover photo as well as some of the other images I use in this book. I am deeply grateful to Jacobo Rodriguez Mendoza for his unfailing and generous support, as well as his encouragement and inspiration. Finally, I would also like to express my gratitude to my family, Johanna, Eckhart, and Moritz Hilbrandt, for their patience and emotional support.

I feel honored to be able to publish this book in the SUSC series and thank Jennifer Robinson and Walter Nicholls for their editorial support. I am also grateful for Erin Troseth's important contribution in copy-editing the final draft of this book, as well as for the support of Wiley.

Chapter 1

Introduction
Housing in the Entanglements of Formality, Informality, and the State

Taking the train from Schönefeld airport, a visitor to Berlin rides through a vast area of urban allotments.[1] Still on the periphery, the train follows the East–West divide that long defined the city, if not much of the world. Straight ahead, at a distance, a passenger can spot the tip of the Berlin TV Tower – the symbol of former East Berlin that marks today's city center. Green garden plots, seemingly endless along both sides of the tracks, are cluttered with small and colorful allotment huts [*Lauben*].[2] I have been asked if these sites are the "slums" of Berlin – or if people live in these huts. Certainly, from a distance, their spatial and social order is difficult to grasp.

This book delves into the everyday governance of housing at these sites. More particularly, it explores the gardeners' scattered, unruly, and precarious dwelling practices as well as the multifaceted and frequently contradictory efforts to regulate them. It examines these negotiations with an interest in learning about the mechanisms through which room for maneuver is gained and constrained in the everyday (re)production of urban order and the exclusions these processes entail.

One way of approaching this task is by framing the practices under examination through the notion of informality. Since the 1970s, researchers have used this concept to describe the unauthorized construction and inhabitation of urban space, particularly in Africa, Asia, and Latin America (ILO, 1972; Hart, 1973; Hann and Hart, 2011). These themes remain, as Tonkiss writes, "a major plot-line in the story of contemporary urbanization" (2012: 55), although today, critical scholarship employs the notion of informality to consider the ambiguities of state regulation, rather than the phenomena that lie beyond the oversight of state institutions (Roy, 2009a; McFarlane, 2012). In this critical understanding, the concept provides a starting point for describing

Housing in the Margins: Negotiating Urban Formalities in Berlin's Allotment Gardens, First Edition. Hanna Hilbrandt.

the scene above through the incoherencies of state and urban governance in regulating housing at these sites.

Another way of approaching the theme of this book is by exploring the enactment of rules in everyday practices of regulatory enforcement. Dwelling in Berlin's allotment gardens breaches the rules of the law, but it is also marked by other forms of intense regulation. Rather than being characterized through spontaneity, the construction of allotment huts is embedded in long-standing traditions of city life. Sheds transgress building codes but are organized strictly on clearly fenced plots. Although buildings are erected without permits, they are systematically serviced with water and electricity. Their residents exceed use rights, but they comply elsewhere with registration commitments. A closer look at the housing situation in the gardens provides insights into the ways in which transgressions are accommodated in the "formal" production of urban order and thereby also points out the institutional ambiguities on which allotment dwelling frequently depends.

Housing in the Margins relates these two approaches and argues that this matters because it accounts for housing and urban governance in a Western liberal democracy in ways that challenge some of the *epistemological* assumptions that have long been engrained in research on cities. With informal housing playing hardly more than a marginal role in scholarship on European, Canadian, or US cities, an exploration of how allotment dwelling is negotiated in Berlin troubles the North–South divisions that underlie much production of knowledge on urban informality and raises questions about the particularity of local experiences and the universality of concepts, including that of informality. I pursue this project with empirical and theoretical objectives: studying *empirically* how Berliners negotiate ways of staying put in allotment gardens and how boundaries around their dwelling practices are drawn, I aim at understanding the production and governance of housing precarity in a relatively rich European city. In *theorizing* these processes of governance, I seek to unveil the possibilities of conceptualizing informal housing in the context of bureaucracies that are commonly understood to regulate thoroughly, coherently, and according to fixed rules.

In the Margins: Allotment Dwelling in Berlin

An abundance of research has documented the history of allotment gardens, but it has rarely associated these sites with informal housing. Most of Berlin's allotment compounds (see Figure 1.1) go back to a period of industrialization and rapid expansion of the city at the turn of the twentieth century. They are frequently referred to as colonies – a term that I adopt and contextualize in

FIGURE 1.1 View of allotment colony in Berlin-Neukölln. Source: Michael Berger.

Chapter 3. As that chapter also details in depth, Berlin has witnessed more than a century of allotment governance in which dwelling on one's plot was variably forbidden and politically sustained. The dwelling practices that persisted throughout two wars, rival political systems, and the increasingly profit-driven use of urban land have left their vestiges in the contemporary city: today's landscape of allotment colonies, 876 compounds with 71,071 garden plots on 2,915 hectares of urban space (SenUVK, 2019: 24), is served by an infrastructure of mini-scale allotment huts, electricity networks, water hook-ups, and telephone lines (Urban, 2013; Hilbrandt, 2015).

By and large, allotment gardens can be characterized as spaces of the lower middle class, though over-proportionally white. Most gardeners are of an older generation that has fostered social networks between allotment holders who have gardened, plot by plot, over decades (SenSW, 2019: 32). Despite repeated exceptions with far-reaching consequences for the acceptability of dwelling, permanent residence on these sites is generally prohibited – today most centrally through the Federal Allotment Law, the Bundeskleingartengesetz (BKleinG). Yet, allotment holders rely on a variety of regulations as they take up residence within allotment huts. To avoid any misunderstandings, it should be stated that allotment dwelling is not a mass phenomenon. In addition to 1,131 gardeners who hold dwelling permits (documentation of the

Berlin Senate, provided in an interview, 18.09.2013), an unknown number of Berliners with other legal statuses permanently reside in colonies, particularly in those that have functioning infrastructures throughout the year, including electricity connections and water pumps. *Schwarzwohnen* [literally: "black" (here signifying clandestine and unlawful) dwelling] remains the exception,[3] although my research has taught me to expect at least one or two permanent dwellers in each colony and higher numbers in some of the colonies at the periphery of the city. Conversely, *Sommerwohnen* [summer dwelling] is a rather frequent practice. It implies moving "out" into the colonies in early spring and returning "back" into the city in late autumn, and possibly subletting one's flat during the stay on the plot, or inhabiting a hut throughout longer vacations, or routinely spending the night.

In the diversity of these practices, the case of allotment dwelling widens understandings of housing precarity in a European city. In contradistinction to studies of homelessness (Mitchell, 1995; Marquardt, 2013), camps (Clough Marinaro, 2017; Pasquetti and Picker, 2017; Picker, 2019), emergency shelter, or some of the work on informal settlements in Asia, Latin America, and Africa, allotment dwelling does not limit the study of housing precarity to an exploration of severe urban poverty. Berlin's allotments – even if some may be inhabited – are commonly seen as orderly and tradition-bound. It is to a lesser extent that allotment gardens also provide refuge for the income-poor – people scraping by on unemployment benefits, or migrant laborers, or pensioners with limited means, for example. Yet the case of allotment dwelling also speaks to growing social divides in which those at the bottom of the income ladder are additionally disempowered through the tensions in European housing markets and their spatial and social effects.

Over the years in which I researched and wrote this book, investment-led policy, housing privatization, and the financialization of real estate have crucially changed Berlin's housing conditions. In the aftermath of the 2007/2008 financial crisis, processes of displacement and the associated deepening of social divides have increasingly appeared to be the order of the day (Aalbers and Holm, 2008; Bernt, 2012; Soederberg, 2017). As a result, Berlin has experienced a resurgence of interest in the "new" housing question (Schönig et al., 2017; PROKLA, 2018). A plethora of urban scholarship (e.g. Holm, 2011; Uffer, 2014) has drawn into sharp relief that Berlin's housing crisis has been politically caused through neoliberal approaches to housing provisioning and the resultant reductions of social housing and rent increases in all market segments; that it is structurally determined through the global financial crisis that moved Berlin's housing stock into the spotlight of capital flows; and that the crisis has been aggravated through the population growth of the city (Investitionsbank Berlin, 2017).

As I argue in Chapter 4, literatures explaining the resulting processes of gentrification and displacement focus predominantly on the political interventions that allow for or hinder gentrification, or on areas that experience gentrification and displacement (Holm, 2010; Schipper, 2018). This includes *qualitative* attention to incoming middle- to high-income pioneers and gentrifiers or *quantitative* explorations of population mobility incidences and rent increases to identify affected areas (e.g. Döring and Ulbricht, 2016). Yet, the debate remains limited in providing an understanding of the affected populations, their housing trajectories, and new forms and locations of residency – in part due to the difficulties of locating displaced residents (although see Helbrecht, 2016). The scarcity of literature on displaced populations is indicative of the lacuna of qualitative studies on housing precarity – including on the many faces of housing practices in irregular conditions. To date, informal housing is hardly recognized as existing in Berlin or in other European, Canadian, or US cities and rarely researched in relation to processes of governance (but see Chapter 4 for a discussion of existing research). Thus, to develop a more complete understanding of housing exclusion, to grasp the practiced relations formal and informal housing have to one another, and to challenge the "intellectual segregation" between these extensive but still largely disparate debates, my discussion of allotment dwelling joins up three strands of work: a global literature on informal housing, the contemporary German housing debate, and more specific and partly historical accounts of urban allotments.

To be sure, my aim is not to establish a direct causal relation between the tightening of housing markets and informal housing practices in Berlin's allotments. Rather, the book approaches questions of the housing crisis "sideways," as Jackson (2015: 3) puts it, through examining one of the "back ends" of the housing crisis – temporary or permanent residency in sites not deemed appropriate for dwelling. This includes discussion of people's lived realities, strategies of staying put, and interim solutions; for instance, when people lessen their rent burden by moving into their allotments over the summer and subletting their apartments during that time. In particular, Chapter 4 offers a rich empirical account of how and why gardeners take up residence within allotment huts. On the one hand, it illustrates the entanglement of formal and informal housing in the dwelling biographies of the allotment's residents. On the other hand, it explores how residents experience their housing conditions in widely varying ways.

This perspective promises two conceptual contributions to understandings of housing precarity. First, allotment dwelling constitutes an object of inquiry through which questions of governance can be explored through processes of negotiation in which informality tends to be tolerated and sustained.

Although I also discuss instances of evictions, allotment dwelling allows examining the normalcy of governance arrangements in which rule-breaking is mostly accommodated by all concerned. Instead of top-down regulation by a heavy-handed state, the case of allotment dwelling permits us to understand how such compromises are collectively secured. Second, and conversely, I maintain that a focus on understanding small-scale negotiation also fosters an understanding of registers of exclusion and boundary work that often remain uncovered in structural accounts of informality and the state. This includes discussion of how ethnic discrimination, self-regulation, and other boundary mechanisms undergird the compromises I previously discussed.

Negotiating Formalities: Postcolonial Urbanism, Informality, and the State

Beyond empirical questions about housing precarity, this book wrestles with the theoretical implications of allotment dwelling and its regulation for an understanding of informality in cities that are commonly understood to regulate thoroughly, coherently, and according to fixed rules. For decades, scholars have argued that informality was a "problem" of the South, in quantity at least, if not in sheer existence. It was seen, as Auerbach et al. put it, as "perhaps the distinguishing feature of contemporary urban life in the Global South" (Auerbach et al., 2018: 262). Yet, informal housing in Berlin's allotments can hardly be understood as a shift in the geographies of power that has fostered the growth of this allegedly Southern phenomenon in a European city – not least because it has had a century-long tradition in Berlin. Rather, an analysis of informality in a relatively rich city of the global North calls for a critical reflection of the concept of informality itself, as well as of the epistemological place and value of that concept in a more global urban analysis.[4]

Critiques of the paternalistic and colonial gaze of theorizing that prescribed informality to the South have long been ubiquitous in postcolonial urban studies (e.g. Comaroff and Comaroff, 2012; McFarlane and Robinson, 2012; Lawhon and Truelove, 2019). But the challenge of "othering" Southern cities continues to "haunt" urban studies (Hentschel, 2015: 80), enlisting cities of the global South into an alleged trajectory of development that presumes one desirable future for all cities, epitomized by the economic hubs of the global North. For the development of a more cosmopolitan urban studies, this debate has proposed forging new lines of connection through more "worldly" (Roy and Ong, 2012; McCann et al., 2013), "planetary" (Brenner, 2014; Sidaway et al., 2014), and comparative methodologies (Nijman, 2007; Robinson, 2011; Myers, 2014). In this vein, authors have attempted to "theorize back," or to postcolonialize the global North by transmitting knowledge from the South northwards (Schindler, 2014a; Hentschel, 2015; Lamotte, 2017; Hilbrandt et al., 2017).[5] This book follows that suggestion: it brings informality – a concept that tends to be used to research cities commonly located "off the map" (Robinson, 2002: 531) of mainstream theory-production – to Berlin, a place normally understood through conceptions of Western urbanism. Yet, this move confronts significant hurdles that may have more to do with the conceptualization of the state in understandings of informality and less with this epistemological approach itself.

As noted, today's more prudent use of the concept of informality in most parts of interdisciplinary urban scholarship has developed a nuanced understanding of the multiple entanglements of informality and the state. First, authors have placed a spotlight on the ways in which the state itself acts informally: by the rule of exception – in other words, suspending the validity of its own order (Roy, 2009a, 2011; Wigle, 2014; Davis, 2018), and by maintaining flexibility in regulation, thereby leaving its citizens in a state of "permanent temporariness" (Yiftachel, 2009a: 90). For instance, Ananya Roy suggests that informality is not a result of planning failure but a mode of urbanization in which "the law itself is rendered open-ended and subject to multiple interpretations and interests" (Roy, 2009b: 80). Moreover, discussions of informality and the state have considered the relation between the two through questions about citizenship, insurgency, and multiple other modalities of struggle and subversion (Miraftab, 2009; Meth, 2010; Porter et al., 2011). In these debates, the state is central as the primary object of contention – an antagonistic force working through the powers of oppression and domination.

Despite their critical contributions, I suggest that these approaches do not travel well into Berlin's allotments. In Chapter 2, I argue that the literature on informality, by casting the state in ways that tend to either underscore its flexible and oppressive use of informality or the ways in which citizens obstruct state powers by resisting it "from the outside," methodologically has less to say about the more interactive practices of negotiation that this book is concerned with, where the roles and interests of "both sides" are more fluid and frequently merge. By constructing informality through the powers of domination and oppression, on the one hand, or insurgency and resistance, on the other, the debate tends to neglect analyzing informality through the quieter registers of change, i.e. the small-scale and incremental powers of negotiation. *Housing in the Margins* focuses attention on these mundane negotiations, drawing on theoretical traditions that place weight on the normative judgments and social embeddedness of those who are negotiating (e.g. Tilly, 1999; Lea, 2008; Lipsky, 2010 [1980]), the legal-material processes of regulatory enactment (Valverde, 2011; Blomley, 2014), the entanglement of institutions in social life (Tilly, 1999; Corbridge et al., 2005; Straughn, 2005), and the ways in which these processes of enactment reflect on and transform wider processes of institutional transformation (Cooper, 1998; Hunter, 2015). Examining allotment dwelling through this lens suggests three contributions to understanding the governance of urban informality in Berlin.

First, by placing weight on the normative judgments, subjective understanding, and social embeddedness of governing actors, *Housing in the Margins* reads informality and its regulation through the ways in which people apply their ambivalent and multiple understandings to processes of governance. For instance, this becomes apparent in Chapter 7, which focuses on the legal work upon which practices of governance rely. Utilizing critical legal studies, the chapter unravels how both regulators and allotment holders employ legal frameworks in regulatory practices to maintain, extend, or restrict outsized huts. Yet, while such frameworks of order constitute a pivotal resource in the making of order, the chapter discusses their operation in practice to understand how order is built through the interpretive mechanisms that shape how rules become "emplaced." In this way, the book seeks a more practice-centered understanding of the interpretive work through which rules operate "on the ground." This fosters an understanding of informality as emerging through the "ordinary stuff" of policy implementation, in which subjectivity, positionality, and individual agency are key.

Second, the case of allotment dwelling highlights that the room for maneuvering through rules lies, in part, beyond the realm of state institutions and is used, and at times coproduced, by civil *and* institutional actors. Chapter 6 makes this point most explicitly when considering the governance of temporary or permanent occupancy from the perspectives of different bureaucrats and allotment holders involved in the transgression and regulation of order. Through this focus, *Housing in the Margins* accounts for a constellation of regulating actors that exceeds the realm of Berlin's bureaucracies and includes the gardeners themselves. Beyond common assumptions about regulatory enforcement as a process in which state actors implement rules, combining the perspectives of all governing actors allows me to consider the ways in which people within and beyond state institutions negotiate room for maneuver in implementing order. Across all chapters, I describe the production of socio-spatial order as a cooperative effort that is shaped by all parties concerned and leads, at best, to a joint although contested arrangement. At the same time, my focus on consensual arrangements raises important questions about the limits of this tolerance and the inequalities that define such a politics of negotiation. The everyday may be a site of small-scale agency, but, as I attempt to show, understanding governance at this scale also unveils the degree to which the various parties concerned with allotment gardening have asymmetric capacities in such maneuvers, and the exclusionary practices that mundane negotiations may also entail – enacted through both civil society and state actors.

Third, *Housing in the Margins* accounts for the minor acts of negotiation in focus here as a means of redefining how urban governance is "lived out." For instance, Chapter 5 confronts this question in its spatial and material dimensions by focusing on the ways in which incremental adaptations of the gardens and their governance have shaped the urban development of the city and its modalities of urban change. Theoretically, the chapter traces questions about urban planning and governance, on the one hand, and coproduction and incrementalism, on the other, in order to juxtapose these forms of transformation. My aim is to unravel how these modalities are entangled in urban development and to tease out how we can understand forms of coproduction, incremental adaptation, or self-built housing in a city of the global North. Across the book, I maintain that understanding informality through the ways in which all those concerned with allotment governance shift legal boundaries and alter the city's urban fabric at the everyday scale allows us to grasp how these practices shape the structures in and through which these practices take place.

Taken together, I suggest that the "payoff" of these theoretical propositions is that they enable us to grasp informality through the *routine* enactment of rules and regulations. In this view, informal housing emerges in and through a normal, not a particular, "mode of urbanization." This understanding requires us to rethink the analytical role and significance of informality in an analysis of urban governance and state enactment. Instead of presupposing the existence of formality and deriving the concept of informality from that, placing weight on *how* transgression and regulation become acted out in negotiation turns the operation of formality itself into an ethnographic question.

In conclusion, Chapter 8 returns to the book's epistemological starting point and reflects on the promises and difficulties of translating concepts from "elsewhere" to Berlin. Drawing its lessons about processes of formalization and informalization both in and beyond the case discussed, the chapter concludes that Berlin's allotments are not an exceptional case but rather a paradigmatic example of governing irregular housing conditions through small-scale negotiations. Rather than seeing informal housing as a distinguishing feature of the global South, I maintain that despite the different analytical route taken here, conceiving of irregular housing through the lens of urban negotiation allows us to build more global approaches to housing research.

Methodology: An Institutional Ethnography of Informality and State Enactment

As with other sensitive issues, researching informality is fraught with methodological, practical, and ethical challenges that require critical scrutiny (cf. Auerbach et al., 2018: 263). The methodological challenge lies in accounting for multiple perspectives and levels of investigation: urban order is enacted through the embodied and situated practices of all concerned, but it is also mediated through institutions, codes, laws, and regulations. My investigation starts from the former; I center this inquiry on the level of situated practices – i.e. place-specific, day-to-day interactions. Yet I explore these in relation to the frameworks of order in which they are embedded by adapting Dorothy Smith's institutional ethnography to the context of urban studies (1990, 1999, 2005). This feminist approach is committed to focus social research on people's everyday lives, and to ground this inquiry in the discursive, institutionalized, or legal relationships within which their practices are embedded. Through this perspective, Smith argues, the study of everyday life can account for the "ruling relations" – relations that enter into and organize social life through unobservable facts that are mediated through replicable texts, discourses, plans, laws, and the like (1990: 6; see Billo and Mountz, 2016 for a geographical perspective on institutional ethnography).

To hold these perspectives in tension requires a mix of approaches. The study combines three data sets: qualitative interviews with bureaucrats and allotment gardeners, ethnographic explorations of the research sites, and textual sources, including statutory texts, the documentation of legal cases, newspaper reports, and archival data. To collect the first set of data, I conducted interviews between July and November 2013 as well as between April and July 2014 and returned to the gardens to update, expand, and refocus this material in April and May 2019. My interviewees included city officials in the Senate Department for Urban Development, the so-called allotment garden administrators [*Kleingarten Sachbearbeiter*innen*], who are administrators at the district level, allotment holders with administrative responsibilities, and residents in the allotments. Across these four groups, I conducted a total of 41 "formal" interviews and an uncounted list of shorter spontaneous interviews "across the fence," as it were.

Access to city officials or functionaries in the allotment association proved to be unproblematic once I had learned that most practitioners already possessed intimate knowledge of the dwelling practices in Berlin's colonies. Not surprisingly, finding allotment holders who permanently lived in their huts was more complicated, and only a mix of strategies allowed me to recruit interview participants. I ended up searching for participants via postcards that I distributed on walks through the colonies; through the gardening associations, which established contact with gardeners they knew were living in the colonies; and while strolling through the gardens, talking about the topic in public, or mentioning my search to friends.

Second, I complemented the interview material with ethnographic observations in order to gain a better understanding of the lived experience of allotment holders. Within the framework of institutional ethnography, my use of ethnographic observations aimed at explicating how institutional frameworks are felt, produced, and contested within and beyond institutional spaces in the everyday (Diamond, 2006; Billo and Mountz, 2016: 7). I aimed to observe the spatialities and social patterns of interaction as well as the material solutions that gardeners find to adapt their huts in response to regulatory efforts. As it is difficult, if not impossible, to "hang out" in the rather private allotments, because the grid structure of the colonies does not tend to provide spaces for the sojourn of external visitors, a good way to enter into the intimacy of the gardens was to walk through the colonies. In practice, my ethnographic data collection thus took the form of observational strolls and a series of *perpetual encounters* that these walks facilitated. This part of my strategy is akin to what Streule (2018: 27–41, 2019) and others (Lee and Ingold, 2006) have described as a mobile ethnography – an approach that captures the materiality, geography, and symbolic representation of a field site through walking. These visits allowed me to establish an overview of the phenomena, facilitated a number of informal chats with the gardeners I encountered, and triggered questions for my interviews. They also provided a means to register the materiality of the buildings and the infrastructures in the colonies, as well as their spatial layout.

In order to further immerse myself in the colonies, I eventually decided to lease an allotment garden and became a member of an association. Although I never ended up living in an allotment, despite my original plan to do so, this strategy of membership still proved to be a fruitful way to gain access to information. Most importantly, the "hunt" for the right hut provided me with an opportunity to get in contact with gardeners, to learn necessary tricks for remaining under the radar, and to get an inside glimpse into the lived experience of allotment dwelling. In my quest for a garden, I struggled to combine the role of a fellow gardener with that of an investigator. Although I was initially worried that any reference to the study would prevent my gaining access to an allotment plot, I nevertheless decided to introduce my role as a researcher, as well as the theme of my project, whenever the opportunity arose. Mentioning my research not only seemed more ethical but also triggered further chats about dwelling practices in the colonies.

It may be difficult to get to the mechanisms through which regulations are understood and put to work "on the ground" through surveying documents, such as laws, contracts, or reports, but the question of urban order is not one that could be answered without these accounts. To understand how spatial order is shaped through these documents, they make up the third set of data in this study. As institutional ethnography is concerned with the ways in which sequences of text coordinate "relations of ruling" (Smith, 1990: 6), this method of investigation is particularly well placed to frame an analysis of documents. Broadly speaking, I concentrated this analysis on two more or less active modalities through which textual discourse shapes socio-spatial relations.[6] On the one hand, I followed a linguistic approach (Dittmer, 2010) to grasp the ways in which documents influence spatial order through the understandings that are embedded in text. On the other hand, I pursued a more contextual approach in order to analyze documents with regard to the ways in which they enter into public life, circulate through different social spheres, and interact with local practices.

Geographically, the primary data collection focused on multiple allotment compounds in four Berlin districts: Pankow, Neukölln, Reinickendorf, and Treptow. I do not explicitly compare the colonies in these districts. The selection aimed to cover a wide variety of colonies across a range of regimes of regulation (with varying degrees of laxity) and locations in the city (across the different historical and legal contexts of the former East and West Berlin). Furthermore, the project is designed as a multi-sited study due to an ethical concern with anonymity, i.e. in order not to compromise specific colonies. To publish on the specificity of one colony or the colonies in one district would have allowed for identifying particular sites and calling individual gardeners or associations into account. When considering particular colonies, I refer to them anonymously. Similarly, I pseudonymized all personal data to ensure the anonymity of my participants.

This book continues across seven further chapters, structured as follows: Chapter 2 presents the book's theoretical perspective. Chapter 3 discusses the shifting political and normative placement of allotment dwelling over a century of allotment governance from a historical perspective. To follow the tracing of these larger political shifts, Chapter 4 turns to the contemporary housing question to explore how and why gardeners take up residence within allotment huts. The subsequent empirical chapters then discuss small-scale negotiations and their wider effects from three perspectives. Chapter 5 considers the negotiation of allotment dwelling in its spatial and material dimensions. Chapter 6 analyses the gardens' temporary or permanent occupancy as a question of governance. Chapter 7 focuses the discussion of negotiability on the legal work upon which practices of governance rely. Finally, Chapter 8 concludes by revisiting the book's key themes.

Summary: Chapter 1

This chapter outlines the book's empirical and theoretical objectives, introduces the study on which the book builds, and explicates the methodological underpinnings of that study. It shows that studying *empirically* how Berliners negotiate ways of staying put in allotment gardens and how boundaries around their dwelling practices are drawn fosters an understanding of the production and governance of housing precarity in a relatively rich European city. In *theorizing* these processes of governance, the chapter unveils the possibilities of conceptualizing informal housing in the context of bureaucracies that are commonly understood to regulate thoroughly, coherently, and according to fixed rules.

Notes

1   Wherever possible, I restrain from translating the diverse German terms for urban allotments, most importantly "Kleingarten," "Schrebergarten," and "Laubenkolonie," as they are materially and culturally not equivalent to what the word "allotment" generally signifies in English. While the official term for a German allotment is *Kleingarten* [literally: small garden], the term used most commonly in colloquial language is *Kleingartenkolonie* [literally: small-garden colony].

2   The German term *Laube* refers to a small-scale roofed building that is typically made of stone or wood, is more solid than a shed, but more lightweight than a house.

3   The term *Schwarzwohnen* is more commonly known in the realm of other informal housing practices in the GDR, but used to designate irregular dwelling practices in allotments as well.

4   The terms "global South" and "global North" are used here as a "concept-metaphors," (Lawhon and Truelove, 2019: 11; see Sparke, 2007, for a similar argument) to point to the global dimension of postcolonial relations rather than to a geographical hemisphere.

5 In this vein, concepts such as "fabricating" (Hentschel, 2015) or "subaltern urbanism" (Schindler, 2014a) have been employed to understand European and US cities.

6 I considered five types of documents: legal statutes and administrative regulations, transcripts or reports of court cases, statutes and pamphlets of the allotment holders, historical documentation of the colonies, and finally, secondary and tertiary material, especially statistical data and media reports.

Chapter 2

Negotiating Formalities
Informality and the Everyday State

This chapter unpicks the relation between informality and the state. The thesis that guides this inquiry is that explicating the ontological assumptions about the state that undergird conceptions of informality can explain some of the limits of the latter concept for an analysis of housing in Berlin's allotments. My related proposition is that specifying these assumptions can help to better grasp and qualify informality's utility in an analysis of state enactment and urban governance. The chapter thus explores the implications of understanding informality through the particular aspect of the state I work with in this book, where the focus lies on how everyday actors negotiate the implementation of regulations in the urban everyday.

The relation of informality to the state has been understood in widely varying ways that are clearly shaped by different ontologies of the state. These underpinnings have rarely been made explicit in research on informality. Yet the ways in which informality is researched and defined are conditioned by how the analytical relations between imaginaries of informality and the state are cast. While informality has long been described as the "other" of states, twenty-first-century scholarship has seen a new generation of urban research advance critical investigations into the multiple interrelations between both concepts, offering more differentiated accounts of the role of the state in the production of urban exclusion. This work has discussed informality as a tool of governance, a negotiable value, a form of state speculation, a means of enacting citizenship, and a mode of resistance (Roy, 2005; Yiftachel, 2009a; Goldman, 2011; Davis, 2018). These perspectives have proven critical in flagging up the forms of exclusion driven by the state, the arbitrary exercise of political power, and the consequential insecurities that those inhabiting irregular housing are prone to face. However, these conceptions do not travel well into Berlin's allotment gardens. More generally put, they pose difficulties for

Housing in the Margins: Negotiating Urban Formalities in Berlin's Allotment Gardens, First Edition. Hanna Hilbrandt.
© 2021 John Wiley & Sons, Ltd. Published 2021 by John Wiley & Sons, Ltd.

operationalizing the ways in which everyday transgressions are accommodated in the institutional work of relatively functioning regulatory processes. My objective is thus not to argue against these diverse approaches. Rather, I aim to extend these debates, grappling with their existing boundaries by analyzing processes that lie beyond their current attention.

Explaining how informality works within or parallel to bureaucracies that are largely accountable, present, and capable requires a more "intimate" analysis of regulatory processes at the level of everyday implementation. Thus, in order to understand the negotiation of transgression and regulation, I take my cue from perspectives on state enactment that stress its *agentic, situated,* and *relational* dimensions. Such perspectives examine the state up-close in order to better comprehend the agency of all parties concerned, foster an understanding of their negotiations from a situated perspective, and analyze how these practices relationally shape and are shaped by how state and urban governance become enacted.

My argument is that this reading of how people negotiate irregular housing conditions in everyday situations is not only more in tune with the ways in which informality is governed in Berlin's allotment gardens than accounts of informality that focus on "states 'with muscles'" are (Boudreau et al., 2016: 2397), but permits us to grasp *the normalcy* of these negotiations as well. The explanatory promise of a focus on these "quieter registers of power" (Allen, 2016: 11) is that it pinpoints modalities of inclusion and exclusion that play out at the everyday scale. Such an analysis not only shows what is up for negotiation and the degree of latitude that is tolerated, but also demonstrates the small-scale *mechanisms* through which power relations work to privilege certain practices and declare others as untypical. In this reading, informality becomes a lens to view the everyday production and reproduction of urban inequalities. Translating the concept in this way may allow us to overcome assumptions of unbridgeable differences between Northern and Southern states. Moreover, it moves us beyond the confines of informality research on the global South, the poor, and the agency of a predatory state.

This chapter continues in three parts. First, a review of informality scholarship serves to explicate the approaches to the state and urban governance that undergird this work. In the next section, my aim to think of informality "differently" involves the mobilization of a repertoire of conceptual angles that deal especially with state enactment at the everyday level of urban regulation. The final section concludes by exploring possible conceptual gains of this perspective for an understanding of urban informality and the negotiation of regulations in the urban everyday.

Research on Informality and Its Accounts of the State

The concepts of informality and the state are inextricably intertwined, although research has defined these links in shifting and fundamentally different ways. A genealogical perspective on the epistemological history of the term "informality" readily explains some of these shifts. While its conceptualization is frequently associated with anthropologist Keith Hart (1973; see also Hann and Hart, 2011) and the work of the ILO (1972; cf. Steenberg, 2016), its first appearance in scholarship has been contested (Rakowski, 1994).[1] Yet, in these earlier conceptual formulations, informality was undoubtedly a (by)product of reading states and state governance in that particular place and particular time (generally meaning research sites in the global South in the 1970s). As it has frequently been noted, earlier, more "structuralist" understandings (Rakowski, 1994) focused on the exclusion of practices of, for instance, any trading, building, dwelling, or transport provisioning from the formal economy. They defined informal practices through their presumed "location" beyond the reach of state bureaucracies, as well as through their small scale, and the idea that they were carried out by so-called "ordinary" people. Thus, despite controversial voices (e.g. Portes, 1983), major parts of this early, more policy-oriented literature framed the concept as a problem of regulatory capacity or administrative oversight that merely concerned under-resourced populations in Southern cities. Similarly, more "legalist" perspectives (cf. Rakowski, 1994) that emerged at the turn of the twenty-first century (de Soto, 2000, 2002) focused on the "entrepreneurial dynamism" (Bromley, 1990: 330) of the "informals" but continued to hold informality to be a sphere outside of the law and, by way of equating both concepts, of the state.

These approaches also forged unhelpful analytical relations between imaginaries of informality and state modernity. Consider geographer Jennifer Robinson's (2006: 4) understanding of modernity "as simply the West's self-characterization of itself in opposition to "others" and "elsewhere" that are imagined not to be modern." In this reading, the early definitions of informality I previously discussed can be seen to have strengthened the idea of Western state modernity while reinforcing assumptions about the difference of the "Southern state." To be sure, the notion of informality as the "'other' of states" was derived from the idea of a "well-developed state" with modern, rational institutions – and imagined to be located in "the Northwestern quadrant of the world" (O'Donnell, 2001: 7). Yet somewhat contradictorily, researchers aligned informality with the supposedly "dis-functioning" and "traditional" states of the global South, despite these states appearing to lack all the previously named definitional characteristics of the Western state. Rather than questioning imaginaries of "Western state rationality" or aiming to understand geographical varieties in the workings of state practices, the use of the term informality in these cases thus reinforced the "othering" of what was cast as "the Southern state."

Critiques of such teleological conceptions of informality and development have since become ubiquitous. I refer to a set of ideas that specifically address the urban dimensions of a wider postcolonial critique that prominent thinkers, such as Dipesh Chakrabarty, Edward Said, Homi Bhabha, and Gayatri Spivak, have advanced since the 1980s. Based on the epistemological contributions of postcolonial theory and led by Robinson's influential contribution, *Ordinary Cities* (2006), urbanists began to debate the essentially parochial nature of urban theory (see e.g. Watson, 2009; Edensor, 2011; Sheppard et al., 2013). Above all, this "Southern urban critique" (Lawhon and Truelove, 2019) challenges the idea of Europe as a signifier of modernity (Escobar, 1995), in relation to which all else is "coming late, lagging behind, and lacking in originality" (Mufti, 2005: 474).[2] In the study of cities, this "teleological imperative" (Krishnaswamy, 2005: 70) had led to a profound imbalance in the production of theory and the pretension of theoretical claims. Consequently, postcolonial urbanists have highlighted the tensions between a wider recognition of historical difference vis-à-vis the universal truth claims of dominant Western approaches while, at the same time, confronting "assumptions of incommensurability" between urban experiences in Northern and Southern sites (Varley, 2013: 125).

In line with this approach, contemporary urban research has increasingly positioned itself against binary understandings of formality and informality. By showing that social spheres are embedded in a complex network of different relations that may be formal or informal to different extents, this literature reconceptualized the nexus of informality and the state. First, accounts that outline the use of informality as a governmental tool have offered useful conceptualizations of the ways in which state institutions assert authority through the use of informality (Yiftachel, 2009a, 2009b; Bear, 2011; de Alba, 2017; Shlomo, 2017; Bénit-Gbaffou, 2018; Tucker and Devlin, 2019). Ananya Roy's (2005) seminal article "Urban informality: Towards an epistemology of planning" was the first in a series of pivotal publications (2009a, 2009c, 2009d, 2011) that highlight the ways in which states use informality to mediate their relations with civil society by continuously rearranging the boundaries of legitimacy (see also Yiftachel, 2009a, 2009b; McFarlane, 2012). These accounts not only point out that the formal/informal labeling serves as a means through which states exert authority, but also that the maintenance of flexible and ever-shifting boundaries between formality and informality, legality and illegality ensures a continuous grip on populations. As Roy convincingly writes, "it is through this logic of informality that the state polices an arbitrary and fickle line between legality and illegality, creating a territorialised flexibility and demonstrating its political potency" (2018: 2243). Moreover, the literature illustrates how state agencies resort to illegal or extralegal means (Goldman, 2011; Ghertner, 2018), thereby creating boundaries between "wanted" and "unwanted" populations (Ghertner, 2010) that frequently work to victimize the poor.

Second, accounts interested in the linkages between informality and state governance are complemented by literature that explore citizens' modalities and mechanisms of claims-making (Chatterjee, 2004; Groth and Corijn, 2005; Benjamin, 2008; Hou, 2010; Elsheshtawy, 2011). In such accounts, these grounded, small-scale registers are researched as ways in which citizens resist modalities of top-down governance. The state is central to these discussions as the subject of multiple forms of subversion, resistance, or subaltern agency that are leveled against institutions, rather than through its own "agentic" qualities. In this view, informality is examined regarding what is taken to be its reformative, resistant, and subversive qualities – as "a counter strategy against dominant modes of production" (2012: 17), as Rainer Hehl frames it.

The work of Asef Bayat (1997, 2000, 2009) on the street politics of Teheran's income poor provides an illustrative example of this perspective. Rather than framing informal practices of subversion as grassroots activism directed against state agencies, Bayat seeks to circumvent the rigid divisions between "active" and "passive," "individual" and "collective," and "civil" and "political" opposition (2009: 26). Those dichotomies, he argues, have restrained scholarly perceptions and limited the opportunity to comprehend those practices that stay under the radar but may precede important social transformations (ibid). Instead, his analytical key – the notion of "quiet encroachment" – thinks beyond the dynamics of suppression and protest. Focused on the continuous engagement of marginalized urban groups, "quiet encroachment" finds everyday politics in the unanticipated moments of negotiation in everyday life. These struggles, Bayat suggests, broaden the domains of what he oddly calls the "informal people" (Bayat, 1997) by improving their positions in the city, by allowing them to gain autonomy from regulatory restraints, and by advancing their access to social goods and economic opportunities.

Both perspectives have redrawn the nexus of informality and the state in crucial ways: they have been pivotal in recognizing types of agency that were previously ignored, and they have critically analyzed the forces behind forms of exclusion and dispossession that have frequently remained invisible. However, the perspective of these studies (on civil insurgency or arbitrary state governance), their empirical focus (on cities in the South), and (most crucially for the approach pursued in this book) their implicit ontological approach to the state imply that they have less to say about the ways in which informality emerges at the interstices of legal ambiguity, institutional discrepancy, and everyday state enactment in Western liberal democracies.

Let me be clear: this is neither to say that informality or the state are different per se in these sites, nor that some of the mechanisms observed in this research would not be transferable (see Tuvikene et al., 2016, for suggestions on how to approach theorization of informality across sites in the global South, East, and West). Instead, I want to point out that these views of informality lend themselves better to analyzing informality in situations in which states act "with muscles" (Boudreau et al., 2016: 2397), and when the predominant research object is the large-scale displacement of informal settlements. In fact, for showing particular injustices in the state's dealing with informality, it might be more appropriate to think about the state in the above ways. Differently put, where the state's governance of informality is driven by heavy-handed eviction, questions other than the small-scale negotiation under examination in this book might be more relevant to pursue – not least, for ethical and political reasons.

I thus list a number of critical points in the spirit of expanding upon these important interventions into the arbitrary and unjust dealings of the state: in such theorizations, the two approaches to informality that I previously outlined in very broad stokes continue to uphold the dichotomy between state and civil society, top-down (oppression) and bottom-up (resistance), and statutory and non-statutory sites.[3] More concretely put, parts of this literature envision the state from a distance as an antagonistic force existing outside of civil realms in ways that underscore either the state's oppressive and flexible use of informality or its encroachment by "informal people" (those outside of the state). In this way, the literature is prone to situate state officials and "ordinary" people in positions from which they respectively either foster destructive and arbitrary oppression or – being subjected to that oppression – react to the state through nonstrategic insurgency. In this reading, agency is precast depending on people's "formalized" roles in (non)institutional sites. Thereby, "good agency" automatically becomes associated with the insurgency of people cast as "informal," and, by way of association, the opposite occurs with "state actors." Moreover, the literature demonstrates a tendency to operate with set assumptions concerning the sites in and through which domination (associated with state offices) and insurgency (associated with informal settlements) is to be sought out.

These points indicate that these perspectives are ill-equipped to analyze registers of power associated with negotiation; their framing implies a more general disregard of the internal workings and everyday operations of states, as well as implicit and preset (mis)conceptions of the rationalities of governing actors. In this way, these accounts leave little room to explore the motivations and rationalities of all concerned agents, including the ambivalent and individual experiences of people acting beyond presumed institutional roles in sites of governance (but see Bénit-Gbaffou and Oldfield, 2011; Radnitz, 2011; Fairbanks, 2012; Boudreau and Davis, 2017; Davis, 2018; Boudreau, 2017). Moreover, how institutional sites or practices of governance are shaped by people's practices in dealing with informality remains unrecognized.[4]

I see two methodological reasons for these constraints: First, insights generated from research on informality have rarely spoken to adjacent fields of research that deal with potentially related concerns in urban, criminological, state, or socio-legal theory, which further hampers a more conceptual debate about the notion (see Haid and Hilbrandt, 2019, for a more detailed exploration of that argument). To my knowledge, literatures on informality have rarely attempted to undergird the concept with different conceptions of statehood or, vice versa, considered the plural ways in which informality – however conceived – plays out in different theories of the state. Rather, the conceptual vagueness of informality has led authors frustrated with the notion to forefront other concepts, such as "speculation" (Goldman, 2011), "fragmentation" (McFarlane, 2018), "occupancy urbanism" (Benjamin, 2008), or "suturing" (Boeck and Baloji, 2016) (cf. McFarlane, 2019: 2). Second, informality research remains limited regarding its geographical scope and preferred objects of investigation – with a majority of its work continuing to examine informality in Southern cities. Research that has turned to countries of the so-called global North has primarily addressed informality in relation to poverty or migration, largely neglecting questions informality poses to the routine of everyday governance (cf. Acuto et al., 2019: 5). My suggestion is thus that explicating ontological assumptions about the actors, roles, and structures of governance that undergird conceptions of informality can help to gain a better grasp of the governance of informal housing in Berlin.

Informality and State Enactment

In the last decades, Marxist, Foucauldian, feminist, and, more recently, new-materialist approaches have theorized the state beyond essentializing imaginaries of an all-powerful government: as multiple and embodied rather than bounded and located outside of the social; as a dynamic process rather than a static body; and as a metaphysical effect or a discursive construct rather than a real entity (Jessop, 2016; Jeffrey, 2013; Painter, 2007; Ferguson and Gupta, 2002; Mitchell, 1999). Although heterogeneous in focus and theoretical commitment, these traditions provide a basis from which to approach the state in the everyday enactment of urban governance through processes of negotiation. More specifically, I base my understanding of informality on accounts that focus on the agentic, relational, and situated dimensions of state enactment. Therefore, I refer to literature that places weight on: state actors and their role in negotiation processes, their normative judgments, and their social embeddedness (Tilly, 1999; Lea, 2008; Lipsky, 2010 [1980]); the legal-material situations of regulatory enactment and modalities of claim-making (Valverde, 2011; Blomley, 2014); and the embeddedness of regulating actors in both society and state institutions as reflecting back on and thereby shaping one another (Cooper, 1998; Hunter, 2015). Running ahead of myself and previewing some of the payoffs of exploring informal housing in this way, this approach provides an alternative reading of informality – one in which informality emerges out of the normalcy through which the state routinely becomes performed. In this reading, regulation and transgression depend on the subjective experience of all governing agents who juggle multiple and frequently contradictory legal orders, and where transgression and regulation frequently do not take place following formally subscribed roles. But to come to this conclusion, let me sketch out this approach and how it shapes our understanding of informality. This book's subsequent chapters will add empirical detail and theoretical depth to different facets of the approach.

In the late 1970s, the empirical work of US political scientist Michael Lipsky (2010 [1980]) challenged assumptions about rigid state hierarchies and bureaucratic silos. Lipsky's focus on the role of day-to-day practices, professional discretion, and individual agency of the "street-level bureaucracy" shifted accounts of state enactment toward an understanding that practitioners in public roles – through their individual lived experiences, normative judgments, and personal ways of going about their work – were central to the governance process. In his view, the implementation process at the "front line" was not simply handing down policy but *constituted* the policy process itself. As Lipsky wrote, "the decisions of street-level bureaucrats, the routines they establish, and the devices they invent to cope with uncertainties and work pressures effectively *become* the public policies they carry out" (ibid: xii, emphasis in origin). Half a century later, Lipsky's work has been criticized as no longer speaking to neoliberal governance arrangements (Durose, 2007). Yet, the view that public policy actors put their powers to play as "persons with commitments" (Jones, 2011: 60), rather than as agents of the state, has shaped contemporary policy implementation debates.

Today's more relational and interpretive approaches to policy implementation have sharpened the view on the agency of workers in public services (Lea, 2008; Hunter, 2015; Dobson, 2020). These approaches displace the distinctions between individuals in public policy and the social and institutional "systems" in which they work by reference to their embeddedness in and through multi-scalar social relations, interactions, and structures. Consider, for instance, Shona Hunter's (2015: 24) conceptualization of "relational politics":

> By relational politics I am referring to the dynamic emotional process through which social categories such as gender and ethnicity get *lived out*, resignified and resisted in the everyday policy process and the ways they act back to reconfigure that very process itself. Thus I am claiming that despite its "under the surface," "hidden" character, relational politics is a powerful driver for the shape of the state, the distribution of power and inequality in "it" and through "it." (2015: 24, emphasis in original)

By tightly entangling the lived experience of practitioners and the structures of the state, Hunter's reading of relational politics suggests two conclusions: First, this understanding renders the state open to everyday transformations. In her relational reading, policy enactment is a pre- and refigurative process, one in which practitioners effectively shape the structures that they enact. Second, a relational view on processes of regulation complicates notions of public officials. In this perspective, policy actors are, as Rachael Dobson vividly argues, neither "cast as institutional automatons who fail to resist because they don't or can't know any better given the saturating power of hegemonic neoliberal governmentalities" nor high-minded do-gooders, "actors doing what they can in difficult circumstances" (2020: 4). Instead, this reading lends itself to imagining street-level bureaucrats, as Dobson notes elsewhere, as "critically humanistic actors: people with varied perspectives who exercise power and agency, and who apply multiple, ambivalent and contested meanings to their constructed worlds" (2015: 694).

In this way, this perspective takes us away from explanations of informality that place weight on, for instance, "cultures of corruption," in which the agency of public officials vanishes behind narratives of all-dominating norms. Instead, it shifts attention to the interrelations through which "governing *subjects*," in Hunter's terms (2015: 3, my emphasis), negotiate structures and situations in their everyday work. Placing the analytical focus on the workers who are doing the governing, and on their normative stance and social embeddedness, takes us closer to an understanding of informality through the ways in which local bureaucracy *understands* the rules and how they ought to be applied. Here, and as I find in Chapter 6, resistance, transgression, and maneuvering lie not only in the contestations of the subaltern, as some of the informality literature posits, but also in the practices of the state's official representatives.

Focusing on the state as negotiated in sites and processes of regulation also implies recognizing, as a more permanent feature of governing, that rules are ambiguous and frequently uncoupled from the situations to which they ostensibly apply. Socio-legal scholars have gone a long way in documenting the plurality of the law and its dependence on legal interpretive practices (Blomley, 1988, 2014; Blomley et al., 2001; Valverde, 2009, 2011, 2012; Delaney, 2010). For instance, as Chapter 7 discusses in depth, for critical legal scholar Boaventura de Sousa Santos, the law only loosely applies to the complexities of all possible real-world situations, as it results from processes of scaling up, projecting, and symbolizing such complexity in ways that provide abstractions that apply to the law's entire jurisdiction. In further complicating the relation between the law and specific sites, critical legal studies assume the coexistence of various legal conventions on the same territory (for example, national law, urban regulations, and local normative orders), thereby undermining the narrow conception of legal formalism (Butler, 2009: 316), i.e. the binary determinism of legality and illegality. Rather, following de Sousa Santos, "we live in a time of porous legality or of legal porosity, multiple networks of legal orders forcing us to constant transition and trespassing" (2002: 437).

As different legal orders intersect, actors need to negotiate one set of rules (e.g. customary law) with another (e.g. state law). Furthermore, they need to apply multiple sets of rules to possibly contradictory real-world situations. This implies, as Melissaris notes, "being attentive both to the plurality of norms but also to the ways in which they are organized in and around practices" (2004: 58). Charles Tilly offers an insightful exploration of the ambivalent mechanisms that govern the "the intersections between abstract, centrally promoted plans and social life on the small scale" (1999: 345), or, to use the title of his seminal article, the interface between "Top Down and Bottom Up" power. Tilly's central proposition (ibid: 350) is that the implementation of abstract projects, plans, or policies is likely to fail in the absence of routine mechanisms that accommodate, mediate, or negotiate contradictory circumstances. In this view, mechanisms such as "polyvalent performance, accommodative bargaining, category formation, intellectual brokerage and improvisation" (ibid: 345) that provide different ways of negotiating conflicting circumstances in processes of governance are central to the functioning of states. Echoing Lipsky's (2010 [1980]) observation, street-level bureaucrats "twist" power (Allen, 2016: 15) when, for instance, they work with contradictions as they adapt rules "on the ground." Understanding the governance and production of informal practices in these terms places more weight, as I will go on to suggest, on the *routine* implementation mechanisms through which all actors translate regulations to specific situations and less on the *exceptional* transgressions that informal housing entails. As Chapter 5 suggests, a discussion of informal housing in these terms also brings the spatial and material modalities of negotiating the city into view: the material transformations and governance of allotment huts and infrastructures are negotiated in relation to the allotments' ambiguous legal framings.

Studying informality by focusing on the everyday negotiation of rules asks us to bring those typically not understood as doing governing work into the analytical frame. And it requires us to include them in ways that go beyond describing the antagonistic relations between state actors employing more "centered" modalities of power, such as domination or manipulation, and civil society actors working against the state through more "mobilized" and dispersed registers of power, such as upheaval or dissent.[5] More useful for an understanding of the negotiated nature of governance is literature that has described interactive relations between state and civil society groups through quiet registers of change. Most prominently, urban regime theory has highlighted how state–market alliances penetrate municipal governance through the political bargaining and factional interest of organized interest groups (Stone, 1993; Kantor et al., 1997; Granados and Knoke, 2005). While these networks steer policy implementation through strategy, mutual recognition, and permanence, others have accounted for the participation of more dispersed and fragmented civil society groups in processes of governing (Davis, 2010; Jaffe, 2013; Schindler, 2014b; Lamotte, 2017). For instance, Ilda Lindell (2008), writing about the governance of markets in Maputo, provides evidence of "fluid" and "unstable" systems of governance characterized, as she writes, "by great uncertainty, unpredictability and precarious alliances with patrons, short-lived agreements and the constant management of conflicts" (2008: 1897). By accounting for the multiple contestations between different groups at work, this fragmented imaginary of how state power is mediated in putting governance to work provides a basis for understanding the internal contestations at play when actors negotiate informal housing.

Still, more central to an understanding of the negotiations at the core of this book are a variety of quiet and frequently dispersed registers of claim-making through which anthropologists have explored the everyday strategies of groups and individuals in processes of governance (Das and Poole, 2004; Auyero, 2010; Fourchard, 2011). These can occur in everyday state–citizen encounters, in which citizens "see the state," in Corbridge et al.'s terms (2005), in the discursive relations in which citizens themselves enact the state (Gupta, 1995), as well as in the ways in which citizens transform the material structures that constitute "the state" (Reeves, 2009: 1283). Jeremy Brooke Straughn's study of "consentful contention" (2005: 1602) is a useful example of these modalities of interaction. His work on the practices of citizens in East Germany led him to describe "consentful contention" as a "genre" of individualistic yet pervasive forms of political negotiation that he took to be flourishing in view of the "inherently paradoxical nature" of post-socialist states. Straughn defines "consentful contention" (ibid) as the interaction between "subordinate actors" and state representatives, in which citizens further their interest on the basis of explicit reference to the ideological commitments of the state. This supplies an analysis of state–citizen interaction that not only breaks with the binary determinism of resistance and suppression – as citizens here too enact the ideology of the state at the same time as they outwit or manipulate state representatives – but also presents actors in and beyond institutions as critical subjects in complex and fluid roles.

In the sense that it accounts for the ambiguous roles of citizens and street-level bureaucrats, the present argument is consistent with Straughn's (2005) analysis. Negotiation, as a family of practices (including, in my reading, multiple other interactive registers of claim-making, such as modalities of bargaining, ways of adapting the law to local circumstances, the gardeners' prefigurative politics, or ways of securing compromises) brings both "sides," with their normative commitments, structural constraints, and situational necessities, into one frame. In offering a more relational and plural understanding of how and by whom power is mobilized and resisted, a focus on negotiation enables an understanding of informality through having a full grasp of the multiple loci and modalities of power through which governance becomes enacted and urban development transformed.

Negotiating Urban Formalities

These approaches do not offer new ways of thinking about the everyday negotiation of regulation and transgression, but they provide novel routes to approaching informality. To recall, my objective was to open up a framework that facilitates operationalizing informality, or, more precisely put, the negotiation of irregular housing practices in an analysis of urban bureaucracies in a Western liberal state. Understanding the enactment of regulations in the agentic, relational, and situated ways outlined earlier has three crucial implications for conceptualizing informality.

First, as this approach accounts for how all governing actors understand rules and how they ought to be applied, in this reading formality and informality acquire meaning in relation to the subjective conceptions through which regulation and transgression are negotiated. That these actors' understandings of formality and informality are always constituted in specific situations makes it necessary to define and theoretically approach formality and informality in relation to these understandings "on the ground." Resisting the assumption that regulations could always be implemented in straightforward ways moves analytical attention away from processes of compliance and toward an analysis of the ways in which rules are translated to specific urban situations, i.e. to the interpretive mechanisms that are the ordinary stuff of policy implementation. In this way, phenomena one could label as informal when analyzed at a different scale or from a different angle appear as cogent or necessary solutions – at times the only way through which rules can be emplaced. These are then not processes lying outside of the state; rather, they point to the multiple ways in which the state regularly becomes performed.

Second, this approach changes understandings of informality regarding how and by whom power is thought to be mobilized in the transgression and regulation of order. Capturing informality through the quieter grammars of power leveraged in negotiations (rather than through the powers of domination and resistance) requires us to consider all actors and their multiple and ambivalent roles in one analytical frame, i.e. to register both how civil society participates in processes of regulation and how the urban bureaucracy works by interpreting rules. In this way, studying informality points to processes of cooperation, where interests of regulators and those being regulated frequently converge. Moreover, this perspective brings everyday politics of inclusion and exclusion into the analytical frame. In contrast to conceiving of informality as "heroic" resistance against the state, accounting for the multiple roles people take up in everyday governance opens up to empirical scrutiny how processes of bordering become reproduced in state–civil society negotiations as well as between groups and individuals on both "sides." As Chapter 6 explains at length, the power to define criteria of incorporation and exclusion – when dwelling becomes acceptable and when it crosses a line – is in part mobilized by the gardeners themselves. This approach thus facilitates exploring how the flexibility of the law and the negotiability of informal arrangements lend themselves to the further marginalization of those already multiply excluded.

Finally, the relational conceptions of state enactment presented here provide a different perspective on the potential of change through "informal" everyday interventions in processes and sites of governance. Informality is frequently associated with transgression and change. Scholars of informality regularly ask if and how these moments become emancipatory. Similarly, the relational reading perused in this book renders the state open to transformation through the work involved in negotiating regulations. In this, "little things pile up" (Povinelli, 2011) to produce continuous change, as Chapter 5 will illustrate. But my conception offers a different reading of the ways in which these "piles" emerge: it leads to an account of change wherein transformation emerges as all actors concerned maneuver through the "structures" they enact. Moreover, from this perspective, transgression is not necessarily emancipatory. Rather, the ways in which actors maneuver around boundaries depend on the power inequalities that imbue spaces of negotiation, as well as on the conditions in which negotiations are set – limiting participation for some, benefiting others, and thereby frequently reproducing entrenched inequalities.

To be sure, this approach moves my frame of reference away from informality. If we understand these negotiations as the normalcy of the state, what meaning does the concept of informality convey in a description of regulatory transgression? Instead of presupposing the existence of formality and deriving the concept of informality from it, this approach places weight on understanding the production of informal housing as part of the normal functioning of the state, i.e. as an inherent aspect of everyday governance. As it translates informality into the vocabulary of state enactment and urban governance, this thinking decenters informality in an analysis of regulation and transgression.

Instead, formality appears in the subtitle of this book. Formality, too, remains a difficult term because its use ultimately reifies a conception of both terms – formality and informality – as opposing, binary principles. However, to put the production of formality at the center of this investigation allows me to circumvent the dichotomy that defines informality through its lack of formality. The processes under scrutiny in this book are then not described as the deviant other, or the negative counterpart of an ordering principle, but as part and parcel of the *making* of order. As these processes depend on a multiplicity of different legal frames (including laws, government programs, contracts, and the like), numerous actors (including state agencies, civil associations, and individuals), different power relations (including social ties, networks, and political allegiances) through which all actors concerned produce a plethora of orders considered to be legitimate, I employ the term in its plural form. I speak about *urban* formalities because thinking about the state at the level of the municipal scale forces us to understand the density of the materialities that are being negotiated, the heterogeneity of the actor constellations involved, the multiple sites of political encounter, and the complexity of overlapping statutory frameworks in multilevel administrations.

Moreover, despite my attempt to decenter in/formality, it is crucial to remember that formality and informality are ideas that are used in the field to certain ends (although in a much wider vocabulary). Formality implies claims to the legitimacy, regularity, or efficacy of order due to a supposed alliance with institutional frames. Rather than the *product* of negotiation, claims to in/formality are, in this sense, a *resource* on which people draw to produce urban order. Thus, while my reading foregrounds the processes of negotiating regulations, these concepts remain useful in an analysis of regulation as they allow us to consider how all concerned actors use these claims in their negotiations.

Summary: Chapter 2

This chapter details the book's central line of argumentation, as well as its underlying theoretical approach. It argues that contemporary literature on informality, by casting the state in ways that tend to either underscore its flexible and oppressive use of informality or the ways in which citizens obstruct state powers by resisting them "from the outside," methodologically has less to say about the more interactive practices of negotiation that this book is concerned with, where the roles and interests of "both sides" are more fluid and frequently merge. To analyze informality through the small-scale and incremental powers of negotiation, the chapter discusses theoretical traditions that place weight on the normative judgments and social embeddedness of those who are negotiating, the legal-material processes of regulatory enactment, the entwinement of institutions in social life, and the ways in which these processes of enactment reflect back on and transform wider processes of institutional transformation. To conclude, the chapter suggests that this reading of how people negotiate irregular housing conditions in everyday situations is more in tune with the ways in which informality is governed in Berlin's allotment gardens than accounts of informality that focus on "states 'with muscles'" are (Boudreau et al., 2016: 2397) and, moreover, permits us to grasp *the normalcy* of these negotiations as well.

Notes

1   See, for instance, still earlier literature on Latin America (e.g. Abrams, 1964). As Marx and Kelling rightly note, "we need to be wary about identifying a singular historical trajectory of debate" (2019: 3).

2   In *Provincializing Europe*, a centerpiece of this debate, Chakrabarty has labeled these conventions as "eurocentristic," denoting that even in

more global ways of theorizing the world, "'Europe' remains the sovereign, theoretical subject of all histories, including the ones we call 'Indian,' 'Chinese,' and 'Kenyan'" (2008: 27; for similar arguments see Mufti, 2005; Connell, 2007, 2014; Hawley and Krishnaswamy, 2008).

3 But see Simone, 2010; Hackenbroch, 2011; Hackenbroch and Hossain, 2012; Lindell et al., 2019, among others.

4 In contrast, for Diane Davis, "a focus on informality provides a lens for understanding urban governance as a system of practises that link citizens, state, and markets" (2016: 6). Davis argues that the ways in which the local state decides to deal with informality (ranging from toleration to suppression) are not only relevant to understanding the priorities of states with regard to order, law, and citizenship, they also work, as she writes, to "restructure … or transform … their own nature and activities" (ibid). The state's dealing with informality can thus be conceived "as a process of state formation, meaning that informality serves as the driving force in determining the nature and contours of the state, and not vice versa" (ibid: 7).

5 See Allen (2003) for a distinction between these different modes of power.

Chapter 3

Footnotes on the History of Housing

Allotment Dwelling in Berlin, 1871–2019

Since May 2012, the most iconic site of Berlin's housing protests has been a small shed located in the middle of a large housing complex in the district of Berlin-Kreuzberg at a junction called Kottbusser Tor. This shed, known under the telling name of *Gecekondu*, is the meeting point of the tenants' initiative Kotti & Co, which protests against displacement in the face of rising rents.[1] With its etymology coming from the idea of a house built in one night, between sunset and sunrise (Ward, 2002: 5), the term Gecekondu is used to describe makeshift housing structures in Turkey. It thus alludes not only to the ethnic mix of the social housing complex but also to housing struggles elsewhere, in Turkey and beyond. What has largely been forgotten is that Berlin's Gecekondu also marks the beginnings of Berlin's struggles over allotment dwelling: only 150 years ago, brutal evictions displaced the first residents of allotment huts from this site.

Allotments have captured the imagination of a wide range of historians around the world (Crouch and Ward, 1997; DeSilvey, 2003; Hobbs, 2012; Urban, 2013; Poling, 2014). Their function has been documented as a space of belonging (Gerodetti and Foster, 2016) and community cohesion (Burn, 2017), as part of the agricultural system (Battersby and Marshak, 2013), and as a project of self-organization and social control (Mack and Parscher, 2017). Only a handful of studies have considered the history of allotments to study questions concerning informal housing (Kuhn, 2006; Urban, 2013), which explains why the 1871 squat at Kottbusser Tor has largely been forgotten. Yet, Berlin's history of allotment gardening was, from its start, entangled in a history of dwelling: unlike the growth of so-called *Armengärten* (gardens for the poor) or *Schrebergärten* (gardens that were based on ideas of physical health, subsistence, and social reform), the city's first wave of allotments occurred in

Housing in the Margins: Negotiating Urban Formalities in Berlin's Allotment Gardens,
First Edition. Hanna Hilbrandt.

the wake of efforts to provide self-help housing.[2] Between 1862 and 1871, incoming migrants settled in so-called *barrakias* [shanties] at Kottbusser Tor, where today's Gecekondu is placed (Lange, 1984: 133; Stein, 2000: 238).

This chapter traces the role of allotment dwelling since the establishment of the *barrakias*: through turbulent years of war, postwar housing shortages, political division, and reunification. I highlight two themes that are particularly pertinent to the narrative arc of this book. First, writing the history of allotments as a history of housing expands an understanding of the ways in which informality is entangled in the social projects and regulatory ambiguities of state agencies. The chapter explores past regimes of planning and governance as well as the social and spatial development of allotment gardening in order to highlight shifting legal imperatives, changing political projects, and local struggles, in which housing was variably forbidden or sustained. This dwelling history hardly follows a teleological development path toward formalization. Moreover, it demands careful attention from urban scholars because it provides an alternative perspective to our current understanding of past housing struggles and mechanisms of housing provisioning since late nineteenth-century Berlin. Hence this chapter's title "Footnotes on the History of Housing": it speaks of a minor history that has been attributed marginal importance but forces us to ask how housing experiences beyond the norm can add to or challenge common understandings of regularization and governance.

Second, a situated historical framing of allotment dwelling provides the ground for a discussion of modernity, obduracy, and development. It allows me to show how past regimes of rule are incorporated into contemporary regulatory projects. As this and subsequent chapters will expose, obdurate urban orders continue to linger, impacting allotment regulation today in ways that are constitutive of modern governance. Despite shifting paradigms of administrative ordering, today's dwelling practices are – at least at times – characterized by outdated norms that continue to prevail. Moreover, narrating the allotment history across time speaks to the imperative of comparative urbanism. It allows me to counter claims concerning the novelty of informality in the global North. Rather than a confirmation of Euro-America moving south (Comaroff and Comaroff, 2012), as the idea of the Gecekondu might also suggest, a historical look at informal housing in allotment huts evidences that informal housing has traditionally been part of multiple unconventional dwelling practices that have existed in spite of, entangled in, or parallel to formal planning efforts.

This chapter follows a chronological structure, into which I weave the two concerns I previously outlined throughout four periods of time. Its first section, "Foundations (1871–1914): Squatting Gründerzeit Berlin," traces the development of Berlin's allotment gardens from their establishment to the First World War. The second section, "Consolidations (1914–1955): Housing During the War Years," documents the intensification of allotment dwelling in the face of housing shortages caused by economic crises and two major wars. In the third section, "Variegations (1955–1989): Dwelling in the Divided City," my focus is on the different laws, norms, and housing practices that became established on both sides of the Wall. "Adaptations (1989–2019): Allotments in the Unified City" then sketches out the adjustment processes that followed German reunification in the face of local variegations and the coexistence of different formalities in allotment gardens. Finally, the conclusion reflects on the implications of these developments for an understanding of the state's projects of housing regulation and the temporalities of urban transformations.

Foundations (1871–1914): Squatting Gründerzeit Berlin

The foundation of Berlin's allotments is closely related to the city's history of industrialization. *Armengärten* [gardens for the poor] had existed since 1833 (Kleinlosen and Milchert, 1989: 14), but they were merely a marginal phenomenon. In the second half of the nineteenth century, Berlin entered into an economic boom that fostered a first broader wave of allotments being established in two ways: on the one hand, allotments were officially integrated into the expansive growth of Berlin's built fabric and rapid industrial development (Landesverband Berlin der Gartenfreunde e.V., 2001: 23). Names of allotment associations such as *Steinreich* [stony grounds], *Wiesengrund* [meadowland] or *Zum Steingarten* [to the stony garden] are reminders of the initial cultivation of land in the course of its urbanization. On the other hand, the immense housing shortage that characterized the period led to the construction of squats in front of the city's former gates that took the form of allotments.

To understand both developments, a snapshot of the urban growth patterns at the time is in order. Between 1857 and 1871, the small capital of Prussia had already grown yearly by 4.8% (Huchzermeyer, 2011: 55), reaching a population of 828,915 (Tissot, 1989: 146). In 1871 alone, the year in which Berlin was nominated to become the imperial capital of the German Reich, 49,986 people migrated to Berlin (Huchzermeyer, 2011: 53). Many failed to find housing.[3] By 1900, the city had 1,900,000 inhabitants (Statistisches Landesamt Berlin, 1999: 25–28), becoming the densest tenement city in Europe (Huchzermeyer, 2011: 4). The housing conditions of the time forced most of those who found housing to endure unhealthy living conditions. The so-called *Mietskaserne* [literally: rental barrack] – a typical tenement building of multiple adjacent blocks separated only by narrow courtyards – lacked fire protection and was subject to skyrocketing rents and astonishing levels of density (Bodenschatz, 1987: 63). As landlords rented beds rather than flats – often to multiple occupants – it housed 3 to 13 inhabitants per heated room (Bodenschatz, 1987: 62). These precarious material conditions were based on a system of arbitrary profit-making in the housing market that was organized through large banks and unchecked housing developers that held the power of monopoly over the land (see also Bodenschatz, 1987: 53 on the organization of housing profits; Huchzermeyer, 2011). Similar to what is seen in today's housing crisis, financial speculation forced large sections of the population into homelessness or to the brink of it, while vacant luxury apartments awaited the arrival of wealthier residents.

The *barrakias* or so-called *Laubenstädte* [cities of allotment huts] that developed outside of the city's recently removed walls in response to this crisis clearly aimed at mitigating the city's housing shortage (Stein, 2000: 240; Poling, 2014: 258).[4] But these horticultural squats can be written into the history of allotments, as Berliners both *housed* and *gardened* on their plots (Landesverband Berlin der Gartenfreunde e.V., 2001: 14). The most famous *barrakia* was developed in 1862, when migrants leased land on the Schlächterwiesen [literally: butcher's meadows] in front of the Cotbusser Tor [now Kottbusser Tor; then one of the city's gates] (Stein, 2000: 240), today site of the Gecekondu with which this chapter began. The French travel writer Victor Tissot describes the relative order established over the decade: "[R]icher occupants found shelter in disused railway carriages. The barracks were set up in four rows. The city had its police and night guards. Shops and ale houses were already present" (1989: 147, my translation). During the *Gründerjahre*, the settlement at the Schlächterwiesen housed 700 people who earned incomes that should have allowed them to house themselves in less precarious ways (Wischermann, 1997: 337–39).[5,6] Despite the fact that the allotment holders paid leases for the land (Landesverband Berlin der Gartenfreunde e.V., 2001: 13), failed negotiations with the mayor at the time brought the period of sufferance to an end with violent street battles and the eviction of the *barrakias* (Lange, 1984: 133–38; see also Tissot, 1989; Richie, 1998: 165; Hobbs, 2012: 269) around the time of the publication of Engels's *The Housing Question* in 1872.[7,8] Interestingly, Kristin Poling reports that these dwelling practices were entangled in ambivalent narratives that mirror contemporary discussions of informality. On the one hand, the settlers were described in a global context of poverty survival to be disassociated with the newly founded German Reich. As Poling puts it, they were seen as "a reversion to primitivism …a symptom of a dangerous and difficult-to-control city landscape" (2014: 262). On the other hand, shanties were alluded to admiringly in discourses around "the rapid development of a young nation" that "celebrated them as miracles of self-organization, evidence instead of an enterprising spirit …fundamental to the new German Empire as a healthy young nation much like the United States" (ibid: 262–63).

Despite the evictions, the number of Berlin's allotment gardeners grew to 40,000 by the turn of the century (Stein, 2000: 245; Landesverband Berlin der Gartenfreunde e.V., 2001: 18). The literature relates this growth to three concerns that go beyond their use for shelter and survival. First, authors explain the emergence of allotments by citing the gardeners' enduring attachment to their former rural lifestyle and their deep suspicion of urbanization. For instance, the title of the first official allotment newspaper, *Der Ackerbürger* [literally: field-citizens] (Jensen, 2005: 319), references an old concept of urban citizenship in which urbanites upheld a rural lifestyle despite living in the city. Other than the overcrowded tenement, the allotments also provided a homestead and sense of belonging. Second, allotments were initiated as a territorialized strategy of appeasing and governing – a biopolitical measure attempting to foster healthier living conditions in the midst of the industrial city. For Micheline Nilsen, they aimed at keeping up the spirit of the working class, and at toughening up young city-dwellers so they could then support the industrial workforce (2014: 83). Moreover, allotments were considered to be a beautifying measure that helped improve urban life through proximity to light and soil (Landesverband Berlin der Gartenfreunde e.V., 2001: 46). Finally, land-based systems of profit-making are key to understanding the growth of allotments. In these early periods, most allotment plots were leased temporarily via a central lessor [*Generalpächter*], a public or private property owner (ibid, 2001: 18). The foundational idea of this system – to put uncultivated land into its most profitable interim use until its further development – made the allotment holders, as Hartwig Stein puts it, "stop-gaps between fallow and building land" (2000: 247, my translation) in a double sense. On the one hand, they had to endure arbitrary pricing with minimal security; on the other, their use cultivated the land and thus increased its value for future sales. In both ways, this anticipates recent debates regarding contemporary urban gardening projects (Rosol et al., 2017).

These beginnings of Berlin's allotment history correspond to the era of German colonialism in Africa (1884–1920). To date, the allotments are frequently referred to as colonies, and the names of some of the oldest gardens, such as Buren, Transvaal, Kamerun, or Kulis speak of this period and, it is said, of the unsatisfied travel urge of the gardeners as well as their patriotism

(Landesverband Berlin der Gartenfreunde e.V., 2001: 24). While Stein (2000: 256) argues that the naming of the allotments references spaces of exploitation, the notion of the colony also alludes to a center–periphery relation. In fact, although allotment land forms green corridors that weave through the city's core, the story of allotments primarily concerns the periphery of the "civilized" city, where gardens provided spaces for food extraction and withdrawal from urban life.[9]

The first decades of the twentieth century fostered the consolidation of allotment culture and a broader political acceptance of the gardeners who soon came to be collectively seen as a movement. Already in 1901, the foundation of the Central Allotment Association united multiple organizational strands including the Red Cross, different reform movements, charitable associations, and previously unorganized tenants who gardened on vacant land. From the perspective of the allotment holders, these early developments constituted a double-edged sword. On the one hand, this fusion strengthened the claims of the gardeners and helped them to organize against the despotism of the lessors. The increasing acknowledgment of allotment gardening provided them with security and opened up a space through which they could maneuver their claims. On the other hand, this security hinged upon their incorporation into political projects of appeasement and social reform. In sum, the decades before the First World War established cultural, social, and material infrastructures of allotment gardening out of very mixed concerns: their development bundled projects of poverty survival, attempts at making a home within the growing industrial metropolis, politics of greening the city, and social reform with strategies of land speculation.

Consolidations (1914–1955): Housing During the War Years

In the first half of the twentieth century, two world wars, their related urban destruction, and periods of economic depression entangled the housing question in Berlin's allotments history yet again. The hardship of the First World War (1914–1918) and its aftermath helped to further remove the taboo of dwelling in allotment huts (Friedrich, 2007: 100). Housing construction had stagnated or declined (Landesverband Berlin der Gartenfreunde e.V., 2001: 43), and the immigration of refugees turned the dwelling practices of the 1870s into a more common practice. In contradistinction to the first wave of allotment squats, where shelter had to be built, the allotment dwellers during the war and interwar periods merely had to refurbish existing huts. Moreover, in difference to the "wild" settlement and violent disputes with the *Baupolizei* (building authority; literally: building police), this period saw no explicit legalization regarding dwelling in allotment huts, but its politics provided wide exceptions and incentives. Instead of progress and development leaving informality behind, the history of the wars reversed, as Marie Huchzermeyer put it, "the chronological determinism that modernism seeks to inscribe into space" (2011: 7). During those years, allotment dwelling was hardly a vestige of a shameful past, but continually normalized as a form of housing.

Already in 1913, allotment holders could count on the benevolent attitude of public authorities. Whereas Berlin's higher administrative court [*Oberverwaltungsgericht*] only allowed overnight stays authorized by a special permit, the minister of public works [*Minister der öffentlichen Arbeiten*] considered *Laubenschlaf* [literally: sleep in one's allotment hut], in exceptional circumstances, a useful promotion of welfare (Stein, 2000: 583). Such flexibilization of dwelling conditions continued as the war drastically aggravated the housing situation, leading this same minister to promote the procurement of allotment sheds to alleviate the housing shortage (Stein, 2000: 583). This development was further institutionalized in November 1918, as the commissioner for housing [*Staatskommisar für das Wohnungswesen*] suggested defining conditions in which huts could be erected without a permit (Landesverband Berlin der Gartenfreunde e.V., 2001: 58). On 25 April 1919, the Ministry of People's Welfare [*Ministerium für Volkswohlfahrt*] designed a decree [*Musterwohnlaubenverordnung*] that permitted dwelling in the huts between 15 April and 15 October provided that inhabitants also had access to housing elsewhere (Stein, 2000: 583). As this decree conceived of huts as housing supplements that were merely to provide a secondary shelter option during the summer months, it fostered political ambiguity. In the winter months, housing was still not permitted in allotment huts, and not only the local districts but also the police increasingly tolerated dwelling in allotments – even during the winter (Voll, 1983: 11). Barely one year later, in July 1920, a decree of the Ministry of People's Welfare instructed the police, which had brutally evicted the *barrakias* in the 1870s, to tolerate allotment dwellers until the end of 1924, even when dwellers had no formal housing elsewhere.[10] Many allotment holders gave up their flats and permanently settled into their huts. Together, these attempts to deal with the influx of people into the allotments created a situation of complicity, if not official incorporation. In 1923, Berlin's colonies counted no less than 35,000 families that were permanently housed in allotments (Richter, 1930: 44). A police decree issued in July of the same year designated housing areas in allotments [*Wohnlaubengebiete*; literally: residential hut areas], and thus institutionally recognized these sites (Figure 3.1).

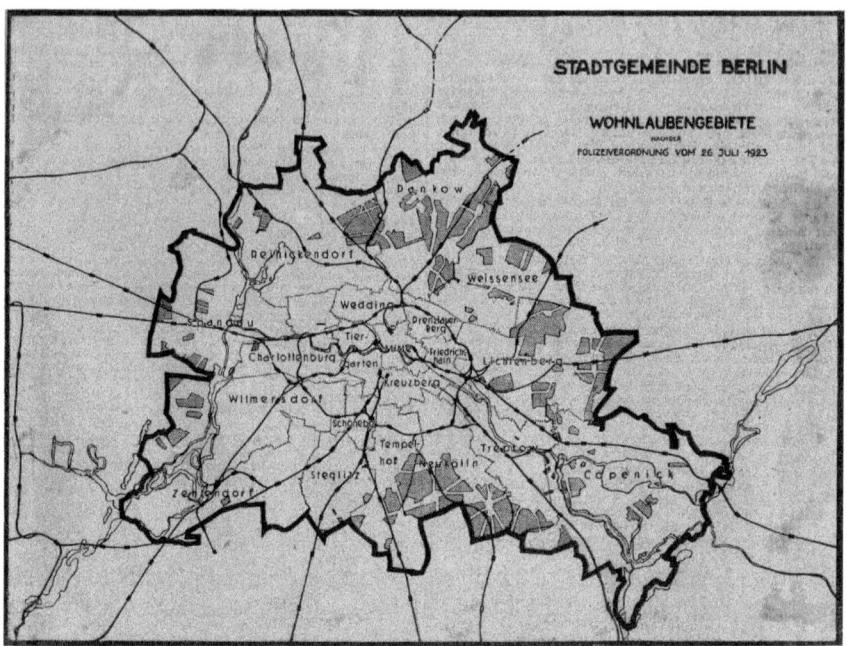

FIGURE 3.1 Allotment housing areas [*Wohnlaubengebiete*]. Source: Landesarchiv Berlin, C Rep. 902 02 05 Nr. 64.

Entangled with these housing histories, the beginnings of the First World War had also led to ideological and organizational changes that both promoted the growth of allotment land and strengthened the social organization in and around the gardens. During these years, allotments became a focus of war propaganda. Political discourses pointed to the gardens as a national strategy of food supply (Nilsen, 2014: 89). As noted by Nilsen, these efforts only obliquely targeted the productive possibilities of the allotments, as most gardeners lacked the necessary seeds to farm effectively (ibid). Rather, as she states, the obsessive propaganda of that time granted allotment holders the feeling that gardening constituted a crucial task through which they were to support the war effort (Landesverband Berlin der Gartenfreunde e.V., 2001: 48).[11]

In 1919, the newly elected Weimar government passed the first of the garden statutes, in the Allotment and Small Tenancy Regulation [*Kleingarten und Kleinpachtordnung* (KGO); my translation]. This piece of regulatory infrastructure not only ended the system of the central lessors (as it set rent caps and protected the allotment holders against unwarranted eviction) but also furthered the gardeners' administrative independence through a civil arbitration procedure and institutionalized numerous rationalities through which the allotments were to be organized, such as the idea that each plot was to be privately used, by only one gardener or family at a time (Stein, 2000: 416; Nilsen, 2014: 95). Although this law had its inherent ambiguities – for instance, around the definition of what was to count as an allotment (Landesverband Berlin der Gartenfreunde e.V., 2001: 71) – it marks the start of a learning process in which lawmakers gradually apprehended how to regulate the gardens. Weimar also institutionalized an administrative agency at the district level – thus moving the allotments into the municipality's realm of responsibility.

In the 1920s, the gardens were to contribute to the recovery of soldiers returning home from the war. Stein argues that particularly the fear of repeating the spread of communist thought had promoted the idea that soldiers were to be recompensed with a homestead: a single-family house with a garden (Stein, 2000: 404–14). As Germany lost the war, the compensations foreseen in the "Homestead Law of the Reich" [*Reichsheimstädtengesetzt*; my translation] were significantly reduced: until the full realization of homeownership, these homesteads could take the form of an allotment (Deutsche Nationalversammlung, 1920).

Berlin had already registered as many as 70,000 house-hunters in 1919, but by 1928 this number had risen to 179,000 (Landesverband Berlin der Gartenfreunde e.V., 2001: 54). Despite repeated attempts to contain these settlements (Rollka and Spiess, 1987: 39), the Great Depression (1929–1939) further broke the taboo of dwelling in allotment huts. Berlin was then a city of poverty, haunted by inflation and economic depression. By 1932, unemployment rates had increased to 5.6 million nationwide (Statistisches Jahrbuch für das Deutsche Reich, 1943: 291). In the face of ever-rising numbers of unemployed and homeless Berliners, the severely strained Weimar Republic passed emergency decrees designed to appease the population. Among these measures, the Reich subsidized allotments for the unemployed; however, as the designated areas were already occupied with "wild" allotments, these measures hardly provided further gardening opportunities (Stein, 2000: 620). Unofficial allotment dwelling continued without rigid sanctions. In 1931, as a municipal official wrote in a contemporary bulletin, "it would be hard to find bureaucracies that would displace him [an allotment holder] from the huts in the face of the current housing shortage. This form of self-help contradicts all legal statutes, but at least it is understandably human" (Landesverband Berlin der Gartenfreunde e.V., 2001: 61, my translation).

The Third Reich's political approaches toward the gardens shifted considerably. The 1932 building exhibition [*Sonne, Luft und Haus für Alle*], hosted in Berlin, promoted the gardens as a political measure about family. Its program stated that the allotment allowed for the educating of a "nature-loving race" [*naturverbundes Geschlecht*] in the midst of the city (Landesverband Berlin der Gartenfreunde e.V., 2001: 76, my translation). Furthermore, the exhibition recommended the possibilities that the gardens offered to increase the "spiritual hygiene" [*geisteshygienische Kräfte*] of urbanites. Gardens were to prevent hedonism and excessive alcohol consumption, which were considered harmful to the masses (ibid). As Florian Urban writes,

> the practices of gardening fit neatly within the blood-and-soil ideology that assigned the German peasant tradition a particular significance. Allotments were aptly construed as promoters of land-bound values for the German race and as counterweight to the ethnically mixed and, according to Nazi dogma, therefore morally depraved big city. (2013: 230)

For Loesdau (2007), the associations and organizational structures established in the Weimar Republic facilitated the replacement of gardening committees through party affiliates, in a standardization process of *Gleichschaltung*. In this way, the influence of the Nazi government on processes through which the political dispositions of the gardeners could be shaped was easily secured (cf. Katsch and Walz, 2008: 11).

The disaster management of the Second World War (1939–1945) mirrored Weimar's ambiguous political attitude toward dwelling in allotment huts. Initially, Nazi Germany institutionalized departments for the rigorous redevelopment of allotments [*Sanierungsdezernenten*], with the aim of eradicating garden dwelling (Schenk, 2011: 5). In May 1934, one-third of Berlin's 140,000 plots were permanently inhabited by 125,000 people (Schenk, 2011: 6), and in June 1935, the Nazis passed a decree that explicitly outlawed dwelling in allotments (Gesetz zur Ergänzung der Kleingarten- und Kleinpachtlandordnung, vom 1935: 805). Yet, allotments were difficult to monitor and control. As Urban writes about these times, "allotment dwellers took to darkening their windows at night so that the police wouldn't notice them" (2013: 222). The housing security of allotment dwellers was also endangered through the residential housing project of the "Imperial City Germania," which led, among other things, to the eviction of the Waggonstadt Plötzensee [literally: wagon city of Plötzensee] in Berlin-Charlottenburg (Rollka and Spiess, 1987: 42–47). It was only in 1943 that the Reich passed a decree that foresaw the use of existing allotments for the purpose of housing (Friedrich, 2007: 103). The 1945 "Guidelines for the erection of allotment huts" [*Richtlinien für die Errichtung von Wohnlauben*] similarly permitted dwelling therein. According to Schenk, the Reich even subsidized the refurbishment of the huts (2011: 9). These building permits were temporary and revocable at any point in order to inhibit the possibility of wild dwelling (ibid). However, Kleinlosen and Milchert report that 60% of the allotments were inhabited during the war and provided accommodation for 80,000 otherwise-homeless Berliners (1989: 48–49).

Similarly, after the war, the hut became a homestead to migrants and Berliners who had been bombed out of their flats. For instance, the allotments in Wilhelmsruh, an allotment area in the north of Berlin, experienced an influx of several thousand inhabitants who repurposed a total of 2,953 allotment huts (Voll, 1983: 27). In June 1945, Berliners were tasked with reporting inhabitable huts to allow the city's district mayors to assign them to homeless Berliners (Schenk, 2011: 10). During this period, the police even helped self-organized alliances of settlers to protect their harvest against theft. In 1945 Hans Scharoun, then the director of the Department of Building and Municipal Housing [*Direktor der Abteilung Bau und Wohnungswesen des Magistrats von Berlin*], instituted rules for the construction of inhabitable huts of up to 30 square meters [*Richtlinien für die Errichtung bewohnbarer Lauben*] to provide safety for the gardens' old and new inhabitants (Landesverband Berlin der Gartenfreunde e.V., 2007: 47). Furthermore, these regulations permitted dwelling in allotment huts that had not initially been designated for housing (ibid: 46). Yet, the five-year period to which the decree was confined passed without major improvements to the housing situation in the rest of the city and without the removal of Berliners dwelling in allotments from their huts (Friedrich, 2007: 103). Figure 3.2 illustrates a typical hut and its occupants in 1952.

These developments unveil that much of today's dwelling infrastructures evolved through legal and administrative ambiguities, at times even through the promotion of dwelling practices through urban bureaucracies. At first sight, this observation speaks to the flexible boundaries between the legal and illegal, regulated and unregulated. But a closer look reveals that regulatory provisions were institutionalized and changed in a piecemeal fashion, by expanding or restricting regulations carefully and gradually rather than in sudden and radical ways. As subsequent chapters will show, regulations then became inert through buildings, infrastructures, norms, and habits of an older generation of today's urbanites who still grew up in an era in which allotment dwelling constituted a common form of housing.

FIGURE 3.2 Allotment dwelling in 1952. Source: Landesarchiv Berlin, F Rep. 290 (09) Nr. 001747. Photo: Peter Cürlis.

Variegations (1955–1989): Dwelling in the Divided City

Postwar housing in Berlin remained precarious for many. In addition to the city's desolate economic conditions, a lack of building material prolonged the housing crisis. Concomitantly, half a century in which the allotment holders maintained traditions, consolidated sociotechnical networks, and expanded their building stock complicated "unbuilding" (Hommels, 2008) the allotments' infrastructures of housing. To the extent that it happened at all, this "unbuilding" took distinct forms on both sides of the soon-to-be-constructed Berlin Wall. In 1948, political disputes fostered the split of the Central

Allotment Association and mirrored the separation of the city and the division of Germany into the German Democratic Republic (GDR) and the Federal Republic of Germany (BRD) (Landesverband Berlin der Gartenfreunde e.V., 2001: 176–177). In tracing these developments, this section explores how different notions of formality evolved on both sides of the politically divided city.

In the GDR, the allotment was seen as a relic and was merely tolerated, given that the labor force was thought to be needed elsewhere, i.e. in the development of the new state (Landesverband Berlin der Gartenfreunde e.V., 2001: 189). In 1959, the East faction of the former Central Allotment Association joined the Association of Gardeners, Settlers and Small Livestock Breeders [*Verband für Kleingärtner, Siedler und Kleintierzüchter"* (VKSK)]. This is an important detail that meant that the allotment gardeners were no longer organized solely around *their* objectives, but were subsumed into an organization that also represented interests of sustenance and housing provision. The VKSK was guided by a mission to develop political, economic, and cultural activities that solidified the foundations of the emerging worker and peasant state; in short, the education of a socialist-minded people (Landesverband Berlin der Gartenfreunde e.V., 2001: 208). In addition, the VKSK aimed at supporting the food supply. As interviewees reported, the gardens had buying stations where gardeners were able to sell their surplus harvest (e.g. interview, 10.06.2014).

The fifties and sixties also challenged the security and usage of the allotments in the city. On the one hand, gardens were demolished, despite their housing functions, to make space for new constructions as well as the expansive areas that were necessary to secure the political border. Many allotment gardeners were evicted, as their plots were incorporated into a buffer zone that demarcated the division of the city until reunification. Remaining allotments on the Eastern side were incorporated into systems of border control. As I learned in interviews with contemporaries, concessions to use the gardens in close proximity to the Berlin Wall were only granted to those party affiliates that GDR bureaucracies felt sure would not "jump the wall" – often members of the state security service, the *Stasi* (interview, 15.04.2014).[12] A permit system restricted entrance into these sites. On the other hand, the allotments increasingly became leisure spaces. With the rise of prefabricated housing [*Platten*] in the sixties, the housing market relaxed only slightly, and the narrow floor plans of the newly constructed flats – the so-called "proletarian lock boxes" [*Proletarierschließfächer*] – as well as the lack of travel opportunities increased the need for leisure spaces in the city. Concurrently, the permissible size of the huts – then named bungalows – was first raised to

30 square meters in 1985 and then to 40 square meters in a later decree (Friedrich, 2007: 104).

Dwelling in allotments was largely tolerated in the GDR. Schenk states that the GDR, or East Berlin for that matter, never issued a law that explicitly addressed allotment dwelling (2011: 12). In the absence of a free housing market, housing was administered by a department [*Wohnungsamt*] responsible for all matters of rent, including the provision of dwelling space. But while state agencies claimed total control of the existing stock (Grashoff, 2019: 549), the everyday realities were, as Mitchell notes, "saturated by a complex network of implicit, unwritten, and negotiable rules which helped to sustain the social edifice" (Mitchell, 2017: 277). Despite an abundance of run-down and officially vacant flats, housing remained a limited resource. Still, in 1990, 382,000 East Germans were without formally assigned accommodation (ibid). Thus, although state institutions technically forbade self-provisioning, practices of *Schwarzwohnen* in the run-down flats of Berlin's central districts were commonplace. Grasshoff estimates the existence of several thousand squatters in East Berlin alone (see also Chapter 4).[13,14]

Similarly in the allotments, administrations frequently granted allotment holders both the possibility of dwelling in their allotment huts and building permits for these huts – even if contrary regulations existed (interview, 29.04.2019). Allotment dwelling hardly contradicted the interests of the state. As allotments provided much-needed housing and lowered the numbers of people on official waiting lists, legalizing dwelling practices and their occupants' registration in the huts came to be common practice (interview, 18.09.2013). For instance, in 1956, the district of Berlin-Treptow registered 2,744 of 9,564 allotment holders as *Dauerbewohner*innen* [permanent occupants] (Schenk, 2011: 13). Grashoff similarly claims for *Schwarzwohnen* in the *Gründerzeit* housing stock that "some housing departments even took semi-legal measures to regularise unauthorised housing" (Grashoff, 2019: 553). In many cases, as he notes, "the element of 'care' proved to be more important than the element of 'total control'" (Grashoff, 2019: 552), thus outlining the ambiguous role of the communist state.

The situation in the Western part of the city mirrored the developments beyond the Wall. Circumscribed by the border and with limited recreational areas nearby, the allotments rapidly developed into leisure spaces (Landesverband Berlin der Gartenfreunde e.V., 2007: 53). However, due to the constrained availability of land, it was difficult to acquire a garden, and success was – as I was told – frequently a matter of bribing (interview, 23.04.2014). Waiting lists became further extended as many allotment colonies fell prey to the construction activities of the postwar era.[15] Planners not only built on allotment land because of the circumscribed expansion possibilities of the city; according to Bodenschatz, the modernization efforts in the sixties and seventies also constituted an attempt to eradicate the desperate housing situation in the "wild" and "unlawful" allotments (1987: 228). Bodenschatz writes of this time as the second Wilhelminian period [*zweite Gründerzeit*], as the expansive construction activities at the time completely restructured the city's periphery, just as it had in the previous period of turbo-growth at the turn of the twentieth century (ibid).

From 1954 on, the lessening of administrative tolerance went hand-in-hand with the stigmatization of the allotment residents, whose political affiliation also became a criterion for the redevelopment (Urban, 2013: 222). The most radical eradication of allotments took place in the course of the construction of a major housing estate, the Märkisches Viertel, which was completed in 1974. As a result of the postwar housing shortage, this site had been home to the largest self-contained area of allotment dwelling in Berlin, a locality called Wilhelmsruh (Bodenschatz, 1987: 232). It was alternately called "Egg Carton City" [*Eierkistenstadt*] or "Little Moscow" [*Klein-Moskau*], alluding to the dilapidated construction materials – often debris from bombed housing – and the suspected political affiliation of its inhabitants (Urban, 2013: 226). Following estimates from 1959, approximately 12,000 people lived in this area, of which two-thirds dwelled on allotment land (Bodenschatz, 1987: 235). All were to be displaced. As Bodenschatz notes, the construction of Wilhelmsruh reproduced two patterns of reconstruction that Berlin had previously experienced with the development of the tenement building. On the one hand, the aggressive modernist urban utopias of the time actively suppressed the "undesirable" history of older structures (1987: 232), sending a 45-year-long dwelling history into oblivion (cf. Urban, 2013: 221). On the other hand, the construction of Wilhelmsruh is marked by a pattern that Bodenschatz (1987) refers to as "social-authoritarian redevelopment" (my translation), in which restorations were initiated by hard-handed policing of the poor under the banner of social welfare.

Despite the fierce but unsuccessful contestation by the allotments' inhabitants, evictions began in 1963, heralding not only an area of tabula rasa reconstruction but also of resistance in the gardens. Since the seventies, the allotment history of West Berlin has also been a history of political organization. Numerous citizen initiatives, action committees, and demonstrations, fighting for the maintenance of the city's allotment land, challenged the public administration. Groening (2000: 171) even claims that the gardeners forced the local government of 1989 to step down because they were unsatisfied with the coalition's allotment politics. At the same time, the institutionalization of the Bundeskleingartengesetz (BKleinG) that was introduced in 1983 to replace the 1919 Allotment and Small-lease

Regulation provided the allotments with some security while also regulating their use. Crucially, this law included provisions stating that a hut was not to be built in ways that would allow for dwelling.[16] Unsurprisingly, these regulations barely conformed to the material and social infrastructure of the gardens, as I will discuss in more detail in Chapter 5. Despite granting some security, the law legally mapped the allotments' unofficial occupants out of the gardens.

In the face of these developments on both sides of the Berlin Wall, the city's eventual unification confronted administrations with coexisting formalities and their inherent ambiguities and contradictions. If this period led to the destruction of parts of the gardens' constructed space, some of the extant infrastructures, as well as a broader tolerance for informal dwelling on the part of the municipalities and the gardeners, continued to leave their traces. They proved difficult to adapt, as the next section will show. Particularly in the east of the city, the end of the communist state opened up a gap in which new demands, projects, and regulations regarding allotment dwelling were soon to be installed.

Adaptations (1989–2019): Allotments in the Unified City

Decades after German unification, Berlin is increasingly understood as a city that has gradually been brought in line with broader neoliberal trends (Eick, 2003, 2011; Bader and Bialluch, 2009). Long assumed to lag behind in the story of globalization, the city has seen many waves of investment and government changes that have attempted to reposition Berlin in the economic and geopolitical center of Europe (Rada, 1997; Krätke and Borst, 2000; Krätke, 2001; Cochrane, 2006a, 2006b; Häußermann and Kapphan, 2013). Much has been written about the particularity of the ways in which these global trends have shaped the city in the past 25 years (Häußermann et al., 2002; Cochrane, 2006a; Bader and Scharenberg, 2010; Merrill and Jasper, 2014). Here, I consider how the city's transformation from a divided island to a presumably global player in the world economy has shaped the fate of allotment land – and allotment dwelling with it. Tightly bound to the dominant trends of the past decades, this fate is embedded in a series of legal, social, and political challenges that came with the transition from a socialist planned economy to a capitalist market economy, particularly around the politics of restitution; it is predicated upon the city's entrepreneurial strategies and dependent on Berlin's social policies, especially its policies on housing. Moreover, this section outlines the social changes that have haunted the city in the wake of this restructuring, such as the increase in poverty and unemployment, and the resultant socio-spatial inequalities.

Above all, the shifting fate of the gardens within a unified Berlin has to be related to the legal and administrative changes that accompanied the inclusion of East Berlin into the political system of the BRD. This "unification" – in fact, a takeover of which the West predominantly dictated the conditions – implied the rapid restructuring of East Berlin's economy, its system of property relations, and its administrational infrastructure, among others. Tracing the development of allotment gardens helpfully illustrates how different understandings of formality collide, become incorporated in each other, and continue to leave their traces today.

Following the fall of the Berlin Wall, the unification treaty [*Einigungsvertrag* (EinigV)] guided the inclusion of the so-called "acceding territory" [*Beitrittsgebiet*] of the GDR into the new federal state. Based on this agreement, the freshly unified republic created a number of legal tools that were to lead the transition from the Eastern system to a nationwide legislation. In the allotments, these broader changes played out in three ways. First, they involved the adaptation or replacement of the outdated state architecture, including its administrative structures and personnel. These adjustments required staff of the bureaucratic apparatus responsible for the governance of the allotment gardens – among them several of my interviewees – to adapt to new rules and roles (e.g. interview 25.04.2014; interview 09.04.2014).[17] However, as I discuss later in the book, this adaptation did not impede a continuation of some of the routines, norms, and habits that had guided such work throughout the 40 years of division.

Second, Germany's unification implied that the allotments in the former GDR had to be integrated into the legal system of the BRD, including its property relations. Particularly, existing rules about permanent dwelling and the inventory of huts that legally exceeded 24 square meters made numerous necessary exceptions that remain in force to date (section 20 BKleinG). Moreover, land and property that had been owned or built before 1948 were to be returned to their previous owners, or to the heirs of those owners, as they were considered the "rightful" proprietors. Communal land was to be privatized (ibid) through the Property Law Validating Statute [*Sachenrechtsbereinigungsgesetz*; hereafter: SachenRBerG, literally: property rectification law] that was issued as part of a far-reaching process of "restitution," through which the rules of the former GDR were to be adapted to the German Civil Code [*Bundesgesetzbuch* (BGB)]. This law functioned for two-and-a-half decades to adapt, as Schmidt-Räntsch points out, "the material legal positions that were developed following socialist principles to the demands of a market economy" (2005: 49, my translation).

When the law expired in 2012, it had created both a set of legal standards that in their variance add complexity to contemporary ideas of formality, and a new "class" of small-scale landowners who participated in the wave of privatization that "rolled over" the East. Today, multiple plots to which I return, especially in Chapter 5, are partly owned by the allotment holders themselves.

Third, the elimination of existing structures was accompanied by a re-evaluation of the everyday culture of the East that touched all walks of life and implied, for instance, the belittlement or devaluation of GDR traditions. The demolition of the Palast der Republik [Palace of the Republic], the seat of the GDR parliament, counts as the most famous case in point (cf. Rada, 2000). In the garden colonies, this re-evaluation not only implied a rethinking of previous categories – for instance, bungalows were renamed into allotment huts, which crucially shifted an understanding of their use – but also a reconsideration of the social relations that had guided internal regulations.

Gardeners in the former East of the city describe the years following unification as a period of anarchism (e.g. interview, 18.06.2014). In the face of all-embracing confusion about the legal situation, many allotment holders speak of bustling construction activities that had become possible through their broader access to building materials (ibid). At the same time, the period was characterized by high vacancy rates in both parts of the city. In the former East, allotment holders used the new freedom to travel and, at times, gave up their plots. In the West, the reunification of the city firstly allowed for its suburbanization (Marquardt et al., 2013: 1547). In that part of the city, Berliners regained recreational possibilities beyond the Berlin Wall and, in part, surrendered their plots.

The rapid restructuring of the city after the fall of the Berlin Wall occurred alongside an alteration of planning norms and investment paradigms. In 1991, Berlin presented the first land development plan [*Flächennutzungsplan* (FNP)] of the united city – an extension of the development plan of its former West. According to Bernt et al., the plan was the result of a "gold rush mentality" (2013: 23) that was marked by high and fundamentally misconceived expectations of the city's future. Above all, it anticipated that the move of the German parliament to Berlin would trigger rapid and extensive population growth and the city's transformation into a global and economic hub, a "gateway city" between East and West (Cochrane and Jonas, 1999; Cochrane and Passmore, 2001; Eckardt, 2005; Colomb, 2012). To realize these expectations, the government fueled planning through the intensive deregulation of the construction market as well as the institution of tax reliefs and dirt-cheap loans that worked to foster real estate speculation (Krätke and Borst, 2000: 130; Shaw, 2005; Bernt et al., 2013: 67). I pick up from here and further expand on the implications of this speculation for Berlin's housing conditions in Chapter 4.

In the planning rush of the 1990s, the fate of the city's allotment land was bound to a political trade-off between the presumed necessity for new housing stock and a political commitment to preserve the gardens. In 1994, when the FNP came into effect after years of struggle, it firstly recorded allotments within this plan and thereby secured approximately 85% of the allotment land (Landesverband Berlin der Gartenfreunde e.V., 2001: 282). Put differently, i.e. from the perspective of the gardeners, 15% of this land, from that date, held the risk of eviction (ibid). While various compulsory purchase orders were issued in the subsequent decade, a first "Allotment Garden Development Plan" followed in 2004 [*Kleingartenentwicklungsplan* (KEP)] and allocated distinct levels of security to the individual colonies. The fate of allotment land in the face of different planning rationalities is the subject of Chapter 5.

Conclusion: Inert Infrastructures, Shifting Standards, and the Temporalities of Urban Transformation

This chapter has traced the gardeners' housing practices in Berlin's allotments throughout 15 decades of urban development to account for self-help strategies, the city's governing efforts, the ambiguities inherent in these efforts, and the vestiges these processes have left in the contemporary city. I focused on two themes.

First, this chapter has traced shifting regulatory projects to learn about the ways in which allotment dwelling was prohibited, tolerated, or sustained. Alongside the changing functions that "formal" planning officially attributed to allotments, the city relied on allotments as a backdrop in the face of multiple housing crises, as a relief scheme for the unemployed, as reserve land for construction, and as a space through which to implement projects of social reform. To be sure, the use of informality continuously changed function.

If the state's regulations variously shaped the underlying conditions, provided incentives, and heavily intervened in allotment dwelling, there is evidence of clear differences in the governance regimes of different periods: in the *Gründerzeit*, state agencies heavily policed informal dwelling in the *barrakias*; during the wars, state intervention was defined both by inherently ambiguous appeasement policies and by outlawing informality; during the years of division, state policy was characterized by "care" (Grashoff, 2019: 552) or toleration in the GDR and as ambiguous politics of displacement, sufferance, and stigmatization across the border in the West. To be sure, the governance of informal housing changed over time. But the processes in the gardens hardly moved toward formalization in a linear way. Berlin's population was repeatedly forced to retreat to irregular housing. Yet, the picture I have drawn here in very broad strokes has only been able to account for the ambiguities of legal regulation, and the discrepancies between the aims of different institutions, in limited ways. This historical narrative lacks a more intimate understanding of the state. Thus, the subsequent chapters turn to present-day negotiations to understand the entanglement of formality, informality, and the state in more depth.

Second, this chapter opens up questions concerning the temporalities of urban transformation. Jennifer Robinson suggests reconsidering "the new" as a basis for urban theorization (2013). Urban studies, Robinson argues, are too often driven by a quest for novel trends set only by a few supposedly paradigmatic global cities (2013: 659). To counter these narratives and disrupt a "progressive or linear historicism, in which one urban outcome or one temporality (the new) can do analytical service for the urban in general," she suggests opening up space for the "co-temporality of past, present and future" (ibid: 666). This chapter has aimed to explore the vestiges of past housing regimes to provide grounds from which to analyze the traces they have left in the contemporary city. While this chapter has shown much dynamism and transformation, I have also illustrated some of the ways in which past orders leave their legacies and continue to have considerable influence in the allotments today. I have particularly pointed to housing infrastructures, as well as long-standing routines and norms, that persisted in the allotments. Consider, for instance, the building stock. The allotment huts, "mutable immobiles" in Guggenheim's terms (2010), were built and permitted in times of severe housing crises, but today they present impediments for rapid urban change. These impediments highlight the inconsistencies in a tidy narrative of modernization and progress, with the coexistence of the traditional and the seemingly backward with repetitive attempts to erase the past. One might typically expect past vestiges of top-down planning to be appropriated by the tactics of urban residents who adapt them to contemporary needs. We will see that in the allotments the opposite is the case: the legacies of past subversion establish barriers to urban planning in present times.

The remainder of this book builds on these two ideas to trace allotment dwelling in present-day Berlin. Since Berlin's reunification, the city's housing market has undergone significant shifts that require asking, yet again, how these trends manifest in the gardens. In addition to the massive reduction of social housing and the ongoing speculation regarding the city's housing stock, the growth of its population has aggravated the situation in the rental market, particularly for low-income tenants (Aalbers and Holm, 2008; Uffer, 2013; Fields, 2018; Aalbers, 2019). In the ongoing legislative period (2016–2021), the new coalition government has declared affordable housing to be its central political aim (Senatskanzlei Berlin, 2016: 21). Yet, in spite of the local government's multifaceted attempts to shift current trends, by the time of this writing, the new coalition government has not yet delivered on its promises. Today's housing crisis has long reached the middle class. Thus, the Gecekondu this chapter began with is not only a necessary space from which to claim tenant-friendly legislations, but the widely overlooked histories of previous dwelling practices in this site also raise questions regarding today's retreat of Berliners into the gardens to mitigate the housing shortage. These questions guide Chapter 4.

Summary: Chapter 3

This chapter sets the scene. Beginning with the housing crisis of the 1870s, it traces the shifting political and normative placing of allotment dwelling over a century of allotment governance through turbulent years of war, post-war housing shortages, political division, and reunification. The chapter highlights two themes that are particularly pertinent to the narrative arc of this book. First, writing the history of allotments as a history of housing expands an understanding of the ways in which informality is entangled in the social projects and regulatory ambiguities of state agencies. Second, a situated historical framing of allotment dwelling provides the grounds for a discussion of modernity, obduracy, and development. It allows me to show how past regimes of governance are incorporated into contemporary regulatory projects. Moreover, in narrating the allotment history across time, it counters claims concerning the novelty of informality in the global North.

Notes

1 https://kottiundco.net/wer-wir-sind
2 The term *Schrebergärten* goes back to Dr. Ernst Innozenz Hauschild, who founded an allotment garden association in Leipzig in 1865, famously named after the social reformer and health campaigner Moritz Schreber (Lorbek and Martinsen, 2015: 103).
3 Poling (2014: 257) speaks of 15,000 homeless Berliners as of April 1872.
4 *Barrakias* or *Laubenstädte* are known to have been established outside the Cottbusser Tor (today Kottbusser Tor), as well as the Landsberger and Stralauer gates; see Huchzermeyer (2011: 54). Poling (2014: 258) also reports of shanties at the Halle and Frankfurter gates (present-day Hallisches and Frankfurter Tor).

5 The period between 1871 and 1873 is known as the *Gründerjahre* (literally: period of foundation), as reparation payments from France following the Franco-Prussian War of 1870/1871 triggered a speculative construction boom and a wave of industrialization.

6 Following Poling (2014: 258), the "city" housed 90 families in 52 dwellings in May 1872, and 2,000 before it was cleared in September of the same year.

7 *The Housing Question* appeared between 1872 and 1873 as a set of articles in the newspaper *Der Volksstaat* [the people's state]. Later publication dates reference edited reprints of this publication; see Engels (1932) [1887].

8 In contradiction to other sources, Poling (2014) claims that the eviction was peaceful.

9 Much gardening vocabulary, such as *Einfriedung* [enclosure] or *Gartenordnung* [gardening order], alludes to the process of taming "wild" nature while expanding the urban territory. The analogy even allows for an allusion to the will to install political order: to educate the *Ackerbürger* [field citizens] to become modern urbanites (see also Stein, 2000: 255).

10 Emergency Police Decree [*Sonderpolizeiverordnung*] of 17.07.1920, section 13.

11 This claim has been refuted by some of my interviewees.

12 This and all other interview translations are mine.

13 The term *Schwarzwohnen* [literally: black dwelling], explained in Chapter 1, is also used for other forms of unauthorized occupation under the communist regime.

14 The district of Berlin-Prenzlauer Berg counted 1,270 *Schwarwohnungen* [literally: black flats] in 1987; the district of Berlin-Friedrichshain 534 in 1979, see Grashoff (2016: n.p.).

15 The area used in West Berlin for allotments was reduced by 30% from 2,864 ha in 1947 to 1,965 ha in 1969; see Kleinlosen and Milchert (1989: 51).

16 Not unlike earlier regulatory measures, the BKleinG prescribes a particular understanding of how the allotment gardens are to be used and understood, but also protects the status of the allotments. Given the urban relevance as well as the socio-political value that German planning ascribes to the gardens, the law grants three exceptions to the German Civil Code (BGB). First, it defines the structural and horticul-

tural use of the allotment by fixing an area of 30% for the cultivation of fruits and vegetables and stipulating the maximum height of the hedges as well as the allowable size and central features of the hut (section 5). Second, it fixes conditions of lease. The BKleinG sets a rent cap that conforms to the land prices of commercial fruit and vegetable gardening (ibid), thus effectively institutionalizing a subsidization of allotment land. Moreover, the law provides protection against dismissal by institutionalizing a regime of liability and compensation. Leases are secured through indefinite contracts, contributing to a long duration of occupancy and a certain degree of inertia. Third, the BKleinG prescribes the institutional architecture of the allotments. Even in 1983, these regulations barely conformed to the actual material and social infrastructure of the gardens in Berlin. They are, in terms of Santos's well-known metaphor of laws and maps (1987), a projection of lawmakers' imagination as they represent the gardens through a "distortion" of the local status quo. Still today, these regulations prevail side-by-side with deviating norms, differently sized huts, and altering usage.

17   This institutional realignment also affected the previously separated allotment associations that were "united," which is to say that the VKSK was incorporated into West Berlin's association. This unified social institution, the Landesverband Berlin der Gartenfreunde, was responsible for 67,000 leaseholders in 738 colonies, as well as 175 settlers and homeowners (Landesverband Berlin der Gartenfreunde e.V., 2018). In May 2018, Berlin had a total of 71,473 leaseholders in 890 colonies that were organized through 18 district administrations throughout the city (SenUVK, 2018).

Chapter 4

Housing in the Margins
Halfway Between Exclusion and Homeownership

Early in the summer of my first fieldwork year, I met a young man in one of Berlin's Vietnamese eateries. I have called him Ron. Ron was in his mid-twenties. He leaned over the table I was sharing with my brother and commented on our ongoing conversation. I had just returned from an allotment in the district, a key site of my research project, and was recounting my hunt for a plot. My plan to lease an allotment and conduct participant observation of the local regulatory practices ran up against challenges: the huts that were currently free to lease were full of asbestos or came with a long list of requirements that had to be met. Ron told me that he had encountered similar problems, but he had found a plot that summer and installed a new, insulated hut so he would be able to inhabit the site permanently. Paying rent for a normal apartment, he reasoned, would no longer allow him to lay money aside to save for his pension. The hut was currently his best option to avoid living at his mum's (field notes, 13.05.2013).

Ron's living conditions are not what one has been taught to expect in a "developed" Northern city. However, his and similar narratives of transgression provide insights into the scope and nature of allotment dwelling and, through this discussion, allow me to consider questions regarding housing precarity in their material, social, and legal dimensions. More particularly, this chapter examines the housing biographies of short- and long-term residents in the gardens and discusses the wide variety of motives, constraints, and experiences that shape these biographies.

In the last decade, a substantial volume of literature that explores the tremendous vulnerability of renters in the face of capitalist urbanization has documented a housing crisis of global dimensions (Kemp, 2015; Aalbers, 2016; Madden and Marcuse, 2016; Schönig and Vollmer, 2018; Rolnik, 2019).

Housing in the Margins: Negotiating Urban Formalities in Berlin's Allotment Gardens,
First Edition. Hanna Hilbrandt.
© 2021 John Wiley & Sons, Ltd. Published 2021 by John Wiley & Sons, Ltd.

This literature captures the ways in which politico-economic structures work to put affordable rental space out of reach for lower-income tenants; it reveals the qualitative and quantitative changes in the social make-up of low-income neighborhoods that follow from these transformations, mostly in terms of "gentrification-induced displacement" (Atkinson et al., 2011: 8; Atkinson, 2015; Berner et al., 2015; Holm and Schulz, 2016; Lebuhn et al., 2017; Soederberg, 2018); and it captures the ways in which people experience these changes in everyday life (Hodkinson and Essen, 2015), as well as how they organize against and resist them (Hodkinson, 2012; Maeckelbergh, 2012; Muñoz, 2017, 2018; Vollmer, 2018, to cite but a few examples).

These research approaches can readily explain Ron's housing constraints in terms of the demographic, social, and politico-economic changes that have led to the widespread exclusion of city inhabitants from access to decent housing. However, critical urban and housing studies have been slow in documenting the wide-ranging forms of housing precarity that sit between studies of displacement and research on homelessness: people who house in irregular housing conditions.[1] How can we make sense of the ways in which urbanites meet their shelter needs without conforming to institutional standards? How can we grasp the voluntary choices people make within constrained markets, the uneven possibilities to make such choices, the room for maneuver people carve out within such constraints, and the multiple layers of vulnerability and risk inflicted on them? What do these experiences imply for an understanding of housing precarity? And can we relate the impacts of Berlin's housing crisis to forms of informal residency in the city's allotments?

This chapter suggests that an exploration of the complexity and heterogeneity of irregular housing conditions holds significant lessons for housing research, with pivotal implications for theorizations of housing precarity. To widen our understanding of the experience of residents who dwell in tension with institutional regulations, I argue that it is necessary to develop a multipronged perspective. First, it must account for the linkages of what might be understood as formal and informal domains that have heretofore been treated independently. Second, it must acknowledge more diverse forms of precarity, including their material, social, and legal dimensions and coincident levels of (in)stability, (dis)comfort, (in)security, and risk from a grounded and place-specific perspective. Third, it cannot take the binary notions of oppression and domination, exclusion and inclusion for granted; rather, it must be sensible to the ways in which processes of discrimination, appropriation, and bordering play out on the ground so as to provide room to acknowledge the place-specific dynamics and ambiguities of precarious housing.

To productively theorize the housing biographies in focus, I take my cue from two discrete debates: housing poverty, on the one hand, and informality, on the other. The former documents extreme levels of material precarity (i.e. poor physical conditions of substandard housing), legal insecurity (forced relocation and constrained tenure expectations), and experiences of eviction from rental housing, particularly for residents at the bottom of the income ladder (Anderson, 2008; Deverteuil, 2011; Desmond, 2012, 2016; Desmond and Gershenson, 2016; Desmond and Perkins, 2016; Purser, 2016; Routhier, 2019). Lately, this work has evolved around the term *housing precarity* (Dwyer and Phillips Lassus, 2015; Greenop, 2017; Lancione, 2019a; Joronen and Griffiths, 2019), with studies examining the flexibilization of rental conditions in, for instance, property guardianship (Ferreri et al., 2016); the policing of alternative forms of accommodation such as squats (Vasudevan, 2011); and the vulnerability of residents in substandard housing (Anderson, 2008; Sullivan, 2017; Durst, 2019); as well as the "hidden housing problem" of evictions (Hartman and Robinson, 2003) and the discrimination against lower-income and minority tenants (Künkel, 2018). This literature shares much ground with literature on *informal* housing (Durst and Wegmann, 2017; Mukhija, 2014; Chiodelli, 2019). Most work that explains informality's relation to housing policy (Lemanski, 2009; Landman and Napier, 2010), municipal regularization and eviction endeavors (Mendez and Quastel, 2015; Weinstein, 2017), struggles against displacement (Weinstein, 2014), and market efforts to capitalize on informal housing (Klaufus, 2010; Soederberg, 2015) addresses residents' multiple forms of precarity as well.

Here, the notion of precarity – frequently used to describe labor conditions within liberalized and deregulated markets (Waite, 2009: 415; Waite et al., 2015) – addresses a condition of structural context as well as "those who experience precariousness" (ibid) and are made vulnerable "relative to contingency and the inability to predict" (Ettlinger, 2007: 320). Beyond focusing on the debilitating conditions the structural context imposes upon low-income residents, some authors – in particular, those giving accounts from the global South – stress the ambiguity of precarity to include the capacitating potential of living at the margins: the inventive, tactical, and strategic practices of people who experience precarity and create capacities to overcome (Jayne and Hall, 2019; Joronen, 2019; Joronen and Griffiths, 2019; Schilling et al., 2019) and negotiate these conditions (Joronen, 2019: 839). While the experiences this chapter reports of echo the double meaning of precarity as both structurally excluding and potentially capacitating, this chapter's title alludes to the residents' marginality – a similarly open-ended term. I use it in multiple ways: to reference an approach to theorization that combines a more structural analysis (Wacquant, 1993) with more relational and grounded accounts of marginality (Datta, 2012), analyzing everyday processes at the margins from the inside out (see Lancione, 2016a for a detailed discussion on the multiple approaches to marginality). Moreover, the margins hint at the geopolitical place of my data collection, mostly on the periphery – both of the city and of housing policies' attention. Finally, the term refers to the residents' marginal practices and struggles within the cracks, or margins, of legal systems.

Building on these insights, this chapter presents a typology of the multiple modalities of informal housing in allotment huts. In response to the scarcity of knowledge on this terrain, I provide an ethnographic account that profiles the residents' housing biographies, the forms of housing they establish across domains of varying degrees of regulation, and the ways in which they experience these conditions. However, before proceeding, to link allotment dwelling to contemporary housing debates it is expedient to address a set of general and specific contextual issues, namely, the German housing market and the state of housing in Berlin, with particular attention paid to precarious housing. The following two sections attempt, first, to build a typology of housing trajectories and, second, to analyze people's experiences of housing. I conclude with the implications of these experiences for questions of housing precarity and the repercussions of Berlin's housing crisis on the city's allotments.

Housing Berlin

Let me start by providing some historical context about the German system of housing provisioning. In the GDR, housing was understood to be part of the state-planned economy (Bouvier, 2002; Buck, 2004). The development of land was at the state's command, rent prices were frozen and amounted on average to 3% of household income (Heinz and Kiehle, 2000), and a state administration allocated housing (Rau, 2012). Yet, although market mechanisms had been set aside, and although new construction in the form of prefabricated housing [*Plattenbau*] was funded extensively, the postwar housing crisis persisted throughout the duration of the regime. The radical shortage of resources and labor, among other challenges, caused continuous cutbacks in the quality and scale of new-built housing, while the old housing stock deteriorated under high vacancy rates (Knorr-Siedow, 2005; Grashoff, 2011, 2019).

Across the border in the West, ample tax benefits, large subsidies, and mortgage interest reductions supported the construction of new-built housing: first, the *Wohneigentumsförderung*, a key pillar of German housing policy, promoted homeownership for the middle classes through state support. The second pillar of West German housing policy consisted of various investment programs aiming at the construction of social housing. To produce social housing, the state either paid investment subsidies to private investors or made low-interest loans available to them (Egner, 2019). Rather than stigmatized or confined to the poor, the rental sector soon came to be characterized as both secure and social (Kemp and Kofner, 2010), and it housed the majority of the BRD's citizens.

Already toward the end of the 1960s, however, the idea that the state should provide access to housing for broad sections of the population was slowly replaced in the BRD in favor of a more market-oriented approach (Jenkis, 1985). This manifested itself, among other ways, in the gradual dismantling of rent control for older flats. In the mid-1980s, a withdrawal from the provision of public housing became more evident – most critically through, first, the abolition of a regulatory provision that had enforced the production of social housing, the so-called *Wohnungsgemeinnützigkeit* [housing for common public interest, my translation], and second, the massive conversion of public housing into private ownership (Droste et al., 2010; Droste and Knorr-Siedow, 2014).

Following the German reunification, processes of market liberalization, privatization, and associated austerity measures continued to undermine housing and employment security. From the 1990s onwards, increasing unemployment rates coincided with the gradual retrenchment of state assistance.[2] Together with the cutback in social housing and the reduction of protections for renters, these developments soon fostered new levels of social exclusion (Mayer, 2009). Berlin, a city of renters, has experienced the effects of these developments in particularly pronounced ways.[3] In 1991, the Berlin Senate still managed 28% of the city's housing stock through its own companies that were concomitantly subject to maintaining rent control (Haeussermann and Kapphan, 2004: 44).[4] Politics of *Behutsame Stadterneuerung* [careful urban renewal] – a renter-oriented approach to planning that was pushed through by the city's tenants and further established with the International Building Exhibition (IBA) in 1984 (Bodenschatz, 1987: 206–10) – had allowed the preservation of much of the tenement housing stock of the *Gründerzeit* (Bodenschatz, 1987). Yet, in the following years, a set of social, economic, and political setbacks dismantled this housing safety net. Let me sketch out the cornerstones of these developments.

In 1991, the decision to move the seat of government from Bonn to Berlin was accompanied by massively overblown expectations of Berlin's future as a global city. It triggered a set of new visions and planning approaches that led to a wide-ranging transformation of the city's building stock that was expanded and refurbished to cater to these expectations (Cochrane and Jonas, 1999; Cochrane and Passmore, 2001; Cochrane, 2006b). This planning hype stands in sharp contrast to the huge tasks the city was faced with, namely to countervail, on the one hand, the end of the federal support payments that West Berlin had received and, on the other hand, the collapse of the manufacturing industry and a related decline in job opportunities (Haeussermann and Kapphan, 2004; Krätke, 2004a: 519). The foreseen growth in the service sector never compensated for this erosion of jobs and economies (Krätke, 2004a: 512, 2004b: 59).[5] Instead, the concomitant and increasing precarization of the German labor market (Brady and Biegert, 2017) soon turned Berlin into "the capital of cleaning crews and security sheriffs," as Krätke and Borst frame it (2000: 44). From 1992 onwards, office rents fell (Krätke and Borst, 2000: 133) and vacancy rates in office space exploded (Krätke, 2004b: 62). The decrease in Berlin's population alongside these developments also led to a decline in housing prices throughout the 1990s. Ten years after reunification, Berlin found itself in a critical debt crisis that reverberates to date.[6]

As has been well demonstrated (Aalbers and Holm, 2008; Holm, 2008; Wijburg and Aalbers, 2017a), this context provided a fertile ground for the housing crisis that the city has been witnessing since the 2010s. This crisis was triggered by three developments. First, a reduction in social housing resulted from the termination of rent caps for market-owned social housing (Uffer, 2014). The privately owned social housing stock remained designated as social housing only as long as credits were being repaid (Holm, 2008: 102). Whenever these periods end, the affected housing stock is released from its time-bound social orientation, thus converted into profit-oriented real estate (ibid). Meanwhile, local politics came to favor private ownership in the considerably neglected tenement buildings of East Berlin and fostered highly subsidized processes of urban renewal that soon led to rising rents (Haeussermann and Kapphan, 2004; Bernt, 2012). Further, the privatization of state-owned housing companies (most prominently the Gemeinnützige Siedlungs- und Wohnungsbaugesellschaft [GSW], later to be owned by the Deutsche Wohnen AG) between the mid-1990s and the mid-2000s reduced significant numbers of social housing units (Moss, 2014: 1443). This privatization can be seen as the immediate reaction to a banking scandal and subsequent debt crisis that the coalition government of Christian and Social Democrats (CDU and SPD) had produced. Beyond this immediate scandal, this wave of privatization has to be read in the context of the city's austerity measures (Peck, 2012). To solve the debt crisis, the subsequent coalition of Social Democrats (SPD) and the Party of Democratic Socialism (PDS, today Die Linke) sold off major parts of the city's holdings, including its communal housing and other prime pieces of real estate, as well as parts of its infrastructure, to private corporate investors (Beveridge, 2011; Lederer and Naumann, 2011: 130; Beveridge and Naumann, 2014).[7]

Second, the global financial crisis of 2007/2008 hit Berlin's housing market particularly hard. Historically low interest rates, volatile stock markets, and the exceptional stability of the German housing market during the crisis moved the city's housing stock into the spotlight of capital flows and led to an appreciation trend that continues to date (Unger, 2017; Wijburg and Aalbers, 2017b). Institutional and private investors have turned to buy, sell, and resell both the tenement housing stock of the *Gründerzeit* as well as the above-mentioned social housing units. As some of the new proprietors are listed real estate companies, whose obligations toward their shareholders inevitably outweigh their commitment to their tenants (Unger, 2017, 2018), the new proprietors have recklessly pushed for profit-oriented strategies. These include the modernization and lucrative resale of housing stock – at times in forms of condominiums – or the exploitation of leeway for rent increases through strategies of housing (dis)investment, such as the reduction of housing maintenance and management, in what Holm calls "discount-housing" (2008). Without doubt, both strategies have crucially impacted the affordability, accessibility, and quality of rental space.

Third, Berlin has experienced unprecedented growth rates that were not anticipated by the city's senate: between 2008 and 2018, Berlin grew from 3,362,843 to 3,748,148 residents (Amt für Statistik Berlin-Brandenburg, 2019: 4), thus gaining 385,305 residents, almost the size of a secondary city. In those same years, Berlin lost approximately 100,000 social housing units, with trends continuing in this direction, as I detail below (Investitionsbank Berlin, 2007, 2017). That these developments have been accompanied by the general polarization of German incomes makes the situation particularly severe for those at the bottom of the income ladder. These include 63,577 refugees who lived in Berlin at the end of 2016, most of whom came to the city in 2015 and 2016 (SenSW, 2017: 10). These three developments which have defined the housing market since 2010 have turned rent costs into a prime cause of poverty.

From 1990 to 2000, Berlin's stock of social housing decreased from 482,000 housing units to 267,000 (Investitionsbank Berlin, 2002: 67). By 2010, this number was further reduced by 37% to 165,000 units (Investitionsbank Berlin, 2012: 35).[8] These reductions have to be read in relation to approximately 1.16 million households (equivalent to 58%) that were entitled to social housing in 2010 (Investitionsbank Berlin, 2012: 36). At the end of 2016, the city was left with a housing stock of 114,915 social housing units out of a total stock of 1,916,517 flats (Investitionsbank Berlin, 2017).[9] This leaves Berlin with social housing stock for 6% of its population, which has a poverty rate of 16.6% (Amt für Statistik Berlin-Brandenburg, 2017: 6).

More recently, the city's economy has experienced an upward trend that is predominantly caused by the growth of knowledge-intensive, construction, and media industries, as well as trade (SenWEB, 2018). Additionally, Berlin has become a hub for creative industries while it is also promoted as the new "start-up capital" (cf. McKinsey, 2010; Lange, 2011). Finally, the "new" Berlin has triggered a boom in tourism (mostly "EasyJet tourism") (Novy, 2013). These developments have further increased the scarcity of housing for those who need to rely on affordable rent.

These developments have left their imprints on the security and affordability of housing. The literature documents what Peter Marcuse calls physical or economic "direct displacement," the "displacement of a household from the unit that it currently occupies" (1985: 205), as a result of harassment (for example, landlords who switch off electricity or heating), rising rents, the conversion of rental units into freehold apartments, or the demolition of affordable housing. A pioneering study documenting the relation between regeneration processes and compulsory evictions in Berlin's neighborhoods has, for the first time, quantified the number of residents threatened with eviction. It finds that 27,858 eviction proceedings were issued between 2009 and 2012 (Berner et al., 2015: 15), particularly in low-income neighborhoods (ibid: 17).[10] Yet, the literature disputes the extent to which displaced populations relocate to the peripheries of the city. To be sure, the "inflow" of poor households into peripheral neighborhoods, in particular into the large housing estates in Nord-Marzahn, Nord-Hellersdorf, and Spandau-Mitte (SenSU, 2015) provides evidence of increasing displacement of poor residents from the urban core. But households also find themselves displaced from living standards, whereby they remain in their neighborhoods at the cost of having to use a significantly higher percentage of their incomes on rent (Häußermann et al., 2002; cf. Häußermann and Kapphan, 2002; Förste and Bernt, 2016).

Geographically, these processes of displacement and gentrification have taken a particular spatial pattern that Holm (2011) describes as a spiral movement of real estate appreciation [*Aufwertungspirale*]. This movement took off in the districts of Mitte and Prenzlauer Berg (cf. Bernt, 2012) and continued on to impact Friedrichshain, Kreuzberg (cf. Holm, 2014), and the northern parts of Neukölln (Huning and Schuster, 2015). In 2016, the districts of Moabit, Wedding, Gesundbrunnen, and Nord-Schöneberg also appeared to be affected (Döring and Ulbricht, 2016: 38). These gentrifying areas tend to be characterized by high poverty rates. In the face of annual rent increases of 4.2% and on the basis of data collected between 2007 and 2012, Schulz (2017: 65–67) estimates citywide displacement rates of 4.1%, whereby gentrifying areas experience rates as high as 6.2%.[11] In the latter areas, this development is accompanied by a drop in poverty rates of about 3.1% (2017: 65); however, this is not because of collective income gains, as one might think, but precisely through that displacement of low-income tenants (ibid).

Today, housing exclusion not only touches the city's low-income residents but also has become the order of the day across higher income ranges (Holm et al., 2017). In addition, the literature documents more indirect patterns of displacement, such as "exclusionary displacement," when former working-class neighborhoods experience processes of closure that inhibit lower-income households from moving into the area (Marcuse, 1985: 206). Such closure becomes evident in the emergence of an alternative and substandard housing market for particularly vulnerable groups, such as refugees (Mattern, 2015). While the use of gymnasiums and lightweight constructions for provisional housing still counts as a peripheral phenomena, Berlin has seen the establishment of a container village for students, who – excluded from the regular market – constitute a lucrative business for investors (Linde, 2015; Mattern, 2018). The increasing number of holiday homes used for temporary housing and the use of centrally located public spaces for the most precarious forms of camping have occasionally introduced the topic of housing informalization into the debate (Hernádi, 2015; Holm, 2017).

Despite these insights and the urgency of recent transformations, existing scholarship fails to answer a number of crucial questions. First, given the nearly exclusive focus on the "G-locations" (Atkinson et al., 2011), i.e. gentrifying areas, the more recent conditions of those displaced, now in their new sites of residency, remain largely understudied and not yet understood (Neupert's 2016 study of a Berlin trailer park and the multifaceted and complex motives and constraints of its inhabitants can be considered an exception here). Second, the literature discusses displacement predominantly in terms of relocation. It pays insufficient analytical attention to the ways in which people find possibilities of alleviating their precarious housing situations. Third, as previously noted, there continues to be a crucial lack of empirical knowledge on forms of informal housing. To address these gaps, the remainder of this chapter offers insights into the housing experiences and motives of those living in allotment huts.

Housing Biographies

It is supposed to be poverty, material precarity, and legal insecurity that best characterize how people come to dwell informally. However, allotment holders living in their huts are from a wide variety of socioeconomic backgrounds across the lower strata of the income range and, similarly, their dwelling conditions and building standards vary. There is no census data on the inhabitants of Berlin's allotments, but a 2008 study of allotment gardens conducted by the Federal Office for Building and Regional Planning (BBR) provides useful statistical data on the characteristics of all allotment holders across the Federal Republic (BMVBS and BBR, 2008). Of the approximately 2.5 million people who profit from an allotment plot (BMVBS and BBR, 2008: 15), 33% are not working (ibid: 5), and 8% of those surveyed are jobseekers, which – in relation to all gardeners of an employable age – amounts to a federal average of 17% and of 26% in colonies of the former East (ibid). Of all gardeners, 55% have a monthly income between €800 and €1,800 per household. Approximately 10% of the gardeners live off less than €800 per household (ibid: 69). Only 7% of all gardeners have a migration background, although the statistical trend describes an increase of gardeners in this "group" (ibid: 68). Although these numbers indicate that gardeners are older, poorer, less likely to be employed, and less (ethnically) diverse than the average resident in Germany, this data can only provide a contextual background against which a fuller understanding of the biographies and motivations of those who move into the gardens can emerge (cf. SenUVK, 2019: 40). The qualitative data of my study indicates three housing patterns.

First, allotment gardens are inhabited by long-term residents. These dwellers may have been born in a garden shed or settled in allotments as a result of previous housing shortages, following the Second World War or during the division of Berlin (see also Chapter 3). Some people I interviewed had been bombed out of their houses, had moved into allotments during the Second World War, and had grown up in larger families in their small huts without further options to move elsewhere. Once these options finally came, the hut had become their home, a lifestyle they had learned to favor vis-à-vis more "urban" forms of housing. A resident I spoke to reported of his neighbor – a permanent resident for decades. The neighbor's family had wanted to move him into a flat when he was diagnosed with cancer. But he decided against the option. "He is an allotment-shed person" [*ein Laubenmensch*], my respondent commented. He could no longer live a flat (interview, 17.09.2013). In a similar case, a resident had been able to continue dwelling informally in her hut because the social welfare office supported making the hut accessible for her wheelchair (interview, 16.08.2013). However, I also encountered stories in which the discomfort of the hut, among other reasons, had led long-term residents to give up their lifestyle (interview, 16.05.2019).

In part, these housing biographies are those of the allotment gardens' 1,131 institutionally recognized "legal" inhabitants (documentation of the Berlin Senate, provided in an interview, 18.09.2013) who have, at various points in history, been granted a dwelling right. Yet, some of the older gardeners who have been dwelling on allotments since the war have never been institutionally recognized through a dwelling permit. Mr. Schmitz, for example, told me that when the opportunity arose, he couldn't afford the increase in payment that this official recognition implied (interview, 10.07.2014).[12] Some of the younger inhabitants have inherited gardens from legally recognized inhabitants and have been the third, fourth, and sometimes the fifth generation to live in allotment huts. Yet, legally speaking, children of permit holders cannot inherit the dwelling right – even if they grew up in the gardens and even if the hut is endowed with a building right (interview, 10.05.2019). I will come back to one of these cases in Chapter 7.

The biographies of long-term residents differ considerably between the former East and West Berlin due to the opportunities created by the SachenRBerG, which were provided only for East Berliners, as I outlined in Chapter 3. In addition to those who used this law to buy or legally lease their plot for the purpose of dwelling, the city recognized the residency of gardeners who had located the "center of their lives" in the gardens before 1990 – mostly people who could not afford to buy their plot. Those who bought or leased their plots through the SachenRBerG have been able to sell this right, and through these sales have brought younger residents into the gardens. But today, many of these residents are older pensioners living on budgets that never allowed them to buy a single-family house.

Second, there is a pattern of biographies in which gardeners gradually extended their seasonal stays in the gardens, to the point where they moved out of their flats entirely during the whole of summer and, at times, permanently as well. For instance, Ms. Peters reported that she had been gardening for 16 years before she was able to take over a leasehold contract:

> I came to Berlin in 1976 and lived in a new housing development until 2013. We permanently lived out here in the gardens between March and October and only returned to the apartment to empty our mailbox and so on. We had good neighbors who also had a garden here. And in 2013, I was lucky and could enter into a leasehold agreement of an older couple. (Interview, 29.04.2019)

In this way, *Sommerwohnen* – moving "out" into the colonies in early spring and returning "back" into the city in late autumn – can lead to steadier inhabitation. Participants suggested that many of the summer-dwellers have a one-room apartment in proximity to their allotments, which they use to register their official address and return to between October and March while, at times, subletting their flat out of financial necessity. The motives for this form of dwelling include, as I will later show, the desire to build a single-family home where the means for homeownership are out of reach, the need to overcome financial bottle-necks, the desire to improve poor living conditions, or the necessity to save on rent – in short, to be able to afford a better quality of life and to overcome severe constraints.

I encountered people who had been forced to move flats, and when newly found flats were only available far from the center of the city, their hut and garden plot became more central to their workplace and other relations of everyday life. Similarly, when relocating, people moved into lower-quality rental stock, fostering the piecemeal withdrawal of gardeners into their huts. They had, in terms of Marcuse (1985), been displaced from their living standard but aimed to evade such displacement by relocating into the hut. Take the example of Mr. Neumann (interview, 17.09.2013). He and his wife had owned a small business in southern Germany, but returned to Berlin when the business ceased to make a profit in the wake of the 2008 financial crisis. Back in Berlin, they found an allotment plot and an apartment in the street they had previously inhabited. In the meantime, however, the housing complex had been bought by a listed real estate company – die Deutsche Wohnen – which had modernized the flats and subsequently raised the rent. Thus, on their return, the couple could only afford a flat with one room less than they previously had. Hence, my respondent moved "out" into the garden between March and October and, in this way, compensated for the loss of living space. Other allotment dwellers who told me that they were self-employed with insecure income streams and precarious labor conditions, or that they were pensioners receiving only meager benefits, used allotment dwelling to similar ends, namely, to compensate for employment insecurities or (in-work) poverty and to widen their financial margins for everyday consumption (interview, 13.08.2013).

However, most people I met, or was told about, who gradually retreated into the gardens to lessen their rent burden were benefit recipients, most of whom had been made redundant in the years of increasing unemployment that began in the late 1990s (interview, 16.04.2019). This context coincides with a 2005 reform of social policy, commonly known as Hartz IV, which decoupled the relation of real rents and housing subsidies, i.e. widened the gap between them. In consequence, real rents increasingly exceed the maximum residential allowance payments – crucially limiting the access of benefit recipients to decent housing. Already by 2005, Andrej Holm predicted that, particularly in the face of increasing modernization efforts and the related price increases of more central flats, such "well organized displacement" (2005: 146, my translation) would force people to move into the prefabricated building stock in Marzahn and Hellersdorf, districts on the periphery of Berlin. Additionally, the above data suggest a relation between this social policy and benefit recipients' displacement into allotment huts.

Other exceptional dwelling biographies can be indexed under this rubric. I learned with interest that property in the gardens does not enter into insolvency estates, so that on very rare occasions people who had gone bankrupt found a last refuge in their huts. Finally, gardeners became dwellers by moving temporarily after significant interruptions in their lives; for instance, when partners sought to separate their living space after a divorce, or young adults moved out of the parental home.

Third, the gardens are inhabited by newly arrived residents who have not had any previous relations to allotment gardening but moved into the gardens out of acute exclusion or strategic choice. Recall, for instance, Ron, the resident with whom I began this chapter, who relocated into the allotment because he failed to find affordable rental space that would have also granted him enough financial security in the future. Exclusion is here not the consequence of eviction, but the superposition of an overall precarity of the living situation with the unavailability of affordable rental space. In his and very few other cases, the search for a garden is more strategically oriented toward finding a space that would allow for the maintenance of everyday life while staying under the radar (interview, 27.09.2018 and field notes, 13.05.2013). I come back to these strategies in Chapter 6.

There is anecdotal evidence of yet other trajectories. These include people who stay in friends' huts in situations of need, and people who had been made to believe that it would be legal to reside in an allotment and had bought a hut on eBay out of naivety and in the face of deception or fraud (interview, 07.08.2013). Interestingly, a respondent moved into an allotment in part to experiment with a more ecologically-minded lifestyle. He concluded:

> I am not saying that this is the most ecological thing one can do. When one lives in a house with, say, seven people, I don't think it would be less ecological than what I do. But in comparison to the 80- or 120-square-meter house at the rural fringe, this is *much* better. How does one want to live? And how do we want humankind to live? And I say: It would be cool if everyone would do the same – 24 square meters, that's it! And a garden … and we would have fewer problems. (Interview, 27.09.2018)

My data is limited regarding cases of acute hardship, because residents on the brink of homelessness are most vulnerable and thus most difficult to interview. My attempts to speak to a group of Romanian working migrants, who had settled in an already evicted allotment colony that stood empty awaiting the construction of a major highway, came to nothing when, I assume, both my respondents and I felt threatened by one another. I spoke to the head of a colony about a case in which a group of Romanian workers had settled in a colony from which they were subsequently displaced (see also Hilbrandt, 2019). For reasons that will become clearer throughout the book, there is evidence that these cases are rare. The increasing costs of allotment huts make them unavailable for people on very limited budgets.[13] Access is further hampered by long waiting lists not favorable to cushioning acute hardship. Finally, those already confronted with various processes of bordering in the labor and housing market – as in the case of the Romanians – tend to encounter further processes of social exclusion in the gardens as well. These processes are the subject of Chapter 6.

Housing Experiences

The individual experiences of dwelling in allotments vary widely. How allotment dwellers discuss their housing situation depends crucially on the voluntariness, comfort, and security of that situation, but most of my interviewees stressed four themes: questions of ownership, feelings of belonging, concerns about (dis) comfort, and notions of (in)security. Let me address each one in turn.

First, allotment holders overwhelmingly emphasized a sense of ownership that the allotments promised. In difference to the relatively constrained usage rights of a city flat, the hut – whether for habitation or not – would offer, as I was told, a sense of autonomy over the use of building and land. Many spoke to me about their diligent efforts to improve the hut, enlarge it, and enhance its infrastructure, and not only due to necessity. For instance, my interviewee Lukas noted:

> And finally, I had the feeling that I wanted to settle down. I realize it is all in the head. So here, I have kind of built a little nest for myself. You can put it that way. And more will be done. But I have already invested quite a lot. It's about making the house a home. I already find it very cozy. And all the ideas I still have. This is only the beginning of more things that I can realize here and I am looking forward to it. (Interview, 27.09.2018)

Ownership is here not only about material property, but also about the accomplishment of creating, demarcating, and enclosing a space that offers an emotional connection.[14] It is here that the term "dwelling" reflects its conceptualization as both "enclosure" (Harrison, 2007: 624) and "event" (Rose, 2012: 758). If the process of dwelling constitutes, as per Harrison, "the spacing of relation" (2007: 643; see also Kraftl and Adey, 2008; McFarlane, 2011c; Rose, 2012), building "a little nest" is a process of crafting a relationship of belonging through the socio-material practice of remodeling the hut into a home.

Second, and closely related to the theme of ownership, most people I interviewed spoke about their experiences of community and belonging. They described the colonies as "a deeply committed community" [*eine feste-ingschworene Gemeinschaft*]:

> Well, in these many years we have known each other so well and families have grown old together. This "practice of collectivity" [*das Miteinander*] is like a little village. [For instance,] there was an empty plot and then the son moved in – everyone who wanted could stay. And this made it possible that the son, a "recreationist" [*ein Erholungssuchender*, someone seeking relaxation rather than a home] could register at his parents' who have property here. This all works well. We look out for one another, the young and the elderly. (Interview, 29.04.2019)

> Well, I would say it's like one big family here. Many don't want it. They go into their gardens and say: "It's enough. I don't want to participate." But at the core, there is one big family and when there's trouble every-one acts together. (Interview, 10.07.2014)

> The garden or the hut, it's just really pleasant! I am out here in the sum-mer and the neighbors … it's all a great sense of collectivity. Better than in the rental flat – there you rarely see anyone … you are hardly recog-nized. (Interview, 16.08.2013)

A respondent told me proudly that when his son had been born in their allotment shed, the association had raised the flag of the colony for one week (interview, 10.07.2014). Allotment gardeners stressed that there would always be something going, in comparison to the isolation of the "urban" flat. This feeling of community is supported through various collective activities, such as women's nights, societies that play card games, voluntary fire brigades, or even a joint savings club (interview, 23.06.2014). However, this romantic portrayal of collectivity and community covers up cases of isolation and neglect that gardeners spoke about only secondarily: cases where people die in their huts or cut off all social relations, or where gardeners with mental prob-lems completely withdraw into their huts. These were not residents I was able to interview, but fellow gardeners reported about such cases of social isolation repeatedly (e.g. interview, 26.08.2014).

Third, the themes of comfort and discomfort present themselves as powerful but ambiguous narratives. On the one hand, gardeners stressed the love of gardening, the comfort the hut offered versus the flat in the city, and the enjoyment of living in close proximity to nature:

> When you have seen your grandma and grandpa in the garden, you just like it. It's just a model of living. (Interview, 29.04.2019)

> Well, when you came from work and walked through the colony … it was like being on holiday. Everything green, the scents and flowers … and when you go to work in the morning and it has rained everything smells incredibly good. (Interview, 29.04.2019)

> I just find it totally cozy … being sort of in the garden all the time. And I find it beautiful. It's not only the ecological and not only the financial. I just like it! (Interview, 27.09.2018)

The German word *Laube* [best translated as "arbour"] stems etymologically from the word foliage [*Laub*] and is, following this connotation, a leafy structure providing only rudimentary shelter. In Berlin, however, even the smaller allotment huts resemble small-scale residential buildings, rather than gardening sheds in the above sense (see Chapter 5). Still, between them there is a wide range of different standards, whereby even in the more "luxurious" huts living conditions are precarious nonetheless: fire hazards, poor provisions for sewage disposal, and makeshift infrastructures, along with legal limitations to properly renovate, for instance, leaking roofs define residential building quality. Frequently, allotments are located on undesirable land; for example, near railways or other noisy or unsalutary uses of land. Rather than romanticizing living in these huts, statements regarding the comfort of living in a hut must be placed in the context of dilapidation and poor infrastructural conditions experienced as well (see Chapter 5):

> Of course, living in Marzahn [a district in former East Berlin characterized by large housing estates] was easier in the winter [than living in an allotment hut]. You didn't have to carry coal and ash. I was familiar with that from back home. But I wasn't very keen. (Interview, 11.06.2014)

Surprisingly, most people I encountered were not ashamed to report that they were living in an allotment hut. Unlike trailer living that is rife with the stigma of "trailer trash" (Kusenbach, 2009; Sullivan, 2018), or other well-known forms of informal inhabitation, allotment dwelling is perhaps too invisible, tucked away, far-flung, and widely dispersed to be charted by popular culture.[15] Asked whether he would be embarrassed to tell others that he lived in his hut, a respondent told me that he would not be ashamed of telling anyone where he lived. Instead, he mentioned security concerns: "How many would you speak to before the news circulates … before it really gets out?" (interview, 27.09.2018).

This concern links to a fourth theme pertaining to different aspects of insecurity, including material, legal, and physical insecurities. To start, allotment holders reported that living in a hut is dangerous to one's health and safety. Used as recreational areas, allotments are certainly seen to promote good health. As dwelling spaces, they are health hazards: they lack access routes for rescue vehicles and have substandard, inadequate fire protection, leading to unnecessary fatalities in the gardens. Respondents noticed that, in cases of illegal occupation, fire incidents in huts tended not to be insurable, exposing residents to possibilities of financial loss (interview, 23.04.2014). Additionally, and to my surprise, the most dominant narrative of insecurity was that of frequent burglaries in the gardens. Walking across any allotment, one encounters numerous signs warning of the "vigilant neighbor," security cameras, and watchdogs. As a respondent told me, "I actually feel quite safe, but burglary *is* an issue. I hadn't thought that … I was told so, and it is *actually a big issue*" (interview, 27.09.2018). Less surprisingly, people spoke about insecurities of tenure when asked if they were afraid of being evicted:

> I honestly have to say yes. Because there is someone at the district level who is very eager to prohibit housing. Well, you can only have the hedge at one meter twenty [height]. And the ovens, I think since 2015 or 2016 that is no longer possible, because of the fire hazard. I get it. Then we just have to heat with electricity. But yes, I am pretty worried … If that [housing prohibition] is carried out, then we get a warning and, if we don't move out, a dismissal. (Interview, 16.04.2019)

Naturally, these experiences are dependent on a dweller's particular legal situation. For legally recognized dwellers, insecurities may center on the continuous status of their colony's land as allotment land; for those in violation of the building code, vulnerabilities center on the maintenance of their huts. Yet others are more at risk of being further displaced. Remarkably, the fear of being completely displaced did not play out as such a strong theme. As I argue in Chapter 6, gardeners and regulators have mostly come to a consensual agreement regarding the occupancy rules about huts. However, the lack of significance attributed to this theme may well go back to restrictions of my data. It seems self-evident that those afraid of further displacement may likely be some of the many gardeners who declined to speak to me in the first place.

These insecurities have to be read in the context of the financial advantages of allotment dwelling. Allotment leases annually add up to around 35 cents per square meter, thus approximately €100 per year for a 300-square-meter plot, with additional expenses for public charges. Even for people on small incomes, the running costs of a hut and a plot are negligible in comparison to a city flat. Thus, particularly younger respondents also mentioned feelings of freedom and flexibility. Those were residents who explained that they were not planning on staying in the huts for long, but that temporarily saving on rent would open up other possibilities for them. Lukas, for instance, told me: "It is a piece of freedom ... Through that you are financially free, less forced to work for your money. Or, you work normally and save for the future (interview, 27.09.2018).

In sum, these experiences may astonish mostly through their immense variety. Clearly, they vary considerably in relation to the residents' income and length of residence, as well as the legal status and conditions of the hut.

Conclusion

When asked about the relation between *Schwarzwohnen* and the housing crisis, Mr. Mayer, a city bureaucrat, told me in 2014: "I would say that relation doesn't exist. No ... we are not there yet!" (interview, 18.06.2014). Five years later, as I finish writing this book and the daily news of the housing crisis in Berlin continues to report on the persistent exclusion of tenants across a widening income spectrum, this answer is ever more unsatisfying. However, to see the reverberation of the crisis in the gardens requires going beyond understandings of gentrification, displacement, and exclusion in order to develop a more fine-grained perspective on housing biographies and the individual experiences of allotment dwellers.

This chapter has tried to typologize the multiple modalities of informal housing in allotment huts as a first step toward recognizing the broad spectrum of housing experiences that sit oddly between being economically excluded and aspiring toward homeownership. Moreover, the housing biographies outlined here bring our attention to the multiplicity of dwelling experiences in allotment huts. Clearly, these different experiences are closely related to the multiple layers of legality – legal occupancy, legal building structure, both, or none, and the related forms of toleration, sufferance, or insecurity attached to them (see Chapter 7). Thereby, experiences of vulnerability, exclusion, comfort, and risk sit plot by plot. Moreover, dwelling biographies vary regarding the length of people's residence. With some biographies carrying the vestiges of past housing shortages and others defined by more recent closures in the market, allotments function as a place of refuge either for more temporary stays or for longer-term residence. In addition, the data is indicative of different motives that animate informal dwelling. These include both need and desire (cf. Devlin, 2019). Poverty migration into the gardens appears to remain an exception. Still, housing biographies that are marked by acute hardship sit alongside a range of other reasons, including the search for comfort, community, ownership, and financial freedom; the need to save on rent in face of financial constraints; and the related quest for more economic stability in light of people's insecure working lives. Allotment dwelling is thus motivated by a set of lifestyle choices, on the one hand, and insecurities and constraints people experience in housing and labor markets, on the other.

The implications of these biographies for our understanding of housing precarity are diverse. Precarity plays out in material, social, and legal dimensions. It cuts across a broad spectrum of income ranges. It straddles, as Simone (2001) puts it, across formal and informal divides. Disentangling these dimensions highlights structures of disadvantage and vulnerability, but also of opportunity, thus requiring that we understand housing precarity beyond concerns about economic exclusion. First, the housing phenomena this chapter has visited include the residential conditions of people with jobs and normal incomes for whom precarity is a question of legal recognition and infrastructure provision. These cases not only highlight that the conflation of informal housing and severe poverty is problematic (cf. Durst and Wegmann, 2017: 295), but also that some people choose to accept legal and material precarity for the advantages the gardens offer as well. Second, a more grounded perspective on precarity underlines the difficulties of negotiating access to allotment dwelling in the first place. Clearly, the barriers in accessing housing in the allotments are fortified not only through economic pressures on land (see Chapter 5) but also through the gardeners themselves. In this sense, different forms of housing exclusion may reinforce one another (cf. Desmond and Perkins, 2016), a theme which will be expanded in Chapter 6. Third, housing in allotments poses questions regarding the potential of the margins (cf. Lancione and McFarlane, 2016; Lancione, 2016b). While the housing biographies discussed in this chapter are indicative of a shortfall of urban citizenship, i.e. the right to adequate housing (in a material, social, and legal sense), the chapter has also highlighted the opportunities and advantages of the transgressions described. As it has been well understood in the literature on informality, self-built housing goes along with forms of empowerment, community building (Turner, 1972), and undue personal advantage, as particularly Chapter 6 goes on to show.

How, then, is the housing crisis reflected in the gardens? First, it has led to renewed claims, leveled by individual gardeners and entire colonies, regarding the toleration of informal housing. "Those whose home we take away here in the gardens," a respondent told me, "you will find them again at the end of the queue [referring to the endless waits necessary to find an affordable "formal" home]. And that is of course very difficult to understand for the people here" (interview, 29.04.2019). Put differently, gardeners lay claims on the toleration of allotment dwelling based on the scarcity of adequate housing options. Second, I noticed a narrowing of possibilities to dwell in allotments in relation to the crisis. In my final phase of interviews, in 2018 and 2019, allotment holders reported that as increasing numbers of outsiders were inquiring into the possibilities of dwelling in the huts, colony officials would closely examine the motives of applicants. These statements suggest an increase in the demand for allotments as places to dwell. But they were uttered to reassure me that people indicating that they might want to house in a hut would be refused access to a plot (interview, 16.04.2019). Similarly, Chapter 5 documents a stricter inspection of the size of a hut in the face of fears that colonies would be rededicated into building land if gardeners were to violate too many rules. In this case, the closure of "formal" housing possibilities may lead to a tightening of "informal" ones as well. Third, and perhaps most crucially, the housing crisis enters the gardens as people are looking to compensate reduced quality of their rental space through the use of their gardens – in part, as a dwelling space. Cases in which displacement from the formal market leads to allotment dwelling might be rare, but they do exist. Perhaps even in higher numbers than those I encountered, given the heightened necessity of this particular group to stay under the radar.

These reverberations pose questions regarding the strategies people use to stabilize insecurity, the ways in which the state deals with situations of precarious housing, and the exclusions and inclusions negotiated within such situations. I address these questions empirically in Chapters 5, 6, and 7.

Summary: Chapter 4

This chapter turns to the contemporary housing question. Against the background of debates on housing precarity and recent trends in Berlin's housing markets, the chapter offers a rich empirical account of how and why gardeners take up residence within allotment huts and how they manage to stay put in them. On the one hand, it illustrates the entanglement of formal and informal housing in the dwelling biographies of the city's residents. On the other hand, I explore how residents experience their housing conditions. I conclude by addressing the relevance of these experiences for contemporary housing debates.

Notes

1   Notable exceptions of studies focusing on informal housing in Europe and North America include research on sheds, dachas, outbuildings, and garages (Brown et al., 2020; Lombard, 2019; Rusanov, 2019), temporary accommodations, such as Airbnbs, sofa-surfing, or property-guardianship (Ferreri et al., 2016; Jayne and Hall, 2019), as well as forms of substandard or self-help accommodation, for instance in overcrowded or subterranean flats, vehicles, or boats (Fairbanks, 2011; Bower, 2017). In addition, scholarship on informal land occupations (Larson, 2002; Ward et al., 2004; Durst and Ward, 2014), a bourgeoning body of work on squatting (Vasudevan, 2015a; Smart and Aguilera, 2017), as well as a wider literature on informality in urban development (Laguerre, 1994; Tanasescu et al., 2010; Smart, 2018) complements more general reviews of urban informality in particular sites (Durst and Wegmann, 2017; Iveson et al., 2019). In Berlin, research has explored campers (Neupert, 2016), squats (Holm and Kuhn, 2011; Vasudevan, 2011, 2015a; Mitchell, 2017), and forms of anarchist living, such as countercultural trailer sites [*Wagenburgen*] (Veith and Sambale, 1998; van Schipstal and Nicholls, 2014).

2   Most importantly, the current Hartz Laws, issued in 2005, significantly reduced the basic social security for beneficiaries.

3   In 2010, only 15% of the city's housing stock was owner-occupied, thus 85% of the population were renters; see Holm (2011: 93).

4   This number includes the formerly socialist housing stock that was added to the stock of Berlin's housing companies; see Uffer (2014: 156).

5   The number of unemployed Berliners rose from 180,000 in 1991 to 273,000 in 1998, equivalent to a rise from 10.6% to 17.9% (Krätke and Borst, 2000: 211; see also Krätke, 2004a: 1547). From 1991 to 2001, Berlin's traditional industries lost 150,000 jobs. Central districts such as Neukölln suffered job losses of 22% (Haeussermann and Kapphan, 2004: 33).

6   By 1995, Berlin's debt amounted to €23bn and was continuing to rise (Uffer, 2013: 154).

7   This included firms such as the German postal service, which owned allotment land that was later to be sold off.

8   It should be noted that these reductions resulted not only from the privatization of the city's own housing stock, but also from the sale of housing owned by the federal government.

9   Social housing units are defined according to the WoBindG (*Wohnungsbindungsgesetz*, literally: the Controlled Tenancy Act, my translation).

10 The number of eviction proceedings does not necessarily correlate with the number of realized evictions, because many residents vacate their flats before the set date of the eviction.

11 Schulz calculates displacement rates on the basis of the estimated effects of real estate appreciation trends and the rates of people moving out of an area (2017: 64).

12 The costs of this lease vary across districts. The law defines that it has to be "commensurate" (section 18.2, BKleingG). Following a lawsuit in 1992, the Federal Supreme Court (BGH) further defined "commensurate" (V ZR 104/91) as in relation to the market value of other building land. An interviewee told me he was paying €62 monthly in addition to the regular gardening fees (interview, 25.04.2014).

13 On the basis of the costs of the plots that are advertised, the blog Grünbedarf (2017) currently calculates the purchasing price of a garden as €32.17 per m^2. With an average plot size of 407 m^2 this amounts to €11,519. As plots are not officially permitted to be sold online, these numbers are, however, hardly representative.

14 The average duration of the leases, between 17 and 19 years, suggests a sense of stability and speaks of such attachment (SenUVK, 2019: 35).

15 This is not to trivialize the force of stigma in the allotment. As we will see in Chapter 6, the stigma of the 'slumification' that is attached mostly to Roma living in allotments plays out in powerful ways.

Chapter 5

The Colony and the Turf
Planning and the Politics of Land Use Change

Toward the northern jurisdictional boundary of the former West Berlin, the city phases out into a fragmented, flat landscape of gyms, cheap shops, youth clubs, gas stations, Greek restaurants, single-family homes, the occasional bus stop, and a number of bakery chains. The key landmark toward the city center is a high-rise satellite city called Märkisches Viertel, reminiscent of former fantasies of modernization that have – as shown in Chapter 3 – led to the bulldozing of previous histories of allotment dwelling to the ground. On its periphery, Berlin's urban fabric remains inconclusive: the materialization of unfinished political projects and former divisions, on which new fears of urban polarization, social marginalization, and increasing ethnic divides play out. One steady and defining property of this urban fabric is a landscape of remaining allotment colonies – residues of previous governing projects that have outlived metropolitan change. Still, the colonies have not been immune to such changes; rather, they are enmeshed in them in crucial ways.

The obvious intersection is planning: for over a century, planning has designated land for allotments, then frequently rededicated this land for other state projects at later points in time. This rededication has predominantly been attributed to private, corporate, or public growth targets that have subordinated the development of allotments to the necessities of the market. Yet, "the usual neoliberalism story" (Ferguson, 2015: 2) seems ill-equipped to interpret a sway of other practices and rationalities that have also shaped the development of these sites, thus making it necessary to consider a second register of urban change. This register is smaller in scale but no less political. It concerns the spatio-material politics of allotment holders, who have incrementally, and frequently in negotiation with urban bureaucracies, crucially shaped the development of allotment land *themselves* through the construction

Housing in the Margins: Negotiating Urban Formalities in Berlin's Allotment Gardens,
First Edition. Hanna Hilbrandt.
© 2021 John Wiley & Sons, Ltd. Published 2021 by John Wiley & Sons, Ltd.

of infrastructures, the expansion of huts, or the overbuilding of green space. This chapter explores the material geographies of allotments as well as the practices and regulatory efforts that shape them, all with a view to understanding how urban planning and governance, on the one hand, and self-production and incrementalism, on the other, are intertwined. In the context of the book's empirical exploration, this chapter's purpose is to picture and explore the materiality of urban change that accompanies allotment dwelling. Conceptually, it pursues two aims.

First, and more theoretically, my aim is to convey some of the ways in which socio-material change can be conceived when thinking about irregular housing in a Western liberal democracy. Research on global-North cities tends to describe urban change in terms of top-down planning with occasional citizen participation. Very rarely has it aimed at understanding the ways in which people reconfigure the city through their own spatial and material practices of adaptation, construction, and inhabitation. The roots of this neglect appear to lie in the scale of these material interventions: "ordinary" people's spatio-material practices are seen to involve only relatively minor interventions.[1] Conversely, literature that captures the material, improvised, and incremental character of dwelling or infrastructure provisioning has long accounted for the more incremental ways in which urbanites themselves transform the urban fabric (Simone, 2010; Boeck, 2012; Silver, 2014; Boeck and Baloji, 2017).[2] That these accounts typically speak of postcolonial urban worlds and marginal forms of city-making weaves an epistemological concern about modalities of knowledge production into the analysis of such urban change. As they have largely remained peripheral to theory-making in global-North cities, they prompt questions as to how and what this analytical lens contributes to an understanding of urban development in Berlin (see Hentschel, 2015 for a similar approach). Second, and more empirically, I set out to show how the two registers of urban transformation introduced above interweave. How does urban planning deal with the allotments from the top down? In turn, how do allotment holders themselves affect the material landscape of the city and thereby participate in shaping urban change beyond the tactics of capital accumulation?

I use the metaphors of the "colony" [*die Kolonie*] and the "turf" [*die Scholle*] to pursue these aims and trace modalities of state planning and the gardeners' small-scale material interventions in these terms. In the first section, the trope of the colony that I introduced in Chapter 3 works to capture urban planning interventions in the allotments. Moreover, it alludes to the relative independence and stubbornness of the development of allotments vis-à-vis other sites in the "metropole" – a more thoroughly governed space. In the second section, the turf provides a second lens that I use to indicate the incremental and small-scale modalities of spatio-material change through which allotment holders transform the colonies in ways that undermine the logics of planning. Not unlike the notion of the colony, "die Scholle" is a wording typical in allotment gardening – a trope for the gardeners' isolation, independence, and withdrawal behind high hedges and within allotment sheds. A rough translation can be found in "turf," with its tone of personal territory. In its allusion to a (however constrained) autonomy, it echoes some of the ideas that undergird the notion of the colony, yet refers to such independence in relation to the scale of the plot. Under the heading of this metaphor, I unveil the influence and agency of urban dwellers in spatializing and materializing their wants and needs, at times in tension with planning norms. In juxtaposing the images of the colony and the turf, the final section confronts the two levels of urban change previously discussed to show how small-scale change piles up to cause larger urban transformation. It not only seeks to highlight how such incrementalism is enmeshed in more "top-down" forms of city-making, but also explores how planning works with the material transformations that the gardeners themselves propel.

The Colony and the Ambiguities of Planning

Berlin's 876 compounds with a total of 71,071 garden plots on 2,915 hectares of urban land (SenUVK, 2019: 24) make up approximately 3.4% of the city's urban fabric (ibid: 9).[3] Of this land, 79% (approximately 2,302 ha) is publicly owned (ibid: 24). The remaining 14,312 plots (approximately 612 ha) are situated on private land (ibid: 24). Although their location hardly follows a striking principle of legible order, allotments tend to be concentrated in the districts of Pankow, Neukölln, Treptow-Köpenick, Reinickendorf, and Charlottenburg-Wilmersdorf (ibid: 24). They are most commonly located in a belt zone outside of the ring road that encircles Berlin's center – not quite yet the city's fringe, but a "proximate periphery." (see Figure 5.1) As in other European cities, allotments are frequently situated near highways, train tracks, or other land uses not favorable to residential construction. Some are lumped together as green clusters or wedges of land along the access routes that lead into the urban center; others form small islands within sealed- and built-up space. The impression that the colonies are alien to other, more urban, uses of land is underscored by their clear-cut demarcation, formed by hedges of conifer trees, height changes, fences and, frequently, hidden entrances. They are, as Simone notes about the periphery, more generally a space "that is never really brought fully under the auspices of the logic and development trajectories that characterise a centre" (2010: 40).

Allotment Gardens

FIGURE 5.1 Diagrammatic map of Berlin's allotment gardens, 2018. Source: Senate Department for Enviroment, Transport, and Climate Protection.

From a planning point of view, the changing landscape of urban allotments is imbricated in two interrelated rationalities: the first refers to social and ecological sustainability; the second concerns the growth targets of housing and the consequential necessities of sourcing land for building. The mechanisms through which the city of Berlin manages these competing land claims reveal the tensions between economic imperatives and environmental aims. Moreover, they highlight how past rationalities and contemporary civic claims play out in decisions regarding their spatial change.

Officially, the city has embraced the idea of allotments. Politicians and scholars alike have argued for the maintenance of allotment lands based on their social and ecological sustainability. Their benefits are seen to be wideranging: in possibilities to foster social integration by creating vibrant communities across lines of difference, in granting a sense of ownership, and in the empowerment of economically vulnerable segments of the population, as well as in gardening's potential to educate (Eizenberg et al., 2016; SenUVK,

2019: 1). Moreover, the allotment gardens are seen to promote ecological sustainability through ecosystem service provision (BMVBS and BBR, 2008), including air filtration, the improvement of the microclimate, and the discharge of rainwater, thus delivering consequential benefits for the health of urban populations. Additionally, the growing of local fruit and vegetables is considered to foster food security and resiliency. Finally, allotments have been praised as a locational factor in urban competition. As part of a "new policy common sense" around "green" development (Wachsmuth and Angelo, 2018: 1), allotments have been incorporated into attempts to revitalize, or, say, entrepreneurialize, the city (Costa et al., 2016: 201) through their ability to raise the quality of urban life for the city's middle class (Eizenberg et al., 2016: 99; Nikolaidou et al., 2016: 5). As they have low maintenance costs, allotments are easily compatible with tight municipal budgets. In consequence, the coalition agreement (2016–2021) of the governing parties – the Social Democrats (SPD), the Green Party (die Grünen) and the Left (die Linke) – promises to maintain the city's allotments (Senatskanzlei Berlin, 2016: 32) or, "if necessary," provide replacement in their proximity (SenUVK, 2019: 1).

In actual practice, however, the imperative of developing land to provide properties for further housing construction looms large, with allotments being, as Eizenberg puts it, a "frail target for implementing growth" (2016: 92). The return of the housing question has crucially heightened the demand for designated building land and turned such land into an ever more expensive asset. The consequences for those at the bottom of the income ladder and the gardeners themselves are well known (Bauwelt, 2018; Hesse, 2018). Between 2008 and 2017, the *average* land price has increased by 348% (Heinz and Belina, 2019: 47). In 2017, Berlin ranked eighth in a comparison of land purchase prices in German cities (ibid).[4] This increase has also raised the share of land costs in relation to total housing price to an estimated 50% to 70% in key locations (ibid: 13). These increased land values have placed pressures on allotments that are compounded by the lack of other land reserves for possible housing construction.

Historically, the city has experienced disputes on the rededication of its greenery time and again (see Chapter 3). The Senate has repeatedly designated new periods of security [*Sicherheitsstufen*] to each colony, which function alongside land-use plans in order to permit greater transparency and ensure long-term plannability. Between 2004 and 2014, 5,924 plots (approximately 7.5% of both private and public allotment land) had already been absorbed by other land uses.[5] Between 2014 and 2018, allotment land declined by 2,117 plots (equivalent to approximately 2.9%) (SenUVK, 2019: 29). This reduction included 511 plots on communal land and was predominantly due to the prolongation of the *Bundesautobahn A100*, a significant ring road (ibid. See Figure 5.2).[6] In the most recent so-called Allotment Garden Development Plan [*Kleingartenentwicklungsplan*], approximately 67.2% of all existing colonies are designated as "permanent small gardens" [*Dauerkleingärten*], which ostensibly declares that these allotment gardens are secured in land-use plans (SenUVK, 2019: 26). An additional 15.5% of all colonies are foreseen to be secured on a long-term basis. All other plots have varying retention periods, and how much longer these various tiers will be retained is a constant debate. Currently, 9.1% of the gardens are "secured" until 2030. For the rest, one could argue that the "unmapping" of land deliberately fosters flexibility to push through alternative claims on land. In 2020, 0.54% of all plots (equivalent to 481 plots) have fallen out of the security of these retention periods (SenUVK, 2019: 26) to be cleared for construction projects, though not for housing (Hönicke and Schönball, 2019). Starting in 2030, the above 9.1% of all gardening land is to be used

FIGURE 5.2 Demolition of an allotment colony in Neukölln, Berlin, 2014.
Source: Hanna Hilbrandt.

for schools, kindergartens, and other infrastructural projects, possibly for housing as well (ibid). The city's current housing strategy (StEP Wohnen 2030) includes a selection of allotments that would be particularly suitable for housing construction (after 2030), although, as the Senate claims, their rededication would preferably be avoided (SenSW, 2019: 14).

In the current housing crisis, the pressure on allotment land has been rising (Honert, 2018; Nowakowski, 2018). In an open letter to the Senator for Urban Development and Housing, a real estate lobbyist and the initiative "Garden Cities Not Garden Gnomes" [*Gartenstädte statt Gartenzwerge*] recently published calculations stating that the city would gain space for 400,000 flats were it to use allotment land for housing construction (Piepgras, n.d.; Loy, 2018). Proponents of this initiative argue that such rededication would be a matter of solidarity: that the right to housing outweighs the right to a garden. They particularly ask that the city repurchase privately owned allotment land (Piepgras, 2018). To undergird this argument, studies have been commissioned to show how such plans could retain greenery so as not to adversely affect the city's sustainable development (Bünger, 2018).

Let's admit that it is tempting to interpret these developments as yet another instance of profit-driven development, and to critique the rededication of allotment land as the exploitation of a possible rent gap and the kind of neoliberal compromise that ultimately disadvantages the allotment dwellers, ecologically sustainable land use, and – given that new-built developments would likely be luxury housing – perhaps most of Berlin's lower-income tenants as well. Yet, while these arguments certainly capture the most prominent discourse around the development of allotments and well-recognizable dynamics in urban politics, such analysis ultimately fails to account for the more fundamental problems regarding the ways in which planning deals with these sites. More concretely put, the development of this land is stuck between outdated norms regarding the use of these spaces and existing infrastructures that establish barriers to transformation and hamper a forward-looking planning strategy for these sites.

Since the early twentieth century, allotments have seen modalities of top-down, territorial ordering of land and nature (Scott, 1998; Schindler, 2015), and even of low-income populations, that were guided by political projects with ecological as well as social aims (see Chapter 3). Today, as DeSilvey notes, allotments are treated as "third spaces" (2003: 444) – incompatible with present-day planning. Breaking down the binary notions of "private and public, production and consumption, labour and leisure" and, as Costa et al. add, "the ugly and the beautiful, the traditional conservative and the modern/ progressive/activist" (see also Crouch and Ward, 1997), allotments are marked by a spatial exceptionalism that makes them particularly vulnerable to "fall between the stools" (DeSilvey, 2003: 444). Hence, no real new vision exists for the allotments that would allow for overcoming a set of contradictions between the projections that are mapped onto allotments and the status quo: established as sites of welfare to alleviate urban poverty, they were catered toward "the poor," while today the governance of these sites lacks a redistributive mechanism to ensure lower-income Berliners access to the gardens. While built, as Nilson writes, to "inculcate moral values in workers" (2014: 14), today, allotments have increasingly become leisure spaces used rather for consumption than for food production. While promoted as sustainable spaces, the building activities of the gardeners have even brought the ecological value of the gardens under dispute (SenSW, 2018).

To be sure, the Bundeskleingartengesetz (BKleinG) protects a vision of the gardens that is entirely out of tune with the status quo. Anique Hommels describes these contradictions as "a clash between a variety of new ideas about urban development and the multifarious viewpoints that are already embedded in a city's existing urban structures" (2005, 2010: 139). Despite the official recognition of allotments, these contradictory viewpoints, as well as competing rationalities of sustainability and growth, have in turn hampered urban politics in imagining the allotments in new ways. At present, stuck between multiple expectations and entangled contradictions, allotments fail to be meaningful elements of planning that would advance a more forward-looking vision for the city's greenery (Drilling et al., 2016: 59). The colony thus remains a stubborn place: an urban enclave with a deficient spatial relation between the semi-public allotments and their surrounding public streets. But beyond this standard explanation of competing interests and aims, it is vital not only to see current development solutions as a question of planning rationalities, but also to enter the allotments in order to understand their modalities of spatio-material change from the inside out.

The Turf and the Negotiation of Incremental Change

Let us then intrude into an allotment colony to visit a "turf" and more closely examine incremental, small-scale modalities of change. Approaching the typical colony, a visitor crosses a parking lot alongside a dusty road. In front of the allotment, a decorated entry gate exhibits the colony's coat of arms. By safeguarding the distinction between urbanization and gardening land, this gate announces a crossing into new territory. Behind the gate, at a distance, a notice board displays the allotments' on-site management board, and next to it, a diagram mapping, on average, 271 plots of approximately 410 m² each (SenUVK, 2019: 26) (see Figure 5.3).

Overcoming the impression that one might not be allowed in, a visitor realizes that the gate can be opened from the outside simply by reaching through its iron bars to the latch inside. Upon entering, the ground is below street level. Plots, huts, and even the trees are of smaller scale; a grid of mud paths connects the plots. Walking through the alleyways of a colony, one can marvel at the immense variety of the huts: an amalgamation of wooden shacks, rustic stone cottages, and mass-manufactured bungalows. Some are two-storeyed, some have a pent roof and others a barrel-shaped top, while still others are really just garden sheds. The character of the colonies also varies across the city: centrally located colonies in particular have less sealed surface; older colonies tend to have more built-up space. Some of the colonies that were planned in the GDR consist almost solely of lined-up huts built from prefabricated construction sets.

In what follows, I explore negotiation within the gardens around the incremental expansion of infrastructures necessary for dwelling. I hone in on a set of internal tensions around such material efforts in order to examine the ways in which incremental spatial change is contested and subject to negotiation. The "turf" appears to be a good metaphor to capture the gardeners'

FIGURE 5.3 Entrance to a colony. Source: Michael Berger.

withdrawals into their sheds and the homeowner culture that has developed around allotment huts and plots. Throughout, my account is inspired by writers exploring makeshift modalities of urban transformations (Rao et al., 2007; McFarlane and Rutherford, 2008; Thieme et al., 2017; Lancione, 2019b). For instance, Teresa Caldeira has recently framed modalities of urban production characterized by autoconstruction and material improvisations as peripheral urbanization (2016). She describes this mode of urban change through its inherent dynamism and heterogeneity in addition to its transversal engagement with bureaucracies. Caldeira reads peripherality not so much in the territorial sense of the word, but rather as something independent of location within a city (2016: 4). For her, this logic of producing space is fundamentally "different from that of the industrial cities of the North" (2016: 4). Conversely, I suggest that the described processes of negotiating the urban fabric constitute similarly peripheral modes of producing space, although I take such socio-technical, decentralized, and bottom-up change to work in negotiation with urban bureaucracies rather than be set against them (see Chapter 6).

To begin to understand the forms of incremental change that characterize the turf, let me recall the inherited roots of the gardens' illegally expanded materiality. Whether people dwell in them or not, Berlin's allotments tend to have a decent infrastructure of telephone connections, electricity networks, water pipelines, postal services, sewers, toilets, and stoves (see Figures 5.4 and 5.5). These infrastructures are, as Bach aptly notes (2010), "the living legacy of contested pasts." An account of Mr. Becker, an allotment garden administrator, summarizes how these infrastructures came about:

> There was always a question about the water connection of the allotment huts. What about toilets? They all had illegal cesspits ... Those who lived in them permanently had a washing machine and a dishwasher. That is of course a massive environmental pollution. And then after years of toing and froing it was somehow permitted that people could build their water-collecting pit ... It was somehow permitted! Same with the telephone! Everything that was conducive to permanent dwelling had been forbidden. And then [the ban] was removed step-by-step – just like the telephone. I have worked through telephone requests, and you always had to name a reason. "Well, my grandma is sick ... !" You can always find something! And then, they received ... a connection. And later *everyone* received a phone. (Interview, 23.04.14)

In some colonies, allotment holders have participated in building up their colonies' infrastructures; others maintain their infrastructures themselves,

FIGURES 5.4 AND 5.5 Interior space of an allotment hut and letter box.
Source: Hanna Hilbrandt.

which has technically enabled them to further advance incremental change and also created a sense of ownership. Paradoxically, at the same time, these processes work to consolidate state space – city-sponsored water pipelines or electricity networks, standardized by federal norms (interview, 27.06.2014).

Today, electricity hook-ups are rarely questioned – although neither the laws nor the city's local administrative guidelines clearly foresaw this infrastructure (see Chapter 7). Similarly, water hook-ups have become standard, with some colonies maintaining their own water supply through local wells (interview, 29.04.2019).[7] I encountered a colony that used to have an on-site shop. Whenever needed, people living in allotment huts can arrange for "at-home" nursing care from medical service providers. As justification for these and other now-normalized transgressions, I was frequently told "You cannot suddenly – 50 years later – change this" (e.g. interview, 18.09.2013). Or, that "in the meantime it becomes consolidated. It is the case in almost every allotment compound that one says, okay … it is … not foreseen in the BKleinG but …" (interview, 18.06.2014). Other contentions went beyond these claims: "Meanwhile the local district says: "See that everything is disposed of decently, that there is a container, etc." On the contrary, if there are plots without containers, they say that they [the gardeners] should finally install something" (interview, 18.06.2014). Legitimacy appears to be characterized by obduracy (Hommels, 2005, 2008), which renders irregular infrastructures thinkable and, in the context of requirement for sustainable waste disposal, even reasonable. In this sense, the "unbecoming" of legality (Hommels, 2010) is not finalized with the change of legislation but must instead be understood as a process in which persistent traditions continue to influence contemporary development patterns.

Despite the illustrated expansion of these *public* infrastructures (see Figure 5.6), the consolidation or expansion of the gardeners' *personal* living space is hotly contested. Materiality figures intensely in these negotiations. In response to my question about his oversized roof, Mr. Neumann, an older resident, described the particular negotiation process involved in maintaining this extension:

Mr. Neumann: Well, this is how it was: here, to the right there is a small terrace with light and then … all the huts were photographed and I was asked to take off the roofing.
H. H.: Did the bureaucracy tell you this? And did you do it?
Mr. Neumann: Well it is … it [the roofing] wasn't ok anymore anyway. And then [the head of the colony] told me: "You have to replace it anyway and then you put up a new one. If you have it in the summer, no one will say anything. But you have to take it down in the winter." (Interview, 17.09.2013)

FIGURE 5.6 Gas tank. Source: Hanna Hilbrandt.

Mr. Neumann's statement suggests a mode of negotiation that links cooperation and transgression and will be explored more thoroughly in Chapter 6.
Similarly, covering up constructions, or rebuilding them along the lines of
some acceptable standard, proceeded in this mode. "My neighbor … she had
to demolish her greenhouse," Ms. Müller told me, "but she is allowed to have
a winterproof tent. And then she just covered the old construction with a tarp.
Clever, right, for an 80-year-old [laughs] … at least she got away with that
tent" (interview, 13.09.2013). This was not the first time I had come across
this construction. The winterproof tent kept following me around. Saunas in
huts, illegal extensions in the back of the plot, or separate, hidden building
structures were readily apparent: some were more permanent; others necessi-
tated continuous maintenance or could be easily relocated.

Not only are these material negotiations concerned with the size and legal
status of a construction, they are also concerned with its appropriate appearance: in fact, some allotment holders keep neat order in mowing their lawns,
and they cherish their weed-free flowerbeds and dead-straight concrete paths.
To echo Ghertner (2010), these efforts could be described as following "a rule
by aesthetics," a rule according to which formality is defined by the physical

appearance of the (however illegally) "planned" city and that, conversely, designates the jerry-built developments of the urban poor as informal – similarly by the quality of their appearance. In both cases, the legal status of these constructions is insignificant in terms of regulation (ibid). Rather for Ghertner, the apparent order of the illegally planned yet "formal"-looking city makes it possible to avoid a rigid enforcement of rules.

Perhaps drawing this parallel goes too far. By no means do I want to suggest that gardeners keep neat order because everyone secretly crosses the line. Rather, in this case, a different "rule by aesthetics" could be learned: order points toward legibility, and legibility prevents intervention, if the proper message can be read. Conversely, not keeping up appearances might possibly become a reason for the bureaucracy to intervene. Thus, a relatively skillful hiding of legal violations through the quality of building materials marks the negotiation of tolerance as allotment holders construct unauthorized modifications, illegally reshape their floor plans, and overstep planning rules.

Looking more closely at the ways in which allotment holders themselves negotiate the boundaries of spatio-material expansions shows that the above rule is also expressed in the governance of cultural preferences, if not outright conflict. Mr. Weber's account of the antagonisms that accompany those material expansions that fall outside the mainstream register of "German allotment aesthetics" is telling in this regard:

> And what, hmmm … increased in the last 15 years is foreigners. I think we have seven or eight, well, uh, Uzbeks and we have many Belarusians, and an Egyptian, uh, not Egyptian but Ethiopian, and a Lebanese in the colony, hmm. Well, everything you can think of. And there it starts. The Lebanese started to build a little mosque, well. And there he goes, who knows at what time, puts out his carpet and then there are also problems. Why can he build an extension? What is this? (Interview, 19.06.2014)

Across most allotment colonies, internal conflicts regarding spatio-material transgressions frequently erupt along lines of ethnic difference that get (re)produced in these conflicts. It is here, where the metaphor of "the turf" ends. Gardeners do extend their huts in secrecy or isolation, but they regulate extensions in negotiation with their peers. As I discuss in more depth in Chapter 6, peer-to-peer regulation works to informally sanction forms of material change that cross a line drawn not only by xenophobic resentment but also to guard and reproduce a normative ideal of traditional allotment culture.

Small Things Pile Up: Rededicating the Colonies

The gradual and material transformations of the colonies are situated within a broader trend of notable urban significance: numerous colonies being rededicated into a new land use classification. These processes of rededication demonstrate how the gardeners' incremental material changes have shifted the character of the colonies, or, one could say, "concretized" the allotments from the inside out. As their development is enmeshed in planning's efforts to reintegrate them into the "official" registers of the state, they force us, as Jill Wigle words it, to "understand … formal planning and informal urbanization as interactive processes" (2014: 578).

These processes become most visible when considering them against the background of the legal changes that accompanied German reunification. As noted in Chapter 3, the SachenRBerG permitted Eastern dwellers to buy the land on which they had built; in the GDR the land was publicly-owned property, but gardeners held their hut, or in many cases a house on their plot, in private possession. As the material augmentations and expansions previously described reached significant dimensions, allotment huts no longer fit into the definitions of the law. This conjuncture not only led to numerous problems regarding planning law, but also the SachenRBerG that guided reunification provided the grounds for broader changes in the ownership of allotment land. Together these processes caused the rededication of numerous allotments.

Already in August 1995, the Senate Department of Finance [*Senatsverwaltung für Finanzen*] suggested that in cases of an accumulation of entitled buyers, whether these colonies could further guarantee the purposes of an allotment colony needed to be subject to critical scrutiny (SenStadt, 2004: 9). Differently put, the Senate asked whether the privatization of plots had moved the colonies into a different land use category. Various court trials put this Senate recommendation to the test (e.g. Bundesgerichtshof judgment of 05.02.2004, III ZR, 331/02, juris). Alongside the above-mentioned city administration, the gardeners themselves pushed for regulatory changes. Between 2004 and 2005, numerous allotment colonies – particularly those with an oversized building stock – made efforts to be rededicated to become housing areas (interview, 18.09.2013). Most gardeners had inhabited these colonies for decades. For them, the adaptation of their "neighborhoods" to the rules of the West signaled significant and disquieting transformations. Those who were officially recognized as permanent inhabitants suddenly had to pay a dwelling fee [*Wohnlaubenentgeld*] that far exceeded their previous lease (Land Berlin, 2009, attachment 2). This and other alterations led them to argue that they could no longer be classified as an allotment colony. To enforce this line of argumentation, they refused to pay their leases. Moreover, they were keen on expanding their current privileges; for instance, by parking their cars on the plots (interview, 18.09.2013). They were, as one could argue, not interested in living up to the obligations of the law, and used the differing circumstances in the colonies, i.e. the material conditions that they themselves had created, as leverage to maneuver their colonies out of the jurisdiction of the BKleinG.

When the city denied their attempts to be granted a different status, the resistant gardeners started paying their leases into a blocked account. This move forced the landowner, the city of Berlin, to claim these losses – the unpaid land rent – in court. In June 2004, a Federal Court decision framed these cases (Bundesgerichtshof judgment of 24.12.2003, III ZR 203/02, OpenJur, 10180) into national legal practice. It authorized criteria according to which a compound was no longer to count as an allotment. Accordingly, the status of a colony could be negated if *more* than half of the plots were used as homes, as of a fixed date in 1990, or if *fewer* than half of the plots were equipped with houses but the colony as a whole resembled a residential estate rather than an allotment compound (Mainczyk, 2005: 244).

As both of these criteria define vague guidelines rather than rigid regulations, it was up to the legal opinion of a local judge to assess each situation and decide whether the adaptation of these colonies to the law appeared to be a realistic possibility, or whether the gardeners' construction activities rather made it necessary to allocate a different land use category to a colony. Ms. Braun, an allotment garden administrator who attended one of these procedures, explained how it went about:

> We had an on-site inspection with the judge in the allotment colonies, in which he walked through the compound and checked: "hut, bungalow, single-family house, hut, hut." And at the end he counted and said, "ok, it isn't one!" And in this way the district lost nine really large compounds. (Interview, 19.08.2013)

The adaptations that would have been necessary in order to apply the categories of the BKleinG to the inspected site appeared to be too unreasonable. The evaluation in the above-described case resulted in an amendment procedure in which the land-use plan was changed so that the allotments finally became a residential housing area. To guide this development and regulate the extensive construction activity in some of the allotment gardens, the legislators also amended the law: the BKleinG was given an annex, which defines the limits of what is counted as an allotment compound.[8]

These legal amendments have caused further problems regarding the urban development of allotment land. To start, these colonies continue to cause inescapable planning problems. Not only is it difficult to adapt them to current housing standards – including zoning requirements regarding fire brigade access – the "recreation compound" [*Erholungsanlage*] status also has never technically existed as a legal category and disrupts accepted notions of German law. "We are a *Wildwuchs* for the authorities," one inhabitant of these colonies told me (interview, 29.04.2019) – a rank growth that is unruly and savage, although at once officially acknowledged and legalized.

Berlin's city council currently plans to build 14 new districts; one of them on the lands of a recreation compound called Blankenburg – a site in which 400 plots are registered for housing. Fierce conflict with the local inhabitants highlighted the city's irresolvable dilemma: although not even rigorous enforcement would solve the planning problems of the recreation compound, its demolition would further restrict the supply of low-income housing. At the time of writing, the situation remained unresolved.

These ongoing rededication procedures happen across the city. In the context of heightened land speculation, market pressures work in conjunction with the material changes described to further endanger allotment land. Following the above legal amendment, the owners of such land can threaten allotment gardeners with the loss of their protected status when too many gardeners defy the law, and this move promises a gain in revenue. This risk finds resonance in the gardens. Mr. Weber, head of a colony located on church-owned land, told me in 2014:

> Well the gardeners … it is often their own fault [that land is repur-posed], because they don't adhere to the rules. Well we know, we have some [gardeners] … they have built up to 100 m². And those are houses! And then, there is little chance [of maintaining the gardens as allot-ments]. (Interview, 19.06.2014)

In this climate, the negotiations around room for tolerance have become harsher. For instance, Landgraf and Kraetsch – the president of the Landesverband Berlin der Gartenfreunde and his lawyer – plead with the gardeners:

> Those that act out of self-interest and do not comply with the legal borders of the BKleinG, for example through oversized structures or

through the refusal to use their gardens for the production of horticultural products … through the parking of vehicles or through dwelling
on the plot, deprive the gardens of the legal protection of the BKleinG.
(2008: 23)

In the context of heightened investment pressure, such threats can be
effective. Even just the fearful awareness of evictions in connection with the
rededication of colonies into building land works to limit the odds of transgressions being tolerated.

At first sight, gardeners' residential construction activities appear to have no
political force. Yet, in showing how their small-scale maneuvers become pertinent at the urban scale, these episodes demonstrate the political power of the
allotment holders as it becomes leveraged in a broader process of change. "Little
things pile up," notes Elizabeth Povinelli (2011: 183), and here an accumulation
of chronic but ordinary moments – "quasi-events" in Povinelli's (ibid) terms –
has altered the status of the compounds. Even if these events, following Povinelli,
"fold into everyday routines" and never appear to have real effects, their aggrega-
tion conjures up change (2011: 14). In this process, it is not the state's governing
rationalities or ordering practices but the allotment gardeners' own, in conjunction with the state's legal system, that cause such change. The loss of allotment
land can thus not only be attributed to the city's growth target or "the global
majority language … of profit" (Stoner, 2012: 17–18). Rather, it is also these
incremental ways – the inner processes of change – that have caused the decline
of allotment land. The new Allotment Garden Development Plan foresees 0.8%
of all allotment land being rededicated in this way (SenUVK, 2019).[9]

Conclusion

This chapter juxtaposed two registers of spatio-material change. First, under
the heading of the *colony*, I analyzed how city planning handles allotments. I
illustrated the ambiguities of the city's strategy of developing allotment turf land,
as it finds itself stuck between growth targets, commitments to ecological
sustainability, and local traditions and norms. Second, regarding these narratives of top-down change, the turf demonstrated how allotment gardeners
further their dwelling possibilities by extending their allotment huts and
solidifying their infrastructures in negotiation with other parties. Finally, I
analyzed how urban planning and the incremental adaptations of the urban
fabric become intertwined and lead to the rededication of the colonies as,
over time, the gardeners' minor tactics shift the character of the colony so
much that, eventually, the city can no longer classify them as allotments.

More frequently than not, analyses of urban political economies of planning and land use have been set against more minor accounts of material incremental change as if they were mutually exclusive explanations (Brenner et al., 2011; McFarlane, 2011a, 2011b; but see Brenner, 2018). Reading these levels of change against one another, by unpacking how large external changes and small internal ones become imbricated, and tracing their wider effects, highlights that urban transformations in the allotments cannot solely be aligned with either the standard story of planning in the wake of neoliberal change or a narrative of informal or transgressive behavior. Rather, the negotiation around the allotments' spatial transformation requires a more nuanced picture that includes an account of the gardeners' self-interest; the bureaucracies' "care" for sustainable development and social housing; the stubborn materialities of infrastructures, plots, and huts; and the reluctance to push for reform, with all of this existing, to be sure, alongside profit-driven claims on building land.

Reading these aspects alongside scholarship about the incremental material changes people make to the urban fabric, which stems most frequently from researching cities in Asia, Africa, and Latin America, is instructive in understanding how "ordinary urbanisms" at the margins work with and are incorporated into forms of planning and urban development. It challenges the claim that "transversal" practices of self-building belong to the global South and provides a broader comparative grasp of the ways in which people participate in city-building. It also permits a more nuanced understanding of the multiple spatio-material practices that play out in negotiating with and enacting state rule. Undoubtedly, the practices that this chapter has described – extending the boundaries of the law, enacting new land use categories, tolerating material transgressions, or taking them to court – escape and transgress the framing of planning (as the most common way in which the state governs materiality and space; Scott, 1998). But it is useful to read such forms of spatio-material change as attempts to negotiate state space. Despite the very minor scale of these transformations, gardeners and local bureaucracies challenge and enact state norms in ways that ultimately shape the state's character and material form. The regulations and transgressions that accommodate informal housing appear here neither as resistance nor as oppression; rather, the case speaks of the ways in which gardeners and the states' "governing subjects" (Hunter, 2015: 3) take on more fluid and ambivalent roles. It follows that it is necessary to see how state power operates in more pluralistic terms in wider constellations of governance. The next chapter disentangles the roles and perspectives of all parties concerned with allotment gardening in regard to how regulations are navigated.

Summary: Chapter 5

This chapter considers the material and geographical relations in which the gardens are embedded by focusing on the ways in which incremental adaptations of the gardens and their governance have shaped the urban development of the city and its modalities of urban change. Theoretically, the chapter traces questions about urban planning and governance as well as about coproduction and incrementalism in order to juxtapose these forms of transformation. Building on interviews and a number of photographs, it aims to unravel how these modalities are entangled in urban development and to tease out how we can understand forms of coproduction, incremental adaptation, and self-built housing in a city of the global North.

Notes

1   The literature working with this lens in global-North cities often chronicles practices of squatting (Vasudevan, 2015b), shelter for the homeless (Lancione, 2019b), and sanitation practices (Lancione and McFarlane, 2016), as well as forms of low-budget or guerrilla urbanism (Hou, 2010; Färber, 2014).

2   Broadly, the aim of these accounts is to decenter and widen mainstream ontologies of urban theory by highlighting the messiness, ambiguity, and provisionality of urban production and account for the ways in which these qualities shape urban change.

3   The total number of 71,071 plots is equivalent to 19.1 plots per 1,000 inhabitants (SenUVK, 2019: 28).

4   According to Heinz and Belina, this tremendous price increase has been caused by the concentration of capital in particular locations, market-conforming land-use policies, urban competition, the current policy of maintaining low interest rates, the sales of public land for budgetary reasons, and land speculation (2019: 9).

5   All in all, the gardeners have "lost" 90 allotment compounds since reunification (Tschacher, 2009).

6   On private land, the most prominent reduction during this period resulted from the eviction of the Oeynhausen colony. From this land, 160 plots were used for housing construction (SenUVK, 2019: 19).

7   Once allotment holders are legally recognized as dwellers, the colony has to provide year-round infrastructural services (interview, 10.07.2014).

8 Additionally an amendment specified regulations regarding the costs of the lease. The BKleinG caps the price of the lease and therewith the rights of the property owner. With the gardeners using their huts as dwellings or extending them beyond the foreseen limit, this restriction could no longer be justified. Thus, the BKleinG was adapted to allow the property owners to raise the lease price (to four times the amount typically paid for land used for commercial agricultural production; SenUVK, 2019: 3).

9 These are not only the cases of the former East Berlin but include land-use changes in the former West Berlin as well.

Chapter 6

Constellations of Consent
Navigating the Politics of Regulatory Enforcement

Although urban bureaucracies have long been described as holders of centralized power, characterized by professionalism and limited room for discretion, contemporary accounts of their workings have undergone a considerable shift. Today, devolution, partnership, and good governance appear to have changed what had been presumably neutral and rigid bureaucracies into strategically operating institutions that are complicit with private corporate interest and act at large in flexible and unaccountable ways (Swyngedouw, 2005; Donald et al., 2014). Much of the literature that deals with the effect such flexibility has had on low-income populations highlights how speculation, negotiation, and backroom deals are entangled in or based on top-down violence, dominance, and oppression (Bear, 2011; Weinstein, 2017). Conversely, this chapter illustrates elements of cooperation, pragmatism, and negotiation in the governance of informal housing. Empirically, it depicts a situation in which all parties concerned with allotment gardening are aware of informal dwelling practices but tolerate these practices as long as a certain balance is maintained. This situation poses questions regarding the making of consent and the boundaries of regulation and transgression: Which infringements undergo close scrutiny? Which processes secure a compromise? And how does consent around the room for tolerating transgression break down?

In providing a theoretical basis from which to answer these questions, Chapter 2 established an approach to the state that understands it as being perpetually produced and reproduced in the everyday practices of actors in and beyond institutions. In particular, I built on literature that suggests the state would lack strategic rationality and solid boundaries. Charles Tilly provides an illustrative version of this perspective that finds regulation to be relationally negotiated rather than imposed in a top-down way. In a short paper (2009) on the everyday operations of states, he proposes the notion of "grudging consent"

Housing in the Margins: Negotiating Urban Formalities in Berlin's Allotment Gardens,
First Edition. Hanna Hilbrandt.

to explore how rulers campaign for the approval of their subordinates. "Democracy," Tilly writes, "thrives on bargaining compliance rather than on either passive acceptance or uncompromising resistance" (ibid: 1). For Tilly, sovereignty is thus acquired and maintained through the grudging consent of the ruled; it is a consent that "manages the tensions [between the rulers and the ruled] and binds the two sides together" (ibid: 7). Such agreement, he concludes, is produced through continuous negotiations.

Beyond the value of Tilly's conclusions for an analysis of *state* engagement, an understanding of the everyday enactment of regulation highlights how *civil society actors* negotiate consent – both with the bureaucracy and among themselves – and exploit potentialities within such consent. Straughn (2005: 1601) calls these acts "consentful contention" to designate forms of political engagement "in which the claim maker enacts the persona of a dutiful citizen, while contesting specific actions or politics of the state." For James Scott, these acts are "infrapolitics" (Scott, 1990), hidden transcripts that undermine state rule. What holds these and other accounts of "everyday resistance" (Certeau, 1988) together is that they describe forms of protest that do not openly defy the state, but perpetually undermine its rule and thereby also trouble the binary of collaboration and contention. Building on this work, this chapter explores consent-seeking in processes of governing as bilateral: not only the ruled but also the responsible state bureaucrats need to consent to a number of compromises. Accordingly, I describe the production of formality as a cooperative effort that is shaped by all those concerned and leads, at best, to a joint, although possibly contested, arrangement. Yet, the claim of consent raises important questions about the boundaries of this tolerance (cf. Lamont and Molnár, 2002). Despite the sufferance of transgressions, dwelling nonetheless becomes a battleground on which disputes about inclusion and exclusion are fought out. In the case of allotment dwelling, the city's toleration relies on a negotiated arrangement that is clearly delimited and protected through contradictory practices of repression, both by state officials and by the allotment gardeners.

These phenomena are all, as I will show in detail below, indicative of the state's relation to informality. To run ahead of myself and hint at some of the conclusions of this book, this understanding of the careful and joint fabrication of consent may help to question a view of informality as delineated singlehandedly by state actors who draw boundaries between legitimate and illegitimate forms of rule. If formality is, as I argue in this book, the effect of such regulatory processes, and regulation is, as I seek to show, not solely produced in a confined sphere of the state, then formality itself needs to be seen as the contested product of the engagement of a broader constellation of actors. A more relational view of the state, which foregrounds a more practice-centered understanding of the making of order, leads, in other words, to a more dialogical reading of formality, as shifting, negotiated, and provisionally arranged through the power relations and networks of wider constellations of governing.

To pursue this line of argumentation, this chapter seeks to analyze regulatory regimes through the mundane practices of governing as found at play across a wide range of actors and, through this, to show how these actors join hands in navigating regulations. More specifically, I trace how political play within these actor constellations produces a range of accepted orders that one might designate as formalities. In order to comprehensively grasp how room for maneuver is pieced together between these actor groups, the following sections explore the rationalities and remits of governing from the point of view of four relevant actor groups: the district administration, the District Association of Allotment Gardeners [*Bezirksverband der Kleingärtner*], the chairpersons of the allotment colonies, and the allotment holders themselves. Across these positions, I highlight two themes: first, the gardeners' strategies to stay put, i.e. their attempts to deal with and stabilize their housing situation, and second, the boundary mechanisms and the ways in which inequalities surface in the negotiations discussed.

Before proceeding, however, a contextual explanation is pertinent. To understand allotment governance, it is necessary to know that allotment land is mostly owned by the city, but leased out at the district level. Allotment colonies are governed by their own administration, the above-mentioned District Association of Allotment Gardeners, which takes over the administration of *all colonies* in one district and typically sublets *single colonies*. The local association of the colonies [*Kleingartenverein*], in turn, subleases these plot by plot. This organizational setup is overseen by a small number of allotment garden administrators who work at the level of the district, represent the city (the landowner), and supervise the work of the gardening associations. Given that the management of gardening land is not a minimal task, this staffing level hardly suffices. Yet in addition, the city of Berlin funds only one position in the city-level administration, SenStadt, to look after the approximately 71,000 plots. Through this organizational setup, the governance of allotment dwelling faces multiple hurdles. Let me start outlining these restraints by pointing to the latitude in negotiating regulatory enforcement at the level of the district bureaucracy.

The District Administration: Beyond the Books, Pragmatism Rules

From an organizational perspective, the units in the district administration of Berlin that are responsible for allotment governance form part of the team in charge of the city's urban greenery, which is consequently engaged in environmental issues rather than concerned with shelter claims. While this setup crucially shapes modalities of governing, allotment dwelling is nonetheless a well-known offense ("we are always aware"; interview, 19.09.2013). Officials might not be in the know about the duration of gardeners' residency or the details of each hut, but as Mr. Werner, a district bureaucrat, ascertains,

> when you really take the trouble to go there in the deepest winter in the morning at six or seven you will see where there's light and you will see where the chimney is smoking and how many cars there are with frozen windows. (Interview, 07.08.2013)

For Mariana Valverde, this "how" of governance is a matter of capacities and rationalities (2009: 144) and, in line with this assumption, different degrees of certainty about allotment dwelling pertain as the individual engagement, enforcement ability, and personal attitudes of bureaucrats vary. In the regulation of allotment gardens, rationalities play out in different ways. Take, for instance, the statement of Mr. Becker, a former allotment garden administrator with a rather relaxed attitude: "If there wasn't something really at sixes and sevens," he noted in an interview, "we didn't immediately demonstrate the power of the state ... well you see it, then you ... um... well ... we are somewhat human too" (interview, 23.04.2014). Whereas his statement speaks for a strong use of discretionary space and a generous understanding of regulation, asked about her control of illegal housing extensions in the allotments of her district, Ms. Richter, who occupies a similar position in the allotment bureaucracy, reasoned:

> I would say I tread on the toes of the District Association of Allotment Gardeners. I really control it, I do! I'm really rigorous in this issue. From the perspective of the District Association of Allotment Gardeners presumably a bit obtrusive, but I stick to it ... when I see something like that, I get on their nerves ...
> H. H.: So you walk through the compounds and check?
> Ms Richter: Of course! Yes! I would say those who are within walking distance, the cards are stacked against them, because when I go [to work] by car and I see something, then ... I would just walk over – say on an afternoon and have a look at what's going on. I take a couple of pictures ... and I'm back in ten, fifteen minutes. And the other compounds, there I simply combine it [regulation walks] with instances when there is construction work, where I would just say ... I'll randomly say, "I'll have a look on-site." Or, I'll check online first, where you can see in the aerial photographs that things may look a bit strange and

you'd like to see it on-site. And then I take the car and drive "out" and have a look. (Interview, 09.04.2014)

Ms. Richter's account of regulation describes her own engagement as rigorous, detailed, and challenging. Although, from her point of view, her commitment to fulfill her institutional role entirely justifies these measures, gardeners consider her means as obtrusive, as they extend the expected realm of intervention. Unlike Mr. Becker, Ms. Richter is not ready to consent too easily to an overstepping of rules. Hannah Jones's (2011) study of policy implementation in the London borough of Hackney explores such commitments in the context of local bureaucracies (Jones, 2011: 60). She suggests with Hunter (2008) that policy documents constitute "a meeting point for ... multiple perspectives" and thus hardly transmit "a definite normative truth about the world, but ... fictions between what 'is' and what 'might be'" (cited in Jones, 2011: 72). Thus, for Jones, the ways in which bureaucrats imagine policies and accommodate the differing assumptions that guide the interpretation of a text crucially shape policy implementation.

Yet, shortage of operational capacity trumps rationality. Despite the personal engagement of some of the allotment garden administrators, the more or less permanent use of a hut as a dwelling space is almost impossible to prove – even in those colonies where large numbers of gardeners reside in their huts. A thorough regulation would imply each employee monitoring a couple of thousand plots. Thus in practice, regulation works, as Mr. Becker adds, by way of stumbling across problems: more in an accidental fashion than a systematic way (interview, 23.04.2014). His contention reflects the testimony of all of my interviewees in similar tiers of the bureaucracy: the tight budgets of local bureaucracies do not suffice to allow for a rigid enforcement of rules (e.g. interview, 25.04.2014). Districts can neither fund more than two positions to manage allotment gardens nor afford to sue their tenants. These restraints turn bureaucrats into confidants of legal transgressions within their jurisdictions. Is this complicity at play?

To be sure, these constraints lead to pragmatism and cooperation. Allotment garden administrators pass on matters of regulation to the District Association of Allotment Gardeners in part because they do not have the capacity to take care of these issues themselves. To regulate the problems that this association does not resolve, the city's allotment bureaucracy has a final measure at hand, which is also a final obstacle. The organizational setup that I previously described implies that local bureaucracies have a contractual relationship with neither the individual colonies nor the gardeners of each plot. As contractual partners of the district association, the ultimate means to enforce regulations is thus to terminate the lease contract with this association and thereby of *all* plots in the district. However, in everyday practices, this is simply not tenable, as no other association could handle the task, as Ms. Braun, a responsible actor in a district bureaucracy, explains to me at length:

> Honestly, it's difficult, really difficult. Of course, we could terminate the contract with the District Association of Allotment Gardeners, or we could sue, but that's all *theory*. Generally, the district association would itself be interested in getting things in order, but they often can't, because … whatever, because someone obstructs things, because something is in their way. I cannot really answer this one hundred per cent. We always try, but sometimes things come to nothing. Other issues are decided in court, but a real handle on things, contractually yes, but factually, we don't really have that. (Interview, 19.08.2013)

The District Association of Allotment Gardeners [Bezirksverband der Kleingärtner] is an organization that has grown over a century and is today a cultural institution. As outlined in Chapter 3, its development is based on the formation of an urban movement strengthened through a period of struggles concerning the privatization of land in the sixties and seventies. Given this tradition and know-how, the organization would be difficult to replace. Despite the many efforts mentioned by Ms. Braun, regulation in practice is thus working with the factual, which, in distinction to the contractual, is doable.

The "how" of governance may be a matter of rationality and capacity. In the present case, the bureaucrats' different rationalities and limited capacity mostly lead to pragmatism. In this arrangement, officers are forced to turn a blind eye or find ways to juggle documents, plans, laws, and the like with the daily restrictions of their jobs. Thereby, they accommodate informal dwelling. To be sure, this accommodation has limits that are negotiated in cooperation with the allotment administration, to which I turn next.

The Allotment Administration: Common Ground

To understand the modalities and boundaries of regulatory engagement and the ways in which formalities are negotiated on the ground, the above-described limits of institutional control have to be considered in view of the institutional arrangements of the allotment administration already alluded to in the previous section. To recall, the everyday governance of allotment gardens is not only handled through the district bureaucracies but also by the gardeners' self-administered associations. These associations function like a political apparatus inserted between the individual gardener and the city's bureaucracy. Their offices are supposed to control the conditions of each plot, to mediate internal conflicts through their own arbitration panel, or to sue noncomplying gardeners. Moreover, these associations assume all relevant managerial functions, such as subleasing individual plots, at two levels of administrative hierarchy. The lower level – the local association of each colony – elects an executive board [*Vereinsvorstand*] that assumes, for example, accountancy functions, and will be discussed in the subsequent section. The upper level, the District Association of Allotment Gardeners, consists of a body of civil experts – often retired lawyers, former employees of local bureaucracies, or other lay professionals. This section is concerned with their regulatory efforts, thereby adding a second perspective on the negotiation of dwelling claims and the limits of such maneuvering.

To start, it is useful to note that this level of regulation is caught between the requirements of the city administration, on the one hand, and the exigencies of the gardeners, on the other. In this sandwiched position, administrators negotiate their regulatory involvement with both of these levels. Consider, for instance, a conversation with Mr. Binder, an experienced district administrator who has volunteered in several posts, worked in his professional life in the city's street-level bureaucracy, and today shares the responsibilities for several thousand plots. When asked about his commitment to regulate, he reasoned:

> The excuses [of the gardeners] are manifold. I know most of them! Even the lawyer says it is terribly difficult to prove *Schwarzwohnen*. And so you leave it! You know that's the way it is; that there are some, but as long as it works somehow, I don't want to say we tolerate it. I can't. But we don't do anything against it. (Interview, 16.08.2013)

Not unlike actors in Berlin's state bureaucracy, Mr. Binder's reasoning indicates the extent to which regulation is driven by pragmatism. The problem of allotment dwelling is not one that promises a solution; hence, it does not urgently require him to get involved. Legal support permits an "informed" kind of looking away. Nevertheless, Mr. Binder is reluctant to describe the administration's tactical practices as tolerant, or, said differently, he is cautious to fix the negotiable nature of dwelling regulation by labeling it as tolerant and thereby declaring his attitude a rule. For Mr. Binder, such pragmatism appears entirely acceptable due to the inaction of all other governing actors:

> If even the local administration [the municipal bureaucracy at the district level] says that it's too laborious to interdict *Schwarzwohnen*,

because it involves too much cost and trouble! ... For example, even the guy at the district office ... says: "Well, I see cars in the winter covered with snow, the chimneys are smoking. Well, then I know what's going on." But he also says, "I don't stand there and freeze my arse off and afterwards I cannot prove anything." ... So I don't need to either! (Interview, 16.08.2013)

Mr. Binder stresses the discomfort of involvement, but more importantly here, the rationality is: the others don't intervene either! This is not to say that tolerance of transgressions is taken for granted. Rather, the inaction of local districts legitimizes the noninterference of the district association and works to normalize infringements.

Yet, the possibility of such toleration depends on a set of preconditions that need to be secured to allow for the administration to remain inactive. Most crucially, this realm of toleration relies on keeping the peace. The case of Ms. Müller illustrates this claim. Ms. Müller had been living in her hut for 25 years to save on rent and to mitigate the risks of self-employment. She had gradually settled into and expanded her hut, and she was not the only one to dwell in her colony. Asked about fellow gardeners in the colony, Ms. Müller reported: "I can tell you that exactly. We have exactly 65 inhabitants. It's simple to see that if you come in the winter and count the garbage bins" (interview, 13.08.2013). However, following a dispute within the colony, a neighbor snitched on her, i.e. he reported her and other colony dwellers to the district association. In consequence, the association asked her to dismantle the gas tank she had used for heating throughout all those years. Ms. Müller reasoned: "The district association had always tolerated that [her use of the gas tank], but presumably they have to follow up when they receive such a charge" (interview, 13.08.2013).

But why was she sanctioned, and effectively forced to leave, while others were able to stay? One way of answering this question is to consider her legal situation. Unlike some of her neighbors, Ms. Müller simply lacked the necessary documents to show that her gas tank was authorized. But key to the end of her tenancy was the creation of a nuisance: Ms. Müller's dispute ended in a TV report, and brought officers into a situation in which they could no longer afford to ignore the denigratory reports filed by her neighbor. As she noted, "at the time, the newspaper was here. And Sat 1 and Pro 7 ... no it must have been RTL [major German entertainment television channels]; they filmed here and it was on the internet – it was a big fuss! So then the district administration went to see who is registered here" (interview, 13.08.2013). Although this might not appear immediately obvious, Ms. Müller herself had called the media, assuming that doing so would support her claims. However, in turning her trouble into a public affair, she crossed the boundaries of local consent in which transgressions could have been managed internally. Officials themselves might not have wanted things to be visible or public, but Ms. Müller's disruption of the rules of the game forced them to act. As noted, the association could not prove that she had been living in the hut. However, in forcing her to dismantle the gas tank, the hut became uninhabitable over the winter months, so that Ms. Müller eventually decided to move out. If the tacit consent I am describing depends largely on the appearance of "peace" in the colonies, no matter how peaceful they may actually be, conversely, too much noise may cause wider troubles for others as well, and thus foster rigid application of rules and regulations. In this line of thinking, keeping the peace widens the boundaries of tolerance.

The story of Ms. Müller would be incomplete without an account of corruption that concerns all levels of administration inside and outside of the allotment administration. Feeling that she had been treated unfairly, Ms. Müller reasoned that others in the colony had never been made to dismantle anything in their own huts because they formed a part of what she referred to as "the gang" – a close and corrupt support network between the association officials, fellow gardeners, and local political figures. I frequently came across accusations of corruption, particularly in relation to sums that had been paid to enlarge huts (e.g. interviews 07.08.2013, 16.08.2013, 23.04.2014, 16.04.2019). And although I was in no position to trace or prove a number of related claims, it would similarly be naïve not to account for the numerous relations of patronage on which allotment dwelling also depends. At least for Ms. Müller, the heavy-handed treatment she received goes back to her position as an outsider to this "gang."

In sum, the perspective of the allotment administration illustrates how the relations between state officials and their cooperating partners in the colonies construct a common ground on which mutual recognition and understanding prevail. Rather than merely copying and adapting to the attitude of city officials, the administrators of the colonies make use of moments of discretion while maintaining a balance by intervening in the most conspicuous transgressions.

The Chairpersons: A *Blockwart* Regime?

Beyond the District Association of Allotment Gardeners, allotment governance relies on elected officials within the colonies – most importantly, the chairpersons of the colony and their team, typically consisting of a deputy, a treasurer, and a secretary. These officials manage internal order, administer a colony's finances, and report back to the upper tier of the association previously described. In addition, posts such as the "allotment specialist consultant" [*Kleingartenfachberater*] – a job that is frequently referred to as "hedge-police" [*Heckenpolizei*] – or official arbitrators work to keep social and material order within the compounds. Mr. Fischer, for instance, is the chairperson of a colony. When I met him in the clubhouse of his colony, he critically responded to one of my first routine questions about his responsibilities in the job by noting that he would be "theoretically obliged through a service contract ... to act as the representative of the district association in a sort of control function and report to the districts ... in a sort of vigilante situation [*Blockwartsituation*]" (interview, 09.07.2014). This skeptical description of his post alludes to what had been the lowest surveillance authority of the Nazi regime. However, the German term *Blockwart* [literally: warden of the block] has survived to date, marking someone as a snooper. Yet, the "vigilante" control at this regulatory level is hardly a function that merely reports from the bottom up. Rather, it adds a third dimension to my claim that regulatory enforcement in the colonies is cooperative work and builds on a consensus that is negotiated by all those concerned, including the *Blockwarte* themselves.

City officials tend to describe this level of regulation as the "weakest" or most unreliable link in the polynomial chain of regulatory efforts: it is the level where a great amount of regulatory work should be done, but this frequently fails to happen. Most chairpersons and their teams are directly involved in the gardeners' everyday lives. They encounter each other during frequent meetings, such as opening ceremonies of the season, children's festivities, or casual chats across the hedge. To be sure, their participation in local affairs goes much deeper than that of a "distant" state official who tends to avoid contact unless problems arise, or who is present through the shadowy control that I previously described. Going beyond the street-level encounters in which citizens "see the state" (Corbridge et al., 2005), allotment bureaucrats not only govern through abstract commitments and rationalities, but also through their tight social relations as neighbors or friends. As Ms. Hartman, an allotment garden administrator, reasoned, it is "because the heads of the colonies are also members and have their plots within the colonies [that] they operate in fairly generous ways" (interview, 09.04.2014). Similarly, Ms. Richter, an allotment garden administrator in a different district, concluded in response to my inquiry into the challenges of regulation that "a major shortcoming of the associations, which I hold against them ... is that the chairs set the example, right? And surely 90% – if they aren't themselves permanent dwellers or proprietors – they support it" (interview,

09.04.2014). However, if these functionaries are able to loosen up and appreciate a certain wiggle room, the generosity that Ms. Hartman describes depends on a number of premises.

First, colony officials work to forge alliances with other parties to widen their sphere of influence in constellations of governance and create room to shape the ways in which transgressions become subject to regulation. Consider, for instance, Mr. Koch's narrative of his colony's strategies to maintain good relations with the political officials of his district:

> We get along well with [our district mayor] … and on the quiet he also knows what's going on here … He would never admit that publicly, for heaven's sake! But he knows what's going on and he also knows that there is peace and quiet here and that we don't make trouble. And as long as we don't cause any difficulties and don't go too far, it's not a problem. … We have also invited [the district mayor] annually to our festivities, also the councilor for construction [*Baustadtrat*].
> H. H.: And what does he say [concerning your residency]?
> Mr. Koch: In fact, he sees it the same way. (Interview, 16.09.2013)

To be sure, this agreement is dependent on close relations to the local officials that allow allotment gardeners to prove they live up to the expected standard. In this agreement, both the openings for and the boundaries of transgressions are clearly stated: gardeners cannot overstep certain bounds, and although the district mayor "knows what's going on," he does not and cannot publicly admit having this knowledge. The question of what it might mean to overstep is one that I will continue to trace in this chapter.

The second premise of tolerance concerns the internal management of the gardeners' transgressions. I frequently noted how colony officials take any issues that arise into their own hands and can, in this way, hold possible regulators at bay. Mr. Koch went on to tell me:

> You know … when there is someone building another storey, I see that from far away. We would never let that go through …
> H. H.: Do you mean that your association regulates this internally?
> Mr. Koch: Yes, we regulate. Yes, of course. To avoid the involvement of third parties: the district association or even the local district. (Interview, 16.09.2013)

Despite the fact that such regulation is officially part of his role, his attempt to resolve transgressions internally also allows colony officials to safeguard and manage their room for maneuver in the "constellations of consent" that this chapter describes. Their efforts to self-manage infringements also permit them to create latitude, in which they can get away with other transgressions (see also Hilbrandt, 2019).

Third, for some, safeguarding boundaries implies managing who is able to take on a garden in the first place – whether they dwell in it or not. Although in some colonies, central management systems regulate applications for a plot, in most colonies, the management board of an association decides upon such applications itself. To understand how processes of boundary-making play out in this process, it is worth quoting Mr. Huber, a chairperson of a colony, at length:

> We have people from Russia and Poland. It is very mixed, I would say. What is important for us is to try to see in the run-up … you know *it's a gut feeling* when you see people and say: "Well, that could work … or it couldn't." These days you have to be a bit more cautions. I have heard it from different colonies that they have very, very bitterly regretted taking on these people from Turkish or Arab origin. They say it doesn't work at all. It's just a different culture. We had it over there [in a different part of the colony] and I was able to control it … well you go on holiday and you know what you are getting into, but here on your own plot or your own colony? That is a bit, I would say … on the threshold of unacceptability. During our last office hours there was someone, I assume he was a Syrian national, when he came in everyone winced. "What the hell is this?" The optics alone were just like an ISIS fighter [*laughs*]. No word of German. He brought along an interpreter. Well, that's when the railway gates came down. There we say no … there I close down and say that doesn't work. (Interview, 16.04.2019, my emphasis)

This was not the only case of racist stereotyping that I encountered in my interviews. Additionally, in 2016, an allotment colony publicly came into disrepute because colony officials were no longer admitting allotment holders with a so-called "migration background" into their associations (Arlt, 2016; Kneist and Röttger, 2016).[1] Going public with these practices breached a taboo even among the associations, especially because the use of allotment land for gardening is justified, in part, with the presumed "integrative" function of collective gardening. The district association distanced itself from these measures (ibid). But Mr. Huber's statement indicates how deeply ingrained racism and intercultural conflict are across a wider number of colonies when defining, for instance, their admission practice. And although the question of admission does not directly answer the question of who is able to dwell, it defines who is to be part of a collective "we" that can then negotiate the tacit consent of dwelling in allotments.

It is evident that the chairpersons of the colonies are themselves not completely free in their maneuvers. Rather, the gardeners discipline their chairpersons too. Mr. Berger, himself a head of a colony, told me about the decades before he took office: "When you hold a plot for so much time, you see people coming and going. Then, there is a new smart aleck [referring to a chairperson of a colony] that you have to calm down and then eventually they also turn out to be terrific" (interview, 10.07.2014). As I was told, calming down elected officials in the gardens also appears to have taken the form of throwing cat food on their cars, spreading paint on their huts, and even more violent interventions (interview, 19.06.2014). Most certainly, officials would not be re-elected if they were to restrict dwelling.

In sum, the "vigilante control" Mr. Fischer described at the start of this section is predominantly not carried out by following top-down measures. Rather, colony officials mediate the conditions of their involvement within constellations of governance, as the devolution of responsibilities to this level increases the flexibility they have in navigating transgressions. These responsibilities, in turn, allow them to configure modalities of regulatory enforcement and the boundaries of participation and inclusion. In this sense, the agency of vigilance appears closer to a notion of vigilantism as the self-rule of community through the everyday governance of security (Wisler and Onwudiwe, 2008) than to the *Blockwart* regulation seen in the Nazi regime.

The Gardening Friends: Pressures on the Ground

In addition to the city's institutional structures and the administrative ranks of the association, allotment holders discipline each other's conduct on-site. Their internal regulation through social ties and mutual control is the focus of my fourth perspective on the constellations that govern allotment dwelling. This view unveils how social relations and neighborhood bonds create pressures to conform to standards of appropriate conduct as well as build moments of tolerance through a set of strategies that shape imperatives of rule.

Let me start by describing these social relations through a pointed "mimicry" that Mr. Fischer added to his account of the *Blockwartsituation*:

The one who lives over there has a very old Transit [*whispers*]. Ford Transit. He stored so much wood on the roof, eventually the roof rack collapsed. Ah … and this one … only ever gets up around noon, although he's a baker [*laughs*] … ah, and, for example, this one, she is

new and a very young woman, a student, has a small child and is separated from the dad and all of that ... and says, okay, actually she wants
to try gardening without watering, that nature provides everything for
itself. Well, I think that's okay, but all the others ... the neighbors ...
umm, well, that wasn't very popular! ... It's this old rationality of order
[*Ordnungsdenken*] that we have long rehearsed and that has, well ...
molded everyone! It's a village ... and once someone has their reputa-
tion, then ... well that's like rumor that is taken through the compound
... There is such a mind-boggling group pressure! (Interview,
09.07.2014)

As Mr. Fischer indicates, conduct is dependent on pressure to conform.
In addition to hedge-to-hedge encounters, the regular festivities, club activities, and horticultural competitions further the tight social relations that
characterize the colonies. His account of the allotments' "village-like" relationships between the gardening friends seems to run counter to descriptions
of the city as a site of alienation (Simmel, 2006 [1903]) that lament the disap-
pearance of community life (Sennett, 1977; Jacobs, 1993 [1961]).[2] In Mr.
Fischer's account, the allotment remains a space of tight social proximity.

In many of the former Eastern colonies, particularly those near the site
of the Berlin Wall, plots had preferentially been given to party affiliates or
those in the GDR's higher ranks of the military (e.g. interviews 06.07.2014,
19.06.2014). According to some of my interviewees, these "selected cadres"
crucially shaped the social pressures and culture of conduct on-site. "Those,
who were then part of the armed forces of those days," a respondent told
me, "they are still with us in the colony. They built, I'd like to say, still a sort
of internal command structure" (interview, 26.06.2014). To be sure, a generational change has shaped these structures, but the "feudal" bonds lend
themselves to a tight system of social control that bears on regulatory
efforts. These peer-to-peer (i.e. hedge-to-hedge) relations also reflect rem-
nants of the dual function of the gardens: on the one hand, as an infrastructure of food supplementation to answer "the stomach question" (*die
Magenfrage,* Nilsen, 2014: 93), and on the other hand, as a project of moral
regulation and social engineering to answer "the lifestyle question" (*die
Lebensfrage,* ibid) or, as Nilson writes, to "inculcate moral values in workers" (ibid: 14). Social relations, in other words, construct a bundle of expectations that are likely to designate what behavior is thought acceptable and
what needs to be followed up on. These expectations, or internal norms,
gain a dynamic of their own. They may support illegal dwelling but may
undermine, for instance, alternative forms of gardening that are tolerated
by bureaucracies. In this sense, the ordering behavior of allotment holders

may be independent of or potentially at odds with the aims of municipal governance or state law.

Allotment holders deal with these pressures to conform through a number of strategies that work to circumvent regulation and allow certain activities to stay under the radar. For instance, they limit the visibility of their practices vis-à-vis fellow gardeners. A respondent told me of his efforts to circumvent being seen accessing the colony:

> I do try to be very strategic and make myself invisible as much as I can. Say, I wake up at 7:30 a.m. and come directly out of my garden – that is a bit strange. Because that is not a time where someone would be done with their morning duties. When I leave at 6:30 a.m., no one is up yet. No one sees me. When I leave at 9:00 a.m. or 10:30 a.m., that is a window of time where people think: "Ah okay, he was here to pick something up and is leaving now." I do think people muse about these situations. (Interview, 27.09.2018)

Moreover, the gardeners' strategies work to bypass control by keeping public knowledge of transgressions at bay. Consider, for instance, Mr. Koch und Ms. Wolf's discussion about their openness toward others. When I asked them if they would talk to acquaintances and fellow gardeners about their living conditions, Mr. Koch responded:

> We spent a lot of time.
> Ms. Wolf: We say we are "out" a lot, particularly in the summer – logically.
> Mr. Koch: Yeah, but toward others … the intimate friends know it.
> Ms. Wolf: Exactly!
> Mr. Koch: But others … it's not other people's business.
> Ms. Wolf: No, it's nobody's business. I agree. (Interview, 16.09.2013)

Their discussion speaks of a reluctance to make their dwelling situation public. As argued in Chapter 4, this reluctance indicates caution, rather than insecurity; and it circumvents the tight social control of their peers.

Moreover, gardeners mediate the access of others to safeguard the boundaries of consent established around the toleration of dwelling. Related measures are readily apparent in an earlier quote of Mr. Koch concerning his regulation of a roof expansion: "those who don't accept that – we don't want them here" (interview, 16.09.2013), thereby referring to a necessary agreement to the internal rules that guide the colony and the exclusion of those who break these rules. As an outsider to the life of the colonies, I frequently experienced such boundaries of access myself. In various colonies, I was immediately told off or asked about my intentions when attempting to photograph houses. While most allotment holders were interested in my project, I noted others closing up – possibly as a matter of precaution – when I was talking about the topic of my book. For instance, in June 2014, I encountered a gardener who was born in an allotment in 1940 and had spent his entire life residing in the colony without a dwelling permit. He had generously promised to organize a get-together of the old permanent inhabitants of this particular compound. Yet, when I returned as we had agreed upon, he had talked through the idea with the chairperson of his compound and I was told that the meeting could not be held. As they noted, "they could not yet divulge all their secrets" (field notes, 14.05.2014 and 05.06.2014).

Delimiting access implies retaining control of outsiders, visitors, researchers, or others who cannot be trusted to consent to the tacit rules of the game; this also touches on thorny issues about racism. As we have previously seen, practices of exclusion become readily apparent in the regulatory efforts of the chairpersons of the colony, for instance in the allocation of plots, but they can also be found at the level of the gardeners' everyday conduct. Consider, for instance, the experiences of Mr. Fischer, a chairperson of a colony. In an interview, he reported of Romanian seasonal workers who had permanently moved into an allotment colony and met the resistance of its members. He noted:

> Well, it's really difficult! … On the one hand there is this threat of "slumification," and as these social structures form, they meet absolute resistance.
> H. H.: How did the neighbors respond to these men?
> Mr. Fischer: Hostile … dismissive … critical, right? … Honestly, I have to say, it's real difficult. (Interview, 09.07.2014)

Mr. Fischer had already worried about the "slumification" of the colony, but the "hostile" and "dismissive" attitude of his peers furthered his fears. During the preceding months, newspapers had inserted this term into the local debate after Roma families had settled in rededicated allotments that were awaiting demolition to make space for the expansion of an urban motorway in the district of Berlin-Neukölln (Mihai, 2013). This discourse finds its context in the 2007 enlargement of the European Union, in which nationals from Bulgaria and Romania were granted freedom of movement, yet remained without the rights to receive full access to work. These work restrictions also repeatedly led to their exclusion from housing markets, and forced them into substandard accommodation or homelessness (Künkel, 2018). Here, I want to point out that the antagonisms and resulting pressure on part of the gardeners reproduced processes of bordering and ultimately led to the dismissal of the men, in contrast to others who were able to stay (cf. Hilbrandt, 2019). It is here where my account resonates with conceptions of informality as the reproduction of confinement (Pasquetti and Picker, 2017; Weinstein, 2017). Clearly, in these cases, the flexibility of extralegality and the negotiability of informal arrangements lend themselves to the further marginalization of those already multiply excluded.

Conclusion

Coming full circle, this chapter takes me back to the case of Ms. Müller, who was forced to leave the colony because she was made to dismantle her gas tank. In the trial she reported about, she sought the support of her neighbors. However, her gardening friends could not help her out, because their dwelling situation was similarly illegal. Ms. Müller told me:

> Well, the problem is really, well, there is a law … but no one is treated equally. This is what happens when you live lawlessly. The people here are aware of that, right. Everyone has something. He has an extension; she has a greenhouse, etc. And when they do something, then immediately … they are afraid that the district association will say: "You have to dismantle this. You live here. You need to …" and all of that. (Interview, 13.08.2013)

Ms. Müller saw me off with a sentence that was difficult to forget. "When you live beyond the law," she said, "you have no protection" (field notes, 13.08.2013). The informal use of their huts to dwell in deprives gardeners of their legal rights. Yet this chapter has shown how space of consent is delineated and stabilized – for some, and according to a defined set of rules. In the examples provided, regulatory enactment is triggered only when problems come to light. It is mostly avoided: colonies reconcile conflicts or neighborly disputes as local matters, they shield legal violations from an outside audience, and they keep their peers in check. Clearly, such stability is not written in stone. But the underlying "trust relations" between bureaucrats and allotment holders have often been built over years. In fact, the prioritizing, stretching, or translating of bureaucratic regulations have perpetually normalized a relatively stable realm of tolerance. Through these processes of repetition, a precedent-based order becomes established in the everyday and institutionalizes the ambiguities in which dwelling is embedded. The presumably unregular nature of informality becomes a knowable messiness that grants relative stability.

In outlining the perspectives of four groups of actors relevant in allotment governance, this chapter has shown that the everyday practices, normative assessments, and social relations on which regulation relies all shape the ways in which order is institutionalized. Moreover, I have suggested that enacting regulations is a joint effort: bureaucracies have little choice but to rely on their partners in the colonies. Allotment holders, in turn, can widen room for tolerance through adapting regulations, but they also need to adhere to the rules of the game. This agency, I find, is neither the unintended minuscule agency of Foucauldian accounts nor the power of collective resistance against a muscular state. Rather, in this case, the gardeners' leverage builds on individual practices and capacities in the everyday enactment of rules. Together, all parties concerned negotiate the modalities of regulatory enforcement to create a space of consent. Consent foregrounds association, but it does not imply approval (cf. Straughn, 2005). This is not to say that all parties actively consent to gardeners' transgressions. Rather, consent is likely to be the contested result of a necessity. It indicates that perpetually "turning a blind eye" delimits a realm of toleration or legitimate inaction, which reifies and thereby institutionalizes rules on the ground.

To be sure, such consent builds on "boundary-maintenance" processes (Misztal, 2002: 145) that operate at different levels (Anthias and Yuval-Davis, 1993; Barth, 1998). And these boundaries go beyond the consensual agreement of "not making trouble," "not causing difficulties" (interview, 16.09.2013), or the imperative not to go too far (ibid) that allotment holders need to meet when they sidestep official regulations. As negotiability tends to depend largely on the ways in which the gardeners create room for maneuver, they also define who is able to partake in these negotiations. In the present case, the room for engagement that opens up in the everyday negotiation of transgressions comes at the price of its uneven distribution, when outsiders are excluded on the basis of racism. To be sure, the literature that speaks of the emancipatory potential of governance from below needs to contend with a reality in which exclusion is also reinforced at this same level of engagement.

These conclusions have significant implications for my understanding of formality. On the one hand, rather than differentiating formality through some boundary set by the law, my discussion points at the ways in which the boundaries of tolerance are established through social practices. It follows that what is inside or outside of a realm of consent not only relies on written statutes or fixed frames but is also determined by the ordinary compromises that negotiations bring about. On the other hand, such an account of enactment implies an understanding of regulatory processes in which formality is mediated through shifting constellations of governance rather than defined from the top down. As I have aimed to show throughout this chapter, prosecution depends not merely on the severity of disobedience. Rather, the possibility to dwell is contingent upon the ability of multiple agents to negotiate an agreement on the perpetuation of the status quo. The enactment of formality builds on these modalities at play and characterizes the notion, as I argue, as an open-ended project that hinges on these constellations of consent. An understanding of formality therefore requires an account of order, state, and law, yet it must also be mindful of the widely distributed room for engagement in the enactment of regulations.

Summary: Chapter 6

This chapter considers the governance of temporary or permanent occupancy from the perspectives of various bureaucrats and allotment holders involved in the transgression and regulation of order. Combining these multiple views allows me to move beyond common assumptions about regulatory enforcement as a process in which state actors implement rules; instead, I consider the ways in which people within and beyond state institutions negotiate room for maneuver in implementing order. On the one hand, the chapter describes the production of socio-spatial order as a cooperative effort that is shaped by all parties concerned and leads, at best, to a joint although contested arrangement. On the other hand, my focus on consensual arrangements raises important questions about the limits of this tolerance and the inequalities that define such a politics of negotiation.

Notes

1   The German census statistically defines Germans to have a "migration background" in the case that they, or at least one parent, were not born with German citizenship (Statistisches Bundesamt, 2018: 12).

2   The gardening friends [*die Gartenfreunde*] is a standard allotment gardening term referring to other allotment holders, or, say, "peers," in friendly terms.

Chapter 7

Working the Legal Threshold
Regulation, Translation, and Boundary Work

This chapter explores the work of various state agencies and allotment holders in enacting rules, with a particular focus on the ways in which these actors navigate and shift rules as they put them in place, thereby fixing or stabilizing legal boundaries. Drawing from debates in legal geographies (Blomley and Bakan, 1992; Blomley, 1994, 2004; Benda-Beckmann et al., 2009) and socio-legal studies (Braverman, 2008; Levi and Valverde, 2008; Valverde, 2009, 2011; Cooper, 2011) introduced in Chapter 2, it asks how legal boundaries are established in the governance of places commonly read as lying beyond the law. These literatures study legal frames not as premises for social relations but as the contested, hybrid, and negotiable products of the wider social context in which they are set. Thereby, they offer a theoretical vocabulary to describe the complexities of the law and of its everyday enactment – themes that scholars exploring the legalization and formalization of land and housing have more frequently addressed in rather empirical terms.

Understanding regulatory work in terms of legal geography paints a clearer picture of the work of designating an object of regulation as inside or outside the legal scope. I take my cue from a research strand that places its focus on legal interpretive practices – processes of translation through which actors adapt the law to a given situation (Cooper, 1998; Blandy and Sibley, 2010; McDermont and Clarke, 2017), in particular to draw boundaries of transgression through employing legal rules. This work has described the bracketing practices of the law – the mechanisms that work to define the threshold that demarcates legal jurisdiction (de Sousa Santos, 1987) and, at times, stabilize the legal/nonlegal boundary (Blomley, 2014). In the framework of this research, legal boundaries are not stable lines but rather zones of intense struggles that modify the law as it is put in place.

Housing in the Margins: Negotiating Urban Formalities in Berlin's Allotment Gardens,
First Edition. Hanna Hilbrandt.
© 2021 John Wiley & Sons, Ltd. Published 2021 by John Wiley & Sons, Ltd.

The sections to follow apply these insights to the study of informal housing. In discussing the multiple and overlapping forms of legality that govern Berlin's allotment gardens and their inhabitation, this chapter contributes to understanding the production of this legal/illegal dichotomy through the maneuvering that regulatory work, i.e. setting this boundary, entails. Following a more precise theoretical framing of legal boundary work, I analyze the different frameworks of order that govern the gardens and the incongruity between them. Subsequently, I hone in on the ways in which actors in the gardens tailor the law and its boundaries in regulating the reduction of the huts to the standard of the Bundeskleingartengesetz (BKleinG) and other legal frames before concluding with an assessment of the relevance of this exploration for an understanding of formality. Across this discussion, I consider a wider array of laws, norms, social conventions, rules, zoning ordinances, contracts, and the internal policies of the associations. I summarize this meshwork of legal ideas under the notion "frameworks of order," a phrase that I keep intentionally vague to include multiple and frequently contradictory rules, which may be stated or unstated, that guide regulation beyond state law.

Boundaries: Plurality, Abstractions, and Legal Interpretive Work

"Liberal societies are," as legal geographer Nick Blomley writes, "heavily invested in the idea of law as an autonomous field, detached from the vagaries of social context" (2014: 141). Socio-legal studies have long challenged this basic conception of legal autonomy and legal certainty or, as Philippopoulos-Mihalopoulos (2010: 4) puts it, of a "positivist concept of the law as immaterial, universal and abstract," and have advanced a more complex analysis of the relation between the law and social space. Let me start by capturing this relation through the notions of legal abstraction and legal pluralism – two pivotal concepts of this debate.

The notion of abstraction captures the relation between the law and social space, as the landmark cartographic analogy of socio-legal scholar Boaventura de Sousa Santos (1987) readily explains. For de Sousa Santos, law distorts reality (ibid: 183) in ways that are comparable to three pivotal procedures of map-making: scaling, projecting, and symbolizing. *Scaling* describes "the relation of distance between the map and the corresponding distance on the ground" (ibid: 283), thereby allowing the map- or lawmaker to increase or decrease the detail of regulatory order. *Projections* flatten the detail of the "curved surface of the earth," thereby producing omissions, compromises, and sameness (ibid: 285). Finally, *symbolizations* abstract from the regulatory objects, thereby creating and naturalizing sign systems (ibid: 285–86). These procedures are guided by the cultural context and normativity of the map-maker. In abstracting from the contextual circumstances to which the law is to be applied, they inscribe "normative fictions" into laws that still come to be seen as neutral. The greater the abstraction, the more adaptation work is required in legal practice to fit the law to the ground.

The notion of legal pluralism complicates the relation between the law and social space. In short, and to recap the discussion of this concept that I offered in Chapter 2, legal pluralism has been defined as the "interaction of many regulative orders based on different sources of authority and legitimacy" (Chiodelli and Moroni, 2014: 163; see also Merry, 1988; Melissaris, 2004). Legal pluralism captures law as "a multicentered field" in which a plethora of quasi-legal practices produce a plurality of legal orders (Barzilai, 2008: 396). This conception decentralizes state law and undermines a clear-cut distinction between formal and informal law. Moreover, it implies that rules do not work on their own but need to be considered through their reciprocal interactions that are dependent on circumstance (Chiodelli and Moroni, 2014: 166). It follows that we can no longer speak of law and legality but, again citing de Sousa Santos, rather need to account for "interlaw and interlegality" – "the complex and changing relation among [different laws]" (1987: 288). In short, by highlighting the entanglement of different legal systems, the concept fore-fronts the relationality of legal enactment vis-à-vis the unequivocal application of any one law.

In explaining the relation between the "worldly" object of regulation and its legal textual referents, both concepts are pivotal to explore the enactment of boundaries that appear to demarcate the law from that which lies beyond its scope of regulation. Legal scholars have approached these boundaries through different concepts. To begin to grasp the production of legal bound-aries, Blomley's idea of bracketing is helpful. For Bromley, bracketing

> entails the attempt to stabilize and fix a boundary within which interac-tions take place more or less independently of their surrounding con-text. That which is designated as inside the boundary must be, in some senses, disentangled from that identified as outside. (2014: 135)

Law, in other words, rests on definitional work that carves out an object of regulation by disentangling it from other relations that are bracketed, i.e. cut off from that definition. This conceptual approach leads away from understanding boundaries as a stable reality and toward bracketing as a laborious process of (re)defining these boundaries. This process requires, to use Blomley's phrasing, "complex and subtle calculations that govern what is, and what is not, to be included within a particular setting" (ibid: 136). It does not, however, turn law into an external "bracketed" reality. Law remains relational in the sense that it reframes "culturally meaningful items that never cease to draw on their external meanings" (ibid: 142). While the boundary is socially constructed, the law maintains a crucial relation to an "external reality" and is, in this sense, a "zone of connection" (ibid: 138). The task of studying the legal regulation of informal housing is then to describe not simply how governance works with a "reality" outside of the law but also the ways in which law and legal enactment work to construct things as inside of or beyond its scope (ibid: 141).

Building on this understanding of bracketing, we can further specify the brackets themselves – the different "frontiers" along which the law is bracketed. De Sousa Santos (1987) describes these "frontiers" as legal thresholds: baselines that demarcate "what belongs to the realm of law and what does not" (ibid: 290). He names three: first, the *detection* threshold sorts out "the smallest detail of the social object that will be considered for regulation," thereby distinguishing relevant/irrelevant objects of regulation; second, the *discrimination* threshold defines the "minimum of detectable differences in the description of the social object that may justify qualitative differences in regulation," thereby separating groups of objects to be regulated in similar ways; and third, the *evaluation* threshold captures "the minimum detectable differences in the ethical quality of the social object (distinguishing legal/illegal)" (ibid: 290–91). Through this tripartite definition, legal boundaries appear as multidimensional rather than as a clear-cut line distinguishing solely between legality and illegality. Compared to national boundaries, legal boundaries are usefully imagined as border regions with specific rules and roles: "sites of conflict, negotiation and exchange," as McDermont and Clarke note (2017: 1390; see also Reeves, 2011), rather than lines separating different territories.

It is tempting to treat these legal approaches and the interpretive moves described as thoroughly distinct from the regulatory work that defines informal housing in both the global South and Berlin's allotments. Practices of interpretations and their inherent boundary work appear to act on a different scale than heavy-handed evictions or massive regularization efforts. Still, the legal interpretative practices and the ways in which boundaries are drawn through them allows an operationalization of the concepts of legal geography to regularization work. This reading enables us to conceptualize regulatory work through a whole set of practices that work/maneuver/extend or fix/stabilize this boundary.

First, and so the standard story goes, regulatory work entails "fixing" the boundary by putting objects of regulation on opposite sides of the boundary.

Practically speaking, this implies outlawing people's dwelling practices by "rigidly" enforcing the ethical threshold, i.e. the legal/illegal distinction. But fixing the boundary by casting objects of regulation as beyond that law can, in de Sousa Santos's terms, also involve dealing with objects that lie beyond the detection or discrimination threshold, and are too small or too particular to be captured in a specific law, and thus require different treatment. Second, regulatory work implies expanding the boundaries of the law, eventually toward the recognition of housing conditions, for instance, by adding exceptions or additional rules at different scales of regulation, thus pushing the boundary elsewhere (see also McDermont and Clarke, 2017: 1387). Think, for instance, of adding bylaws. Bylaws broaden the discretionary threshold of the law, thereby placing the object of regulation closer to the realm of legality. Similarly, granting land-use permissions or legal property titles changes the object of regulation to move it closer to or into the brackets of the law. Third, and conversely, granting legal exceptions normalizes a wider threshold between the law and the object of regulation. Fourth, as legal pluralism suggests, regulatory work can imply drawing on a different boundary. For instance, bureaucrats enact order by reaching out to different rules, which, in turn, need to be accommodated alongside the regulations commonly used to guide a particular context. In this way, regulations are strategically composed. Finally, spatio-material practices work to place the object of regulation closer to the boundary zone or the legal threshold of the law. Think, for instance, of the institutional efforts to extend infrastructures. These efforts change the object of regulation itself. Similarly, residents' own efforts to consolidate irregular housing conditions and change the material fabric can imply moving these conditions closer to or within the brackets of planning bylaws.

These different sets of boundary work rely on "bordering practices" (Côté-Boucher et al., 2014); some are more tactical, others more strategic (de Sousa Santos, 1987). What holds them together is the room for maneuver inherent in drawing boundaries – the interactive and discretionary dimensions of legal enactment. Boundary work thus highlights the ways in which urban practitioners interpret, use, and contest the meaning of frameworks of order in their everyday work. With these legal concepts and their operationalization in mind, let me turn to the allotments. In the governance of allotment dwellings, the law, its amendments, and certain protocols are always present. However, these documents are overlaid with individual interpretations and narratives of their enforcement, as bureaucrats work in their personal ways to make these texts productive through operationalizing the concepts outlined above – combining different laws, interpreting abstractions, and drawing legal boundaries.

Allotment Dwelling and Its Legal Context

Turning now to the gardens, let me start by clarifying the legal context of allotment dwelling and its wider sphere of bylaws and juridical as well as customary rules, codes, and contractual relations to characterize the legal complexities that govern the irregular inhabitation of one's hut. My aim in this section is to characterize the legal boundaries and legal ambiguities that govern the gardens. But given this chapter's focus on legal interpretive work and the drawing of legal boundaries, this analysis will, at times, overlap with the next section, which is more directly concerned with how these laws play out as they are put to work in everyday situations.

Most importantly, German allotment gardens are governed by the BKleinG, a law that is concerned with the structural and horticultural use of the allotment, as well as the conditions of its lease. Following de Sousa Santos, it can be described as a "geocentric" law, as it regulates the utilization of the allotment by regulating the nature of the space (2002: 432). The BKleinG protects the use of the gardens for noncommercial purposes, in particular for the production of horticultural produce for subsistence, as well as for the gardeners' recreation (section 1). Consequently, its underlying norms uphold the idea of greening cities and of fostering urban health. Given this focus, the BKleinG is not particularly concerned with questions of dwelling, although it does regulate the uses of the allotment huts (section 3). But the legal restrictions that concern these constructions are brief: the BKleinG describes the standard of the hut as "simple" [*einfach*]. A German allotment hut cannot exceed a floor space of 24 square meters including a roofed porch (sections 3, 2). Neither may it – through the character of its furnishing and installations – be designed for *permanent stay* [*zum dauernden Wohnen*] (ibid). Given the relative ambiguity of that term, dwelling lies thus somewhat ambiguously between the ethical threshold, i.e. the legal/illegal boundary, and the detection threshold, i.e. beyond the definitional detail of the law.

As the everyday governance of allotments is primarily a municipal responsibility, Berlin's administrative regulations [*Verwaltungsvorschriften*] (Land Berlin, 2009) are of considerable importance for an understanding of the legal interpretive work that governs allotment gardens: they further define the purposes of the allotments [*Kleingärtnerische Nutzung*] (section 4) as relaxation and the production of horticultural produce for subsistence (Land Berlin, 2009). They limit the height of the hut to one storey and dictate further details, for instance, the character of its roof (ibid: section 11.1).[1] Concerning the regulation of dwelling, they explicitly interdict the use of the plot for residential uses (ibid: sections 4 and 5), with the exception of the dwellers mentioned in Chapter 4 who were granted permits under different historical arrangements (ibid: section 12; see also Chapter 3). These regulations also establish that the leaseholder (the allotment association) must take action first by warning, then dismissing or subsequently evicting unlawful dwellers – with the help of the court, if needed (ibid: section 12.3).

As previously noted, permanent stay in allotments is almost impossible to prove; thus, the above measures are hardly called upon. Regulation thus resorts to a law that has a different remit: the Federal Registration Law. This law obliges all residents in Germany to locally register their whereabouts at an existing address. The collected data is administered in the form of a register of residents [*Melderegister*] by local municipal authorities [*Bürgerämter*] and, one could argue, works to make the complexities of the citizenry legible, i.e. statistically intelligible, and thereby manageable. Technically, the Federal Registration Law does not address allotments. The public registry falls under the responsibility of the registration office [*Meldebehörde*], which also does not forbid registration in allotments. However, it has become common practice among allotment administrators to check the register of citizens to detect illegal registrations under the address of the gardens. This indicates that regulatory frames need to be activated, i.e. known, understood, and successfully applied, highlighting the often "latent" power (Allen, 2004: 20) of these frames. Actors actively resort to this law and combine it with allotment rules to delimit practices of dwelling.

A set of outdated rules complicates enacting these regulations. The responsible institutions accept constructions as lawful if former administrations have granted official approval. This also applies to buildings that have "actively" been tolerated [*aktive Duldung*] by the building inspection as well as to those buildings that lack a building permit but can prove that they were built during periods in which their size was in accordance with the standard then in force. For instance, huts erected before 31 December 1958 are granted a size of 60 square meters because the municipality assumes that a permit would have been given by the respective administrations of that time. Similarly, huts built before reunification remain materially lawful [*materiell rechtmäßig*] in cases where they live up to the standards of the GDR (section 7.1, Land Berlin, 2009). Theoretically speaking, these regulations refine the detection threshold.

Adding to these regulatory complications, the SachenRBerG, already introduced in Chapter 3, legalized dwelling for some along with altered conditions of lease. To recall, the SachenRBerG led the restitution process that worked to translate the legal and material reality of the GDR into the legal sphere of the BRD. On the one hand, it presumed that those who had built on the land earned the right to purchase the property, and because those individuals were likely to have nurtured the grounds and invested in them for decades, the law significantly reduced the price of the land (Matthiessen, 2005). On the other hand, the SachenRBerG was to protect people's living conditions in the face of the unsettling experience of uncertainty that governed the conjuncture at the time (ibid). It did so either by granting the current users the acquisition of the land for half of its estimated value or permitting the lessee to sign a 99-year leasehold contract at half of the common interest rate, allowing the lessee to pay off the loan in a piecemeal way.

Interestingly, the law was underpinned by the so-called "principle of subsequent subscription" [*Nachzeichnungsprinzip*]. Accordingly, it included those cases in which investments were made that were "factually" and "materially" illegal but enjoyed toleration, legitimacy, or sometimes protection by the governmental authorities of the GDR. To be sure, the newly regulated plots created further legal contradictions. The now legalized but oversized constructions may conflict with building codes; for instance, regarding the zoning regulations of access roads. At the same time, they contradict planning law, as many of the allotments in question are located on land not designated for residential uses (section 35.3, BauGB). Thus, although the overall aim of the law was to do away with GDR rule, in the allotments the law rather worked to amend the legal boundaries of BRD law.

To grasp the full range of frameworks of order that govern allotment dwelling, these written and institutionally acknowledged regulations have to be considered alongside a set of club rules and oral agreements. The latter concerns mutual understandings that have become institutionalized in terms of a common jargon. For instance, the label "socially acceptable reduction" [*sozialverträglich zurückbauen*] speaks of a wider consensus that the costs for a possible reduction of a hut should be limited (interview, 18.06.2014). The "generational solution" [*Generationenenlösung*] (interview, 07.08.2013) describes the aforementioned cross-generational reduction through which huts are disassembled in a step-by-step procedure. Allotments that have exceeded the remits of the law through their extended building structure have been relabeled as "recreation compounds" – a term that is not legally defined (see Chapter 5). While Berlin's administrative regulations specify the boundaries of the law, these rules work to extend legal boundaries and widen the realm of what is taken to be formal.

Moreover, local rules build on long-standing oral traditions, which are taken into account alongside the BKleinG. Consider, for instance, how Mr. Berger, a colony president I previously introduced, describes the extension of legal frames:

> For us, it's really different, because we are an old colony and run according to the "Rixdorf model" [*Rixdorfer Modell*] … This dates back to

when Professor Doctor Manegold was district mayor. He said that these
are old colonies, because we used to have so many permanent inhabitants from wartimes. And then you cannot say all of a sudden, "well, we'll
tear this down" and the small huts now need to have 24 square meters
or something like that. So it's about the old building stock that you
continue to maintain …

H.H.: And the "Rixdorf model" determines the kind of reduction work
to be done? A kind of prolonged security?

Mr. Berger: Exactly, yes, longer security. (Interview, 10.07.2014)

After the interview, I found out that this model dates back decades and
was never officially institutionalized. However, it extends the boundaries of
what is considered to be formal. At least in Mr. Berger's and other adjacent
colonies this outdated political idea is frequently mentioned, appears to enjoy
local legitimacy, and works to guide regulatory enactment. These rules go
back to a process of legal translation and at the same time they are its object –
they require further adaptation and negotiation as they are implemented in
the allotments. As the rules of this game are inscribed into local narratives
only, their validity is spatially confined.

Against the background of this legal conjuncture, the next section turns
to the level of mundane regulatory decision-making to explore how these
ambiguities play out through processes of interpretation, translation, and the
drawing of legal boundaries. Thereby I follow an interpretive approach that
restrains from associating the weight of the different regulations that this section has introduced with governmental hierarchies and instead aims to
empirically see how all involved in governing use frameworks of order in
processes of regulation.

Navigating Boundaries

The above regulations have created varying legal standards for allotment
dwelling. To discuss how these rules are translated and boundaries drawn in
everyday practices of governing, it is useful to consider how the outsized
building stock that exists in most of the allotments becomes adapted through
the very *practice* of governing. Although allotment garden administrators
rarely link the regulation of allotment infrastructures to the curtailment of
dwelling, regulating huts of undue shape and size certainly has this effect.
Typically, the modification of oversized huts follows a standard procedure:
two assessors visit a plot and write a protocol that fixes a number of reduction
requirements, such as the removal of illegal trees or supplemental constructions.

This protocol defines an estimated transfer fee, which depends on the work that is necessary to meet these requirements as well as on the value of the property on the site, including trees and buildings owned by the departing leaseholder. These requirements force the new tenant to deconstruct the parting tenant's illegal and often run-down property. Sometimes officers rely on the previously mentioned "generational solution" to postpone the fulfillment of these requirements through an agreement in the sublease contract until the end of the tenancy. This amendment allows the gardeners to maintain, for instance, an oversized hut but forces them to dismantle this hut upon the termination of their lease (interview, 06.07.2014).

However, how these processes play out in specific situations involves, as this section shows, incessant negotiations. In considering how these regulations are interpreted when translating them to specific situations in which boundaries of tolerance are drawn, I consider two such cases that vary in the ways in which interpretive authority plays out: in the first, negotiation around the extension of a hut allows allotment dwellers to temporarily widen their room for maneuver, whereas the interpretive authority remains shared but contested. Second, I discuss a case in which the bureaucracy retains legal interpretive authority as it restricts the possibilities for dwelling.

Mr. Schramm, one of the allotment garden administrators I interviewed (25.04.2014), had been recommended to me as a bureaucrat who knew the regulations well. He had long worked in the former East Berlin and was now employed in one of the city's western districts to oversee the managerial work of the allotment association. When I met him and spoke of my subject matter, I encountered open ears. He immediately brought up multiple instances in which gardeners had adapted the law and negotiated a local solution for a regulatory concern. A particularly interesting example involves a case in which a lessee took over a plot with the obligation to dismantle the extension of the site's allotment hut. In the course of the renovation, the gardener came to realize that the wall that the extension shared with the allotment hut was defective and could no longer be used. From his perspective, the wall had to be built anew. Having successfully pursued this renovation, to Mr. Schramm's indignation, the lessee went on to replace another wall and then another one until only a single original wall remained.

From the perspective of the bureaucracy, the renovated hut ended up being a new construction that exceeded the appropriate size and thus clearly crossed the legal/illegal threshold. In compliance with standard procedures for dealing with such concerns, the district administration asked the association of allotment gardeners to sue the offending owner. When the association met this demand, the judge ruled in favor of the lessee, to the surprise of the district administration. This decision fixed the status of the hut on the legal side of the evaluation threshold, to use de Sousa Santos's term. The court reasoned that the hut would have been impossible to use without reconstruction, and the work that had been done was hence to count as a legal renovation. For Mr. Schramm, this "skewed argumentation" (interview, 25.04.2014) ignored the fact that a new construction of that size would have never received a building permit – as it breached the specificities of the BKleinG.

In the interview, I wondered if the unexpected ruling of the court was a matter of misinterpreting the definitional criteria inherent in the law, but Mr. Schramm responded unmistakably: "What counts as a new construction is stipulated very clearly: more than 50% of the supporting substance, and it's a new construction. This [the renovated old hut] would have definitely been a new construction." In this perspective, the flaw in decision-making appeared to be a problem of regulatory pluralism whereby, from the perspective of Mr. Schramm, the judge resorted to the wrong kind of norm. But Mr. Schramm hit the ball right back:

> They [the court] also stated that the lessee could use this construction until the end of its remaining operational life. Well, I'm going to interpret this decree – the judge also has his possibility to interpret, right – I'm interpreting that the old hut would have maximally had a remaining lifetime of 10 years. The new hut can thus stand for 10 years maximum until the end of the lease … Then, I'll stand on the doormat again to demand its demolition. (Interview, 25.04.2014)

Unwilling to accept the status quo for too long, his interpretation adds details to regulatory orders that move the detection threshold. In planning to demand the demolition of the hut in the future, Mr. Schramm's interpretation of the judge's ruling brings a new boundary into view in order to restrict the extensive building activities. Bureaucrats, just as all others involved, are using the law "as persons with commitments" (Jones, 2011: 60).

The ruling had an epilogue: after the court had decided in favor of the tenant, the allotment holder rebuilt the fourth wall – although this remaining wall had been decisive in the court's decision not to classify the hut as a new construction. In this revised state, the ruling was no longer valid, as it had crossed the boundary extension that the judge had granted. However, at the time of this writing, it remained to be seen if the district association would be ready to engage in another legal dispute. In this case, boundary work relies significantly on a play with categorizations, which for Blomley (2014: 140) is a "particularly important … framing technology." In his view, categorization is a crucial process of meaning-making, as the fit of a category is "not always a yes/no question, but one that works outward from a prototypical core, allowing for degrees of association and similarity" (ibid). Understanding categorical distinctions in this way highlights struggles for definitional power. This ability is typically ascribed to the state and its power to frame legal categories in a normative way. In the present example, however, gardeners also perform definitional work by mediating categories to fit their own needs. Similarly, in interpreting sentences or enacting definitions like "life-length," bureaucrats mediate and seek to fix the meaning of legal categories.

Switching scenes to a different regulator's office on the outskirts of the former East Berlin allows me to further explore a set of legal interpretative practices and respective boundary mechanisms. In contradistinction to the processes of negotiation I previously discussed, in this case the interpretive authority remained largely with the local bureaucracy. In April 2014, I interviewed Ms. Richter, who had prepared a number of cases to explain how she dealt with the transgressions in the gardens. In one especially notable example, a permanent dweller who had passed away bequested her oversized hut to her adult grandson (see Figure 7.1). The transfer of this hut led to a dispute concerning the legal nature of the situation, which, as in the previous example, highlights how room for maneuver emerges and is negotiated, as well as how boundaries become fixed. Yet here, the interpretive authority remains with the local bureaucracy.

Before I turn to discuss the legal negotiations around this inheritance, a contextualization of this particular legal situation is in order. The grandmother was one of the few remaining allotment holders who held a dwelling permit, paid dwelling fees, and was registered by the bureaucracy. Such residents enjoy relative housing security. The legality of their huts further distinguishes the legal situation of these permanent dwellers: while some huts are endowed with dwelling permits, others have been illegally extended or built. These allotment holders can pass on their property (the hut), but they cannot bequeath their dwelling permits, as these rights are bound to the person rather than to the hut. Even if gardeners have grown up in an allotment hut, as they move out of a compound, their dwelling rights immediately cease. Nevertheless, the grandson was keen to inherit his grandmother's right to dwell. Yet, given the above regulations, the death of its only legal resident also terminated the possibility of using the hut as a dwelling. Additionally, the building permit only covered parts of the hut. However, given its extended size, the construction was also not suitable to serve as an allotment hut. The grandmother's death had thus caused a situation in which the law intervenes in the liberty of people to use their property in the only reasonable way.

However, in these cases, administrations can grant exceptions, or, say, they can extend the boundaries of the law in favor of the allotment holder: as a matter of bureaucratic judgment, the dwelling permit can be inherited if the

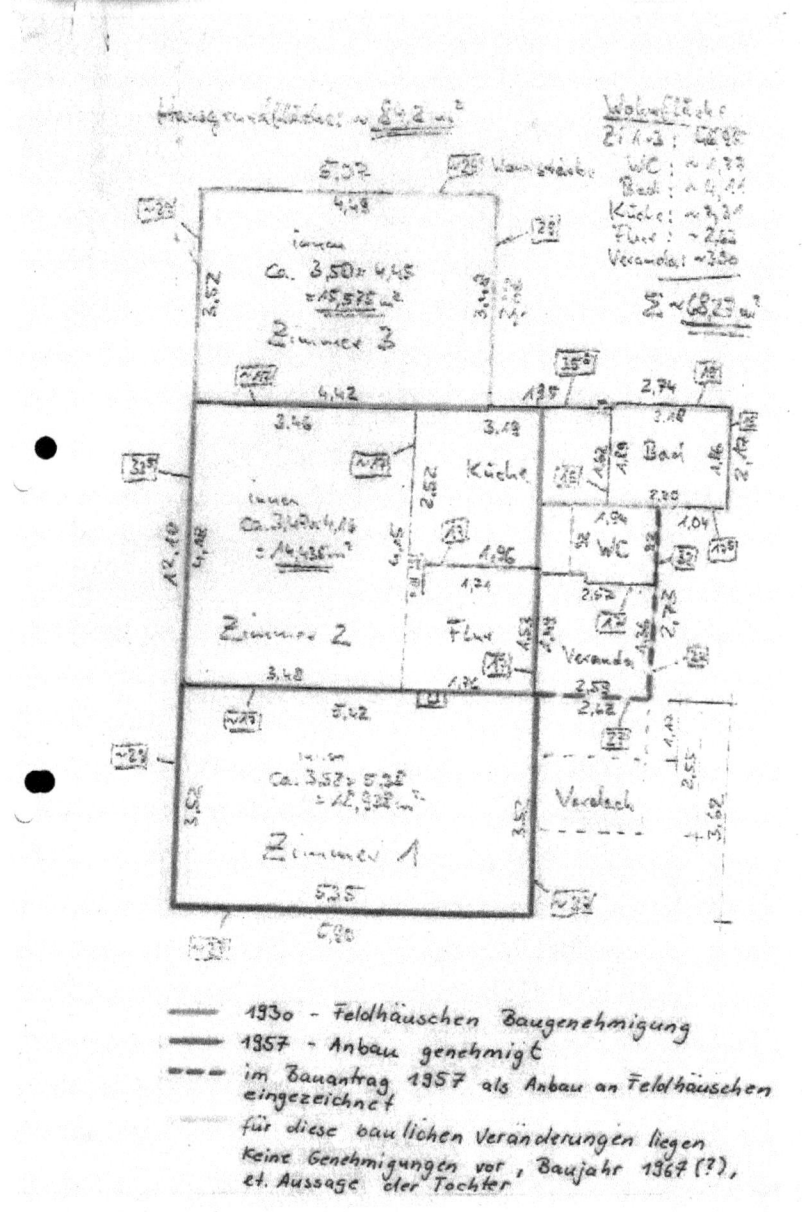

FIGURE 7.1 Photocopied floorplan of run-down allotment hut. Source: Interview, 09.04.2014.

conditions of the hut are taken to be *adequate* (interview, 09.04.2014). These contradictions thus require the bureaucracy to redefine the boundaries of accepted tolerance on a case-by-case basis.

So the negotiations began. Given the dilapidated standard of the hut, the district administration was willing neither to grant the dwelling permit nor to tolerate the oversized building. Moreover, this administration was in a good position to demand a partial demolition, as its former owner had extended the house without permission, thus unequivocally crossing the legal/illegal threshold.

The floorplan I was given (see Figure 7.1) illustrates how the building grew over the years. Although a hut was authorized in 1930, and an application for an annex was filed and the annex built in 1957, a further extension was erected in 1967 without any official permit. Consequentially, the administration demanded the demolition of at least this last part of the hut:

> This was a point where we said, well … he has to decide: either he takes this [the 1967 annex] or the sheds, although the sheds have building permits, but he cannot have it all: it's either-or … Because a dwelling permit – given the state of construction – we just cannot grant. And he then decided, okay, he will remove both annexes, but keep the sheds, because as a gardener he can make good use of them. (Interview, 09.04.2014)

As in cases we have seen before, here, the building becomes the technology to regulate dwelling. Yet, the workings of this technology still remain negotiable. In fact, fixing legality implied in this case a bargaining between different sections of the built structure. Interestingly, the grandson, who had anticipated this procedure, became involved in these processes of bargaining through remodeling the hut. Ms. Richter, the bureaucrat responsible, told me: "They had already started to renovate, but the fact is, they [the building administration] not only examine what it looks like, but the structural conditions" (interview, 09.04.2014). Nevertheless the grandson's renovations required the bureaucracy to involve building experts from a different department to provide sufficient evidence to fix the boundary. Ms. Richter explained:

> I only see what it looks like, but the colleague … can see that … there is only simple flooring; that there is no insulation; that there are only simple windows, the entire electric connection … everything was not according to standard. And they see that! (Interview, 09.04.2014)

Prohibiting dwelling through the interpretation of legal frames is thus, as Ms. Richter's assertion shows, not an arbitrary procedure. Rather, she sought support from a different agency to enhance her interpretive authority. Although the grandson's renovation of the hut worked to place the object of regulation closer to a zone of legality in which it might be permissible to dwell, the materiality of the hut (see Figure 7.2) allowed the bureaucracy to narrow the legal threshold around a normative categorization of an adequate housing standard. As the result of these negotiations – the ban on using the hut as a dwelling – clearly shows, the bureaucracy thereby retained the definitional authority.

In both cases presented here, all actors concerned with allotment gardening mediate the application of the law through processes of meaning-making as well as material processes of incremental change in order to move the legal/illegal boundary. In this way, the enforcement of a set of boundaries frames legal orders into rules that are more apt to fit the messy circumstances on the ground. These processes thereby allow for the setting of priorities and the exclusion of certain practices by designating them as beyond the threshold of legal frameworks.

FIGURE 7.2 Photocopied image of hut. Source: Interview, 09.04.2014.

Conclusion

This chapter has highlighted how actors maneuver frameworks of order, translating them to specific situations and thereby drawing boundaries between what is permissible and what is precluded. Specifically, it has explored some of the qualities of the frameworks that govern allotment dwelling as well as the mechanisms through which rules are enacted as people go to court, reconstruct walls, and apply legal categories. On the one hand, my discussion characterized the overlapping and, at times, contradictory frameworks of order that govern allotment dwelling and produce a variety of legal situations. On the other hand, I pointed to the ways in which legal frames are put to work in everyday processes of regulation. This discussion traced processes of meaning-making and boundary work necessary to implement the law in the first place. Together, these sections underline two points.

First, the processes of maneuvering and boundary work I have described do not constitute something that is beyond these frames of order that govern allotment gardening; instead, they are a crucial feature of the law and necessary for it to be made productive. One could argue that the gardeners defy the law as they shape frameworks of order by translating legal abstractions to fit a problem at hand. But to speak of defiance or noncompliance requires rules to be clear-cut. Given the discrepancies inherent in the rules I discussed, translation is endemic to the legal governance of allotment dwelling: to implement these rules, actors will need to negotiate. Echoing the socio-legal scholarship I discussed, the case shows that situations of greater legal ambiguity both *require* and *permit* more extensive interpretive work. Second, as the law is "performed into being" (Blomley, 2014: 142), it points to spaces of political agency at the level of everyday governance. Using the legal thresholds, allotment holders and bureaucrats alike actively widen or employ spaces of negotiability, or, say, everyday engagement. This process is defined by normativity and competition around the interpretative authority between the gardeners and the administration as well as between different state institutions.

Discussing the implementation of legal boundaries thus raises concerns about agency and contestation, and the power differentials between negotiating actors. The two disputes I discussed in this chapter highlighted that regulatory authority lies not only within the state. Rather, the gardeners also act as "active agents" who participate in legal practices (Azuela and Meneses-Reyes, 2014: 169–70). In adapting the rules on the books, individuals gain leverage so that the enactment of rules appears as a place for agency. If this engagement may decenter the imperatives of regulations, it neither demands changes in the structure of political regimes nor alters the power of institutions. Still, that does not mean that the modalities of maneuvering I encountered cannot alter the status quo. As Chapter 5 has shown, the processes of interpretation and boundary work depicted here pile up to cause larger change.

These observations have broader conceptual consequences for my understanding of formality. To start, they imply that the rules on the books may specify the legislator's intended effects, but that does not mean that they constitute formality. Rather, the mechanisms I have described lay bare what Ms. Braun described as the difference between "the contractual" and "the factual" in an interview I discussed in Chapter 5 (interview, 19.08.2013). This difference highlights the gap between the normative illusion of regulatory frames ("the contractual") and that which is practiced on the ground ("the factual"). For an analysis of governance, it is useful to avoid presupposing the effects of these frames. Rather, it is necessary to focus on their operation in practice, as it is through their application that their contingencies play out. In this sense, the enactment of regulations through the social processes I have outlined hardly lies beyond formality. The solutions that are found on the ground may be adaptations of the law, but they gain legitimacy and are treated as the formal order on-site. These are the processes that fabricate formality, and an understanding of the notion in terms of an abstract and autonomous sphere therefore misses the point. Rather than presupposing a fixed and unrivaled status – contrasted to informality as its negotiable other – a closer look at the enactment of laws suggests that formality itself is inherently flexible and plural. It illustrates that informality and formality themselves are both the effects of a normative (rather than a neutral) procedure.

Summary: Chapter 7

This chapter explores the legal work upon which practices of governance rely. Utilizing critical legal studies, the chapter unpacks how both regulators and allotment holders employ legal frameworks in regulatory practices to maintain, extend, or restrict outsized huts. Yet, while such frameworks of order constitute a pivotal resource in the making of order, the chapter discusses how they operate in practice to understand how order is built through the interpretive mechanisms that shape how rules become "emplaced." In this way, the book seeks a more practice-centered understanding of the interpretive work through which rules operate "on the ground." This furthers an understanding of informality as emerging through the "ordinary stuff" of policy implementation, in which subjectivity, positionality, and individual agency are key.

Note

1   In addition, new constructions need to meet Berlin's building code (BauOBln), and this necessitates the authorization of a building inspection [*Bauaufsicht*] as well as the approval of the lessor.

Chapter 8

Conclusion
The "Gallic Village"

> Mr. Berger: Imagine a "Gallic village." This is how … I always describe the colony […].
> H.H.: Umm … And why a "Gallic village"?
> Mr. Berger: Well, I always describe it like this, because we are right in the middle here … in the thick of it and … here the rules of the game are different.
> H.H.: Yes?
> Mr. Berger: Here the clock still ticks differently. And I take good care that this is the case. (Interview, 10.07.2014)

Following Mr. Berger, the "Gallic village" is "in the thick of it": "right in the middle." But as people work to protect their room for maneuver and their own pace of urban change, for him, the rules of the game differentiate it from other urban sites. Nevertheless, this chapter concludes that unlike René Goscinny's village of indomitable Gauls, Berlin's allotment gardens are not truly an anomalous place. Instead, this book found them to be a paradigmatic case of everyday negotiation of informal housing and urban governance that permits us to explore the possibilities and limitations for transgressive housing practices that such action entails.

Housing in the Margins has examined the "Gallic village" in the midst of a European capital. It has analyzed the temporal, spatio-material, peopled, and socio-legal dimensions of the ways in which transgression and regulation are negotiated as rules are emplaced. This analysis has highlighted improvisations, accommodations, and other modalities of adaptation through which all parties involved with allotment governance transform top-down rules by putting them into practice; furthermore, it has described how these actors delineate spaces of negotiation and place limits on tolerance. Here, this

Housing in the Margins: Negotiating Urban Formalities in Berlin's Allotment Gardens,
First Edition. Hanna Hilbrandt.
© 2021 John Wiley & Sons, Ltd. Published 2021 by John Wiley & Sons, Ltd.

chapter ventures into a set of tentative conclusions about the book's key themes: First, I link my thinking about negotiability to questions concerning the possibilities and limitations of agency in processes of transgression and regulation. Second, I draw conclusions from the analysis of allotment dwelling about informal housing in Berlin as well as about more normative concerns with the planning challenges that emerge from these housing practices. Third, I revisit the attempt to employ the concept of informality to marginal housing practices in Berlin, and I close with reflections on the promises and challenges of this epistemological move for informality research in cities of the global North.

Negotiating the Enactment of Urban Regulations

With its focus on unauthorized dwelling, this book has explored a subject matter at the core of informality research, but it has done so with a shift in perspective. In Chapter 2, I suggested strengthening informality research through conceptually engaging with the understandings of the state that undergird current thinking about informality. In expanding such thinking, *Housing in the Margins* approaches informality on the basis of literature on state enactment that stresses what I characterized as the agentic, situated, and relational dimensions of the state: a close-up view that accounts for the normative judgments of all actors involved in enacting regulations, for the legal-material situations and interpretive work on which the negotiation of regulations is based, and for the way in which this work shapes and is shaped by social structures.

These lenses sharpen our understanding of the processes through which the state is enacted and formality produced in everyday governance. To this end, I focused in on the micro-scale of transgression and regulation, analyzing the ways in which state and civil society actors negotiate who impacts the production of order, how rules are to be used, and what is and is not to be tolerated. The spaces of agency that emerge in these negotiations are an important arena through which urban development is implemented and contested. They disrupt, in Clarke's words, the "very functional account of the machinery of government as an apparatus that processes ideas, intentions, interests or ideologies and delivers the desired results" (2012: 209). They provide a pivotal opportunity to explore, as Newman points out, "how and where politics is or could be enacted" (ibid: 10).

Examining the mechanisms and sites of a "relational politics" (Hunter, 2015) of small-scale negotiation helps to qualify and delimit the scope of agency people have at their command in navigating regulations. This book equally found room for maneuver in the conflictive and cooperative interaction of all concerned. By accounting for the engagement of a wide set of actors, including allotment dwellers, neighboring gardeners, heads of colonies, and the local bureaucracy, it indicated how bureaucracies and gardeners join hands to rule through pragmatism and compromise – in a joint, although contested, effort in which "constellations of consent" put formality in place. In this, the involvement of civil society actors, who negotiate with the district administration, is disjointed, individualized, and fragmented; at the same time, these negotiations are embedded in "ruling relations" (Smith, 1990). Conceptualizing the various actors involved, the structures of institutional power, and the enactment of rules as relationally constitutive of one another (Hoggett, 2001; Dobson, 2015; Hunter, 2015) fosters a reading of these "ruling relations" as emerging in and through social networks, normative understandings, and situated necessities. On this basis, we can think of individuals as gaining leverage by appropriating, interpreting, and accommodating rules. This includes the quasi-legal work of interpreting laws, standards, social conventions, zoning ordinances, and the like by moving and fixing legal boundaries. In this line of thinking, the various ways of enacting new land use categories, tolerating transgressions, and fighting regulations in court ultimately shape how governance materializes in everyday negotiations. Reading informality in this way produces an account of agency distinct from scholarly approaches that take governance to be the realm of strategically organized state, civil society, and market collaborations (as for instance urban regime theory might suggest) because it finds agency in the negotiation of individuals. Similarly, because this approach puts predefined roles into question and thereby troubles the binary of domination and contention, it varies from readings of informality as enacted through top-down rule by states creating "gray" spaces in arbitrary ways or as the insurgency of civil society actors.

Following from this account of agency, negotiability could be framed as an enabling tool or as a resource that may be put to work to cushion or reconfigure the pervasive influences of market-driven regeneration processes. But *Housing in the Margins* has also illustrated the inherent exclusions that undergird everyday state enactment. Finding agency in a politics of negotiation thus needs to scrutinize what goes uncontested and what is designated as unacceptable. Clearly, everyday leverage gained in negotiations is not necessarily redistributive. For instance, the negotiability in focus compounds the problem of equitable access to housing and land. Consider that the extensive construction activity of some of the gardeners prevents poorer households from gaining access to allotments, as newcomers with small incomes are unable to afford acquisition costs of up to €15,000. In these cases, allotment holders have transformed the colonies from state-subsidized welfare institutions into leisure spaces for households with higher incomes.

Therefore, the effects of negotiability require critical assessment. The maneuvers I have outlined add necessary amendments to smooth regulatory work, but they can also advantage individuals in unfair ways. Room for negotiation hinges both on resources and people's relative place in "constellations of consent," yet it also depends on the context of such negotiations – politico-economic pressures on housing and land, local party politics, or the personal commitments of governing actors. To be sure, even at a larger scale, state power is, as Roy writes, "reproduced through the capacity to construct and reconstruct categories of legitimacy and illegitimacy" (2005: 149), but it is – at least in theory – checked and balanced through institutions. Everyday negotiations introduce less transparent modalities of claim-making. But these undue and exclusive personal gains, as well as opportunities for agency, are all part and parcel of the ways in which governance is put to work.

Clearly, the negotiations, interpretations, and small-scale transgressions that skirt the "letter of the law" are endemic to everyday state action. But it is less clear when and how the use of such leverage builds up to produce change. *Housing in the Margins* has indicated how the negotiation of transgressions normalizes a relatively stable realm of tolerance. Thereby, mechanisms such as perpetually "turning a blind eye," the gardeners' self-regulation, and processes of "boundary-maintenance" (Misztal, 2002: 145) delimit a realm of toleration that reifies and thereby institutionalizes a set of transgressive practices that come to be seen as normal in everyday situations of governance. In this reading, negotiability is not, as some informality literature insists (Roy and Sayyad, 2004: 5), a feature that marks informality as distinct. Drawing this conclusion is more than simply a restatement of the dangers of dichotomous thinking, because it defines formality, too, as a contested product of enduring negotiations. *Housing in the Margins* tells its story from the viewpoint of formality to take up the challenge to reflect on the notion in a way that advances not only an understanding of transgressions but also accounts for the making of urban order within the everyday work of state bureaucracies.

Housing and the Everyday Politics of Difference

My second concern has been to understand the (re)production and governance of irregular housing practices in Berlin. I addressed the paucity of research on informal housing in cities with well-resourced bureaucracies as well as the North–South dichotomy that persists in researching this topic. And my aim was to bring this case of informal dwelling into a wider discussion of precarious or marginal housing.

To do that, it is crucial to account for the multidimensional nature of allotment dwelling, or, differently put, not to reduce precarity to its material dimension. The book has characterized allotment dwelling through the wide heterogeneity of the dwellers, their housing conditions, their socioeconomic backgrounds, their forms of organization, and the spatial characteristics of dwelling practices. To begin, the physical appearance and material conditions of allotment dwelling vary. While some allotment holders have built comfortable homes, others inhabit more precarious makeshift huts. Yet even in the former case, one should not be deceived by the apparent comfort of little stone cottages and concrete-block bungalows. Dwelling in allotments is unsafe and substandard: huts burn down when illegal ovens spark fires, ambulances cannot pass through the small alleys of the compounds, and the material quality of the huts and their location in the city tend to invite burglary.

Second, the socioeconomic background of the dwellers differs widely. Given the quality of dwelling infrastructures, one might readily assume that allotments are spaces of refuge for the have-nots and excluded. However, it is not solely the income poor or people in vulnerable situations who inhabit allotment gardens. Allotments are spaces of refuge, but at the same time, lower-middle-class Berliners have built relatively comfortable homes and lives. More than just a survival strategy, for some, allotment dwelling can be explained through feelings of attachment, and a sense of belonging based on strong traditions and norms.

Third, allotment dwelling can be characterized through its form of political organization. Dwelling practices are individualized, though rather than being disruptive, they predominantly aim to stay under the radar. Despite a strong tradition of collectively protesting the rededication of allotment land, allotment dwellers are largely apolitical in the sense that they lack a political agenda related to dwelling – partly due to the "hidden character" of their dwelling practices that inhibits social organization (see also Durst and Wegmann, 2017: 295). Still, the tight social relations that characterize the allotments have an impact on allotment dwelling through collective norms that govern the tolerance of nonconforming practices and at times reinforce processes of exclusion.

Fourth, allotment dwelling is marked by spatial relations. Unlike, for example, Roma camps, which are visible though frequently located at the geographical margins of the city (e.g. Picker and Pasquetti, 2015), the "Gallic village" is in the "thick of it," yet spatially dispersed and largely invisible.

These multiple "faces" of precarity or irregularity are governed more by negotiation and tolerance than by rigid intervention. Due to the relatively minor magnitude of the phenomenon, allotment dwelling is, most generally put, somewhat outside of the consideration of the "responsible" agencies, not least because these bureaucracies are rather more concerned with greenery than with housing conditions. Moreover, as it is largely hidden from the public view, allotment dwelling rarely becomes a political concern. Alongside the relatively minor scale of the phenomenon and a public opinion of it as largely unproblematic, the position of the administration is readily explained through a double bind: the need to hinder the urbanization of the gardens, on the one hand, and lack of intervention possibilities, on the other.

The implications of considering housing precarity in these multiple dimensions are plentiful. In contrast to the treatment of squatting or rough sleeping – frequently seen as public nuisances to be controlled and at best hidden away – allotment dwelling, perhaps because of its versatility, tends to be treated with relative "care" and cooperation. This political handling can also be explained through the actor constellations in and through which governance proceeds. Through the organizational setup of the allotments, the gardeners themselves are involved in their governance. As they both widen the room for tolerance and cut off wider transgressions, I have argued that all parties involved govern in "constellations of consent" rather than of conflict. Moreover, traditions of dwelling, existing property and housing permits, as well as infrastructures that permit for dwelling, widen the gardeners' possibilities to stay settled in Berlin's allotments.

But this heterogeneity also comes with its own dynamics of exclusion. Despite the case-by-case character of the negotiations and the lack of common procedures or policies toward dwelling, the bureaucracies' dealings with allotments depend on conflictual negotiations around where to draw a line. Throughout this book, I have pointed to the ways in which boundaries are maintained around the bureaucracies' social standards and norms of tolerance, on the one hand, and through the practices of the gardeners, on the other. To be sure, these two forms of governance are entangled. As I have argued elsewhere, gardeners also build on the bureaucracy to reinforce boundaries of exclusion (Hilbrandt, 2019). Recognizing the nuances in the multiple forms of claims-making, exclusion, and quests for personal advantages makes it harder to formulate normative claims. For some of the inhabitants, informal housing only becomes problematic in the rather exceptional case that the land of their colonies is earmarked to undergo urban renewal. But the housing crisis gives rise to renewed concerns about the vulnerability of those excluded from housing markets, and about their possibilities of finding emergency shelter in the gardens. From the viewpoint of the allotments, these dwellers are disadvantaged in three ways: they find themselves excluded from formal markets, have severely limited opportunities to find shelter in the gardens, and lack the support of housing rights advocates lobbying for them. But although the organization of privilege for some has fairness implications for those who belong to disenfranchised groups, it is certainly the former of these issues that seems the worst: concerns about equity and justice in the wider housing market.

In the absence of affordable housing alternatives, cracking down on allotment dwelling is not an option. But what requires tolerance on the level of the everyday seems untenable through the lens of juridical vigor. The view that dwelling in allotments should be a panacea for housing, as some have suggested, is ethically disconcerting. As Jane Larson notes, "to legitimize informality is to accept substandard conditions for some that violate generally applicable norms of dignity, health, safety, or fairness" (2002: 159). It turns some people, crudely put, into second-class citizens. Quoting Richard Delgado, Larson adds that "policies predicated on tolerance of informality in housing production may be 'pragmatic' but can never be justified 'as a matter of social principle … [Such] theory is explicitly predicated on a legal acceptance of otherness, difference, and perhaps inferiority'" (ibid: 160–61). From a social justice perspective, the right to adequate housing cannot be traded for an informal entitlement.

Still, from a planning perspective, Berlin's allotments require socio-spatial reform. The avowed objective of current allotment politics is to maintain the status quo of the gardens to foster ecological sustainability, and by extension, the quality of urban space. Yet current politics overlook the status quo in the gardens and inhibit the possibility of finding planning solutions that might actively deal with and resolve pressing but contradictory demands on land. The "Gallic village" is hardly a frontier of innovation. Its historical legacies appear to be challenging contemporary interventions. It largely resists external influences and relies on continuity, inertia, or obduracy. Still, allotment gardens today have become spaces of leisure. Unlike earlier periods, in which policy prioritized the access of the unemployed, the 1983 Bundeskleingartengesetz (BKleinG) law no longer constitutes a redistributive policy, as it entails no specification as to who is entitled to profit from the minimal lease. But a reform of the BKleinG remains improbable. Not only are allotments locked into the consciousness of the city as sanctuaries for the working classes and as valuable cultural institutions, but also the pressure of the housing economy and politically organized gardeners provide additional reasons not to reform the law. Consequently, past rationalities continue to rule and require their adaptation in everyday negotiations. A daring reform of planning that would press for new typologies and organizational schemes might allow for integrating adequate housing solutions and social fairness issues with concerns about ecological sustainability.

Translating Informality: Promises and Challenges for Further Research

This book has started from the challenge of translating a concept that is predominantly built from research in the global South into a Northern city in order to open up a more global conversation on a long-standing theme: informality and its relation to everyday practices of urban governance. But how helpful is it to discuss informal housing in Berlin through the lens of Southern urbanism? This question, or the idea that processes in cities elsewhere should inform an understanding of European, Canadian, or US cities, is not free of contradictions. To conclude, let me therefore reflect on some of the challenges and possibilities that I encountered throughout my own process of translation.

To translate implies the transfer of meaning. It requires the holding of at least two places in tension and is, in this sense, a relational term. Thus, to "theorize back" or "postcolonialize Berlin" (Hentschel, 2015) implies rendering spaces commensurable. But, translating also speaks of otherness. "Theorizing back" builds on the assumption that places are different, and to decipher them within the same analytical frame makes it necessary to use an intermediary, namely to translate. Authors have explicitly addressed this problem. Ananya Roy, for instance, urged scholars not to essentialize the global South and its diversity as a new privileged worldview (2015). But frequently and for political reasons, the archetypes of the global South (e.g. informality) are read as the soon-to-be prototypes of the global North. For example, Sheppard et al. note that "current urban experiences in Asia and Africa … foreshadow North American and European urban life" (2013: 898). In these accounts, the directionality of development trajectories that have previously been deduced from the global North to analyze the South are merely reversed, insisting stubbornly on one singular development scheme. Such "spatialized logics of inversion" (Peck, 2015: 171) go hand in hand with a tendency to translate predominantly those ideas from the South that concern poverty, gangs, or corruption and use them to understand the growth of inequality in the global North. A "Southern take" translates, in this sense, into a focus on the "badlands of the republic" (Dikeç, 2007) or on the subaltern agency of the poor.

Instead of following yet another trope, Ann Varley asks scholars pursuing global comparative urbanism to consider the following two questions: "How can we take on board the imperative not to assume unbridgeable differences without assuming and valorizing sameness? How can we recognize a lack of convergence without either pathologizing or fetishizing difference?" (2013:

125). By thinking across difference in relational ways, we can make it productive. Or, as Mohanty puts it, "in knowing differences and particularities, we can better see the connections and communalities" (2003: 505). Moreover, difference helps us to revise, contrast, and expand theoretical approaches. Regarding the concept of informality, this implies using it not in search of similar practices "elsewhere," but as a starting point of discussion. It is in this sense that the approach to informality pursued in this book relates to research on informal housing elsewhere – even if the approach differs considerably from common forms of researching informality, as Chapter 2 has shown.

In arguing that the negotiability of urban governance is a necessary dimension of institutional processes – whether located in the North or the South – I have aimed to expand these understandings through a "genre" of informality, where transgression and regulation emerge in negotiation. In this understanding, both the transgressive practices described and their negotiation appear neither as the result of state failure nor through the arbitrary governance of the state itself, but as a corollary to processes of the state or, one could say, an inherent characteristic of making states work. Although this reading differs from the informality accounts discussed in Chapter 2, I refer to them in the spirit of extending these debates. Moreover, these differences do not imply that I take informality to be different in Southern sites, but that the context of my study demands asking different questions than the ones scholars researching contexts in which informality is defined by largely unaccountable state institutions might be interested in. Rather than discouraging us to enter into conversations across places, conversations are necessary to unearth these differences in the first place.

The word "translate" conveys yet another meaning: following its Latin word origin [*translatus*, past participle of *transferre*, to transfer], it implies to move something toward another place. The German word for translate [*übersetzen*] conveys this meaning still more directly. Composed of *über* [trans-] and *setzen* [to set] it literally signifies to "carry across" or, more figuratively, "to head for a new shore." "Theorizing back" proceeds from the idea that a postcolonial perspective makes it possible to develop approaches that differ from those deeply embedded in the experience of European, Canadian, or US cities. Additionally, it assumes that the experiences of cities that have been less visible to Western academic analysis make it possible to imagine alternative narrations and new analytical paradigms. McFarlane (2010: 734) aligns the notion with the concept of indirect learning: translation, he writes, "embodies a sense of creative possibility that does not reduce learning to direct transfer." As translations require devising novel terminologies and redefining actors, units, or registers, they allow for a process in which new conceptions may occur. In this sense, they are likely to allow the translator to head for new shores.

Connecting the governance of Berlin's allotments – commonly seen as orderly and tradition-bound – to strands of debate based on researching Southern cities, such as Lagos, Mumbai, or Mexico City, may appear a circuitous route. To be sure, Western concepts describing state–society relations offer theorizations of the relations of governance and transgression that may align closer with the negotiation of housing in Berlin's allotments than descriptions of informality that stem from these sites. The work of translation consists exactly in connecting these debates despite their varied actors, units, and registers of analysis and in learning from these connections. To bring Western conceptions of governance together with a discussion of Southern scholarship on informality is thus more than an appreciation of urban post-colonial debates. Rather, it allows reading a European case study through a more global lens and perhaps takes another step forward in making our conceptual language more adequate to describing the twenty-first-century city.

Summary: Chapter 8

This chapter returns to the book's epistemological starting points. First, it links the book's discussion about negotiability to questions concerning the possibilities and limitations of agency in processes of transgression and regulation. Second, from the analysis of allotment dwelling, the chapter draws conclusions about informal housing in Berlin as well as about more normative concerns with the planning challenges that emerge from these housing practices. Third, it revisits the attempt to employ the concept of informality to marginal housing practices in Berlin, and it closes with reflections on the promises and challenges of this epistemological move for informality research in cities of the global North.

Glossary of German Terms

German terms	English translation
Amt für Wohnungsbau	Housing agency
Armengärten	Gardens for the poor
Baugesetzbuch	Federal Building Code
Baupolizei	Building authority
Bezirksamt	District administration
Bezirksverband der Kleingärtner	District Association of Allotment Gardeners
Bundesgesetzbuch (BGB)	German Civil Code
Bundeskleingartengesetz (BKleinG), 1983	Federal Allotment Law
Bundesrepublik Deutschland (BRD), 1949–1990	Federal Republic of Germany/West Germany
Dauerbewohner*in	Permanent dweller
Dauerkleingärten	Permanent allotment
Deutsche Demokratische Republik (DDR)	German Democratic Republic (GDR)
Erholungsanlage	Recreation compound
Gründerzeit	Wilhelminian period
Kleingartenentwicklungsplan (KEP)	Allotment Garden Development Plan
Kleingarten Sachbearbeiter*in	Allotment garden administrator
Kleingarten und Kleinpachtordnung (KGO)	Allotment and Small-lease Regulation
Kleingartenverein	Local association of an allotment colony
Kolonie	Colony
Landesverband Berlin der Gartenfreunde (LBdG)	Association of allotment gardeners on the state level
Lauben	Allotment huts
Meldebehörde	Registration office

Housing in the Margins: Negotiating Urban Formalities in Berlin's Allotment Gardens, First Edition. Hanna Hilbrandt.
© 2021 John Wiley & Sons, Ltd. Published 2021 by John Wiley & Sons, Ltd.

German terms	*English translation*
Melderegister	Register of residents
Sachenrechtsbereinigungsgesetz (Sachen RBerG)	Property Law Validating Statute
Scholle	Turf
Schrebergarten	Allotment garden
Schwarzwohnen	'Black' or illegal/unlawful dwelling
Senatsverwaltung für Finanzen	Senate Department of Finance
Senatsverwaltung für Stadtentwicklung und Wohnen (SenStadt)	Senate Department for Urban Development and Housing
Senatsverwaltung für Umwelt, Verkehr und Klimaschutz (SenUVK)	Senate Department for the Environment, Traffic, and Climate
Sommerwohnen	Summer dwelling
Stadtrat/Stadträtin	Municipal councillor
Verband für Kleingärtner, Siedler und Kleintierzüchter (VKSK)	Association of Gardeners, Settlers, and Small Livestock Breeders
Verwaltungsvorschriften	Administrative regulations
Vorstand der Kleingartenvereine	Executive board of the allotment garden associations
Wohnlaubenentgeld	Dwelling fee
Wohnungsamt	Housing department

References

Aalbers, M.B. (2016) *The Financialization of Housing: A Political Economy Approach*, Routledge Studies in the Modern World Economy, Taylor and Francis, London, New York.

Aalbers, M.B. (2019) Financial Geography II: Financial Geographies of Housing and Real Estate. *Progress in Human Geography* 43.2, 376–87.

Aalbers, M.B. and A. Holm (2008) Privatising Social Housing in Europe: The Cases of Amsterdam and Berlin. In K. Adelhof, B. Glock, J. Lossau, and M. Schulz (eds.), *Urban Trends in Berlin and Amsterdam*, Geography Department, Humboldt University, Berlin, 12–23.

Abrams, C. (1964) *Man's Struggle for Shelter in an Urbanizing World*, MIT Press, Cambridge, MA.

Acuto, M., C. Dinardi, and C. Marx (2019) Transcending (In)formal Urbanism. *Urban Studies* 56.3, 475–87.

Alba, F. de (2017) Challenging State Modernity: Governmental Adaptation and Informal Water Politics in Mexico City. *Current Sociology* 65.2, 182–94.

Allen, J. (2003) *Lost Geographies of Power*, Wiley Blackwell, Malden.

Allen, J. (2004) The Whereabouts of Power: Politics, Government and Space. *Geografiska Annaler. Series B. Human Geography* 86.1, 19–32.

Allen, J. (2016) *Topologies of Power: Beyond Territory and Networks*, Routledge, Abingdon and Oxon.

Amt für Statistik Berlin-Brandenburg (2017) Regionaler Sozialbericht Berlin und Brandenburg 2017 [WWW Document]. URL https://www.statistik-berlin-brandenburg.de/produkte/pdf/SP_Sozialbericht-000-000_DE_2017_BBB.pdf (accessed 24 August 2018).

Amt für Statistik Berlin-Brandenburg (2019) Statistischer Bericht. Einwohnerinnen und Einwohner im Land Berlin am 31 Dezember 2018 (Potsdam) [WWW Document]. URL https://www.statistik-berlin-brandenburg.de/publikationen/stat_berichte/2019/SB_A01-05-00_2018h02_BE.pdf (accessed 23 February 2019).

Anderson, M.W. (2008) Cities Inside Out: Race, Poverty, and Exclusion at the Urban Fringe. *UCLA Law Review* 55, 1095–160.

Anthias, F. and N. Yuval-Davis (1993) *Racialized Boundaries: Race, Nation, Gender, Colour and Class and the Anti-Racist Struggle*, Routledge, London and New York.

Arlt, S. (2016) Unfrieden in der Kolonie „frieden": Rassismus in Kleingartenanlage. Deutschlandfunk, 6 July [WWW document]. URL https://www.deutschlandfunk.de/rassismus-in-kleingartenanlage-unfrieden-in-der-kolonie.1769.de.html?dram:article_id=359211 (accessed 22 June 2019).

Atkinson, R. (2015) Losing One's Place: Narratives of Neighbourhood Change, Market Injustice and Symbolic Displacement. *Housing, Theory and Society* 32.4, 373–88.

Atkinson, R., M. Wulff, M. Reynolds, and A. Spinney (2011) Gentrification and Displacement: The Household Impacts of Neighbourhood Change. [WWW document] https://www.ahuri.edu.au/__data/assets/pdf_file/0007/2122/AHURI_Final_Report_No160_Gentrification_and_displacement_the_household_impacts_of_neighbourhood_change.pdf (accessed 6 May 2019).

Auerbach, A.M., A. LeBas, A.E. Post, and R. Weitz-Shapiro (2018) State, Society, and Informality in Cities of the Global South. *Studies in Comparative International Development* 53.3, 261–80.

Auyero, J. (2010) Chuck and Pierre at the Welfare Office. *Sociological Forum* 25, 851–60.

Azuela, A. and R. Meneses-Reyes (2014) The Everyday Formation of the Urban Space. In I. Braverman (ed.), *The Expanding Spaces of Law: A Timely Legal Geography*, Stanford law books, Stanford University Press, 169–89.

Bach, J. (2010) "They Come in Peasants and Leave Citizens": Urban Villages and the Making of Shenzhen, China. *Cultural Anthropology* 25.3, 421–58.

Bader, I. and M. Bialluch (2009) Gentrification and the Creative Class in Berlin-Kreuzberg. In L. Porter and K. Shaw (eds.), *Whose Urban Renaissance? An International Comparison of Urban Regeneration Strategies*, Routledge Studies in Human Geography, Routledge, New York, 93–102.

Bader, I. and A. Scharenberg (2010) The Sound of Berlin: Subculture and the Global Music Industry. *International Journal of Urban and Regional Research* 34, 76–91.

Barth, F. (ed.) (1998) *Ethnic Groups and Boundaries: The Social Organization of Culture Difference*, Waveland Press, Long Grove, IL.

Barzilai, G. (2008) Beyond Relativism: Where Is Political Power in Legal Pluralism? *Theoretical Inquiries in Law* 9.2, 395–416.

Battersby, J. and M. Marshak (2013) Growing Communities: Integrating the Social and Economic Benefits of Urban Agriculture in Cape Town. *Urban Forum* 24.4, 447–61.

Bauwelt (ed.) (2018) Die Bodenfrage 217.6.

Bayat, A. (1997) Un-Civil Society: The Politics of the "Informal People." *Third World Quarterly* 18, 53–72.

Bayat, A. (2000) From "Dangerous Classes" to "Quiet Rebels" Politics of the Urban Subaltern in the Global South. *International Sociology* 15, 533–57.

Bayat, A. (2009) *Life as Politics: How Ordinary People Change the Middle East*, Stanford University Press, CA.

Bear, L. (2011) Making a River of Gold: Speculative State Planning, Informality, and Neoliberal Governance on the Hooghly. *Focaal* 61, 46–60.

Benda-Beckmann, F. von, A. Sarat, K.V. Benda-Beckmann, and A. Griffiths (eds.) (2009) *Spatializing Law: An Anthropological Geography of Law in Society (Law, Justice and Power)*, Ashgate, Farnham.

Bénit-Gbaffou, C. (2018) Unpacking State Practices in City-Making: In Conversations with Ananya Roy. *The Journal of Development Studies* 54.12, 2139–48.

Bénit-Gbaffou, C. and S. Oldfield (2011) Accessing the State: Everyday Practices and Politics in Cities of the South. *Journal of Asian and African Studies* 46.5, 445–52.

Benjamin, S. (2008) Occupancy Urbanism: Radicalizing Politics and Economy Beyond Policy and Programs. *International Journal of Urban and Regional Research* 32.3, 719–29.

Berner, L., A. Holm, and I. Jensen (2015) Zwangsräumungen und die Krise des Hilfesystems: Eine Fallstudie in Berlin [WWW Document]. URL https://www.sowi.hu-berlin.de/de/lehrbereiche/stadtsoz/forschung/projekte/resolveuid/705d470c70b8479d8e582de202476822 (accessed 8 May 2019).

Bernt, M. (2012) The "Double Movements" of Neighbourhood Change: Gentrification and Public Policy in Harlem and Prenzlauer Berg. *Urban Studies* 49.14, 3045–62.

Bernt, M., B. Grell, and A. Holm (eds.) (2013) *The Berlin Reader: A Compendium on Urban Change and Activism*, Transcript, Bielefeld.

Beveridge, R. (2011) *A Politics of Inevitability: The Privatisation of the Berlin Water Company, the Global City Discourse and Governance in 1990s Berlin*, Springer, Wiesbaden.

Beveridge, R. and M. Naumann (2014) The Berlin Water Company: From "Inevitable" Privatization to "Impossible" Remunicipalization. In M. Bernt, B. Grell, and A. Holm (eds.), *The Berlin Reader: A Compendium on Urban Change and Activism*, Transcript, Bielefeld, 189–203.

Billo, E. and A. Mountz (2016) For Institutional Ethnography: Geographical Approaches to Institutions and the Everyday. *Progress in Human Geography* 40.2, 199–220.

Blandy, S. and D. Sibley (2010) Law, Boundaries and the Production of Space. *Social & Legal Studies* 19.3, 275–84.

Blomley, N. (1988) Law and the Local State: Enforcement in Action. *Transactions of the Institute of British Geographers* 13, 199–210.

Blomley, N. (2004) *Unsettling the City: Urban Land and the Politics of Property*, Psychology Press.

Blomley, N. (2014) Disentangling Law: The Practice of Bracketing. *Annual Review of Law and Social Science* 10, 133–48.

Blomley, N., D. Delaney, and R.T. Ford (2001) *The Legal Geographies Reader: Law, Power and Space*, Wiley Blackwell, Oxford and Malden.

Blomley, N.K. (1994) *Law, Space, and the Geographies of Power*, Mappings, Guilford, New York.

Blomley, N.K. and J.C. Bakan (1992) Spacing Out: Towards a Critical Geography of Law. *Osgoode Hall Law Journal* 30.3, 661–90.

BMVBS and BBR (2008) Städtebauliche, ökologische und soziale Bedeutung des Kleingartenwesens. Forschungen 133 (Bonn) [WWW document]. URL https://www.bbsr.bund.de/BBSR/DE/Veroeffentlichungen/ministerien/BMVBS/Forschungen/2008/Heft133_DL.pdf?__blob=publicationFile&v=2 (accessed 31 July 2020).

Bodenschatz, H. (1987) *Platz frei für das Neue Berlin!*, Transit Schwarzenbach, Berlin.

Boeck, F.D. (2012) Infrastructure: Commentary from Filip De Boeck: Contributions from Urban Africa Towards an Anthropology of Infrastructure. Cultural

Anthropology Online [WWW document]. URL http://culanth.org/curated_
collections/11-infrastructure/discussions/7-infrastructure-commentary-from-
filip-de-boeck (accessed 25 September 2020).

Boeck, F.D. and S. Baloji (2016) *Suturing the City: Living Together in Congo's Urban
Worlds*, Autograph ABP, London.

Boeck, F.D. and S. Baloji (2017) Positing the Polis: Topography as a Way to De-
Centre Urban Thinking. *Urbanisation* 2.2, 142–54.

Boudreau, J.-A. (2017) *Global Urban Politics: Informalization of the State*, Urban fu-
tures, Polity, Cambridge and Malden, MA.

Boudreau, J.-A. and D.E. Davis (2017) Introduction: A Processual Approach to Informalization. *Current Sociology* 65.2, 151–66.

Boudreau, J.-A., L. Gilbert, and D. Labbé (2016) Uneven State Formalization and
Periurban Housing Production in Hanoi and Mexico City: Comparative Reflections from the Global South. *Environment and Planning A: Economy and Space*
48.12, 2383–401.

Bouvier, B. (2002) *Die DDR – ein Sozialstaat? Sozialpolitik in der Ära Honecker*,
Veröffentlichungen des Instituts für Sozialgeschichte e.V., Braunschweig, Bonn,
Dietz, Bonn.

Bower, R. (2017) Forgotten Plotlanders: Learning from the Survival of Lost Informal
Housing in the UK. *Housing, Theory and Society* 34.1, 79–105.

Brady, D., T. Biegert, and Deutsches Institut für Wirtschaftsforschung, DIW Berlin (2017) The Rise of Precarious Employment in Germany. SOEP Papers on
Multidisciplinary Panel Data Research at DIW Berlin [WWW Document].
URL   http://www.diw.de/documents/publikationen/73/diw_01.c.567683.de/
diw_sp0936.pdf (accessed 31 July 2020).

Braverman, I. (2008) Governing Certain Things: The Regulation of Street Trees in
Four North American Cities. *Tulane Environmental Law Journal* 22.1, 35–60.

Brenner, N. (2014) *Implosions/Explosions: Towards a Study of Planetary Urbanization*,
Jovis Berlin, Berlin.

Brenner, N. (2018) Debating Planetary Urbanization: For an Engaged Pluralism.
Environment and Planning D: Society and Space 36.3, 570–90.

Brenner, N., D.J. Madden, and D. Wachsmuth (2011) Assemblage Urbanism and
the Challenges of Critical Urban Theory. *City* 15, 225–40.

Bromley, R. (1990) A New Path to Development? The Significance and Impact of
Hernando de Soto's Ideas on Underdevelopment, Production, and Reproduction. *Economic Geography* 66.4, 328–48.

Brown, A., V. Mukhija, and D. Shoup (2020) Converting Garages into Housing.
Journal of Planning Education and Research 40.1, 56–68.

Buck, H. (2004) *Mit hohem Anspruch gescheitert – Die Wohnungspolitik der DDR*, LIT
Verlag, Münster.

Bünger, R. (2018) Wohnungen statt Kleingärten: Baubeginn nicht vor 2021.
Der Tagesspiegel, 2 July [WWW document]. URL https://www.tagesspiegel.
de/wirtschaft/immobilien/wohnungen-statt-kleingaerten-baubeginn-nicht-
vor-2021/22750394.html (accessed 27 June 2019).

Burn, D.J. (2017) The Social World of Allotment Gardens: An Ethnographic Account of Formations of Social Cooperation. PhD thesis, Newcastle University.

Butler, C. (2009) Critical Legal Studies and the Politics of Space. *Social & Legal Studies* 18, 313–32.

Caldeira, T.P.R. (2016) Peripheral Urbanization: Autoconstruction, Transversal Logics, and Politics in Cities of the Global South. *Environment and Planning D: Society and Space* 35.1, 3–20.

Certeau, M.D. (1988) *The Practice of Everyday Life*, University of California Press, Berkeley and Los Angeles, CA.

Chakrabarty, D. (2008) *Provincializing Europe: Postcolonial Thought and Historical Difference*, Princeton studies in culture, power, history, Princeton University Press, NJ.

Chatterjee, P. (2004) *The Politics of the Governed: Reflections on Popular Politics in Most of the World*, Leonard Hastings Schoff Lectures, Columbia University Press, New York.

Chiodelli, F. (2019) The Dark Side of Urban Informality in the Global North: Housing Illegality and Organized Crime in Northern Italy. *International Journal of Urban and Regional Research* 43.3, 497–516.

Chiodelli, F. and S. Moroni (2014) The Complex Nexus Between Informality and the Law: Reconsidering Unauthorised Settlements in Light of the Concept of Nomotropism. *Geoforum* 51, 161–68.

Clarke, J. (2012) The Work of Governing. In K. Coulter (ed.), *Governing Cultures: Anthropological Perspectives on Political Labor, Power, and Government*, Palgrave Macmillan, New York, 209–31.

Clough Marinaro, I. (2017) The Informal Faces of the (Neo-)Ghetto: State Confinement, Formalization and Multidimensional Informalities in Italy's Roma Camps. *International Sociology* 32.4, 545–62.

Cochrane, A. (2006a) Euro-Commentary: (Anglo)Phoning Home from Berlin: A Response to Alan Latham. *European Urban and Regional Studies* 13, 371–76.

Cochrane, A. (2006b) Making up Meanings in a Capital City: Power, Memory and Monuments in Berlin. *European Urban and Regional Studies* 13, 5–24.

Cochrane, A. and A. Jonas (1999) Reimagining Berlin: World City, National Capital or Ordinary Place? *European Urban and Regional Studies* 6, 145–64.

Cochrane, A. and A. Passmore (2001) Building a National Capital in an Age of Globalization: The Case of Berlin. *Area* 33, 341–52.

Colomb, C. (2012) *Staging the New Berlin: Place Marketing and the Politics of Urban Reinvention Post-1989*, Taylor & Francis.

Comaroff, J.A. and J.L. Comaroff (2012) Theory from the South: Or, How Euro-America Is Evolving Toward Africa. *Anthropological Forum* 22, 113–31.

Connell, R. (2007) *Southern Theory: Social Science and the Global Dynamics of Knowledge*, Polity Press, Cambridge, Malden.

Connell, R. (2014) Using Southern Theory: Decolonizing Social Thought in Theory, Research and Application. *Planning Theory* 13.2, 210–23.

Cooper, D. (1998) *Governing Out of Order: Space, Law and the Politics of Belonging*, Rivers Oram Press, London and New York.

Cooper, D. (2011) Reading the State as a Multi-Identity Formation: The Touch and Feel of Equality Governance. *Feminist Legal Studies* 19, 3–25.

Corbridge, S., G. Williams, M.K. Srivastava, and R. Véron (2005) *Seeing the State: Governance and Governmentality in India*, Cambridge University Press, Cambridge and UK.

Costa, S., R. Fox-Kämper, R. Good, and I. Sentic (2016) The Position of Urban Allotment Gardens Within the Urban Fabric. In S. Bell, R. Fox-Kämper, N. Keshavarz, M. Benson, S. Caputo, S. Noori, and A. Voigt (eds.), *Urban Allotment Gardens in Europe*, Routledge Taylor & Francis Group, London and New York, 201–29.

Côté-Boucher, K., F. Infantino, and M.B. Salter (2014) Border Security as Practice: An Agenda for Research. *Security Dialogue* 45.3, 195–208.

Crouch, D. and C. Ward (1997) *The Allotment: Its Landscape and Culture*, Five Leaves Publications, Nottingham.

Das, V. and D. Poole (2004) *Anthropology in the Margins of the State*, SAR Press, Santa Fe and New Mexico.

Datta, A. (2012) *The Illegal City: Space, Law and Gender in a Delhi Squatter Settlement*, Gender, Space and Society, Routledge, Taylor & Francis Group, London and New York.

Davis, D.E. (2010) Irregular Armed Forces, Shifting Patterns of Commitment, and Fragmented Sovereignty in the Developing World. *Theory and Society* 39.3/4, 397–413.

Davis, D.E. (2016) Informality and State Theory: Some Concluding Remarks. *Current Sociology* 65.2, 315–24.

Davis, D.E. (2018) Reflections on "The Politics of Informality": What We Know, How We Got There, and Where We Might Head Next. *Studies in Comparative International Development* 53.3, 365–78.

de Soto, H. (2000) *The Mystery of Capital: Why Capitalism Triumphs in the West and Fails Everywhere Else*, Basic Books, New York, NY.

de Soto, H. (2002) *The Other Path: The Economic Answer to Terrorism*, Basic Books, New York, NY.

de Sousa Santos, B. (1987) Law: A Map of Misreading: Toward A Postmodern Conception of Law. *Journal of Law and Society* 14.3, 279–302.

de Sousa Santos, B. (2002) *Toward a New Legal Common Sense: Law, Globalization, and Emancipation*, Cambridge University Press, Cambridge and UK.

Delaney, D. (2010) *The Spatial, the Legal and the Pragmatics of World-Making*, Routledge, Abingdon and New York.

DeSilvey, C. (2003) Cultivated Histories in a Scottish Allotment Garden. *Cultural Geographies* 10.4, 442–68.

Desmond, M. (2012) Eviction and the Reproduction of Urban Poverty. *American Journal of Sociology* 118, 88–133.

Desmond, M. (2016) *Evicted: Poverty and Profit in the American City*, Crown Publishers, New York.

Desmond, M. and C. Gershenson (2016) Housing and Employment Insecurity Among the Working Poor. *Social Problems* 63.1, 46–67.

Desmond, M. and K.L. Perkins (2016) Housing and Household Instability. *Urban Affairs Review* 52.3, 421–36.

Deutsche Nationalversammlung. (1920) *Reichsheimstättengesetz: Gesetz-Nr. 7529, RGBl.*

Deverteuil, G. (2011) Survive but Not Thrive? Geographical Strategies for Avoiding Absolute Homelessness Among Immigrant Communities. *Social & Cultural Geography* 12, 929–45.

Devlin, R.T. (2019) A Focus on Needs: Toward a More Nuanced Understanding of Inequality and Urban Informality in the Global North. *Journal of Cultural Geography* 36.2, 121–43.

Diamond, T. (2006) "Where Did You Get the Fur Coat Fern?" Participant Observation in Institutional Ethnography. In D.E. Smith (ed.), *Institutional Ethnography as Practice*, Rowman & Littlefield, Lanham and Boulder, 45–64.

Dikec, M. (2007) *Badlands of the Republic: Space, Politics and Urban Policy*, Wiley Blackwell.

Dittmer, J.N. (2010) Textual and Discourse Analysis. In D. DeLyser, M.A. Crang, S.C. Aitken, L. McDowell, and S. Herbert (eds.), *The SAGE Handbook of Qualitative Geography*, Sage, London, 274–286.

Dobson, R. (2015) Power, Agency, Relationality and Welfare Practice. *Journal of Social Policy* 44.4, 1–19.

Dobson, R. (2020) Local Government and Practice Ontologies: Agency, Resistance and Sector Speaks in Homelessness Services. *Local Government Studies* 18.14, 1–21.

Donald, B., A. Glasmeier, M. Gray, and L. Lobao (2014) Austerity in the City: Economic Crisis and Urban Service Decline? *Cambridge Journal of Regions, Economy and Society* 7, 3–15.

Döring, C. and K. Ulbricht (2016) Gentrification-Hotspots und Verdrängungsprozesse in Berlin: Eine quantitative Analyse. In I. Helbrecht (ed.), *Gentrifizierung in Berlin: Verdrängungsprozesse und Bleibestrategien*, Urban Studies, Transcript, Bielefeld, 17–43.

Drilling, M., R. Giedych, and L. Ponizy (2016) The Idea of Allotment Gardens and the Role of Spatial and Urban Planning. In S. Bell, R. Fox-Kämper, N. Keshavarz, M. Benson, S. Caputo, S. Noori, and A. Voigt (eds.), *Urban Allotment Gardens in Europe*, Routledge Taylor & Francis Group, London and New York, 35–60.

Droste, C., P. Berndt, and T. Knorr-Siedow (2010) Study on Housing Exclusion: Welfare Policies, Housing Provision and Labour Markets: Country Report for Germany [WWW Document]. URL http://www.urban-plus.eu/fileadmin/user_upload/Homelessness_Germany_final.pdf (accessed 4 July 2020).

Droste, C. and T. Knorr-Siedow (2014) Social Housing in Germany. In K. Scanlon, C. Whitehead, and M.F. Arrigoitia (eds.), *Social Housing in Europe*, Wiley, Chichester, 183–202.

Durose, C. (2007) Beyond "Street Level Bureaucrats": Re-interpreting the Role of Front Line Public Sector Workers. *Critical Policy Analysis* 1.2, 217–34.

Durst, N.J. (2019) Informal and Ubiquitous: Colonias, Premature Subdivisions and Other Unplanned Suburbs on America's Urban Fringe. *Urban Studies* 56.4, 722–40.

Durst, N.J. and P.M. Ward (2014) Measuring Self-Help Home Improvements in Texas Colonias: A Ten Year "Snapshot" Study. *Urban Studies* 51, 2143–59.

Durst, N.J. and J. Wegmann (2017) Informal Housing in the United States. *International Journal of Urban and Regional Research* 41.2, 282–97.

Dwyer, R.E. and L.A. Phillips Lassus (2015) The Great Risk Shift and Precarity in the U.S. Housing Market. *The ANNALS of the American Academy of Political and Social Science* 660.1, 199–216.

Eckardt, F. (2005) In Search for Meaning: Berlin as National Capital and Global City. *Journal of Contemporary European Studies* 13, 189–201.

Edensor, T. (2011) *Urban Theory Beyond the West: A World of Cities*, Routledge, Abingdon and New York.

Egner, B. (2019) Wohnungspolitik seit 1945. *Bürger und Staat* 69.2/3, 94–101.

Eick, V. (2003) New Strategies of Policing the Poor: Berlin's Neo-Liberal Security System. *Policing and Society* 13.4, 365–79.

Eick, V. (2011) Policing "Below the State" in Germany: Neocommunitarian Soberness and Punitive Paternalism. *Contemporary Justice Review* 14.1, 21–41.

Eizenberg, E., S. Tappert, N. Thomas, and A. Zilans (2016) Political-Economic Urban Restructuring: Urban Allotment Gardens in the Entrepreneurial City. In S. Bell, R. Fox-Kämper, N. Keshavarz, M. Benson, S. Caputo, S. Noori, and A. Voigt (eds.), *Urban Allotment Gardens in Europe*, Routledge Taylor & Francis Group, London and New York, 91–112.

Elsheshtawy, Y. (2011) Informal Encounters: Mapping Abu Dhabi's Urban Public Spaces. *Built Environment* 37.1, 92–113.

Engels, F. (1932) [1887] *The Housing Question*, Martin Lawrence, London.

Escobar, A. (1995) *Encountering Development: The Making and Unmaking of the Third World*, Princeton Studies in Culture, Power, History, Princeton University Press, NJ.

Ettlinger, N. (2007) Precarity Unbound. *Alternatives* 32.3, 319–40.

Fairbanks, R.P. (2011) The Politics of Urban Informality in Philadelphia's Recovery House Movement. *Urban Studies* 48, 2555–70.

Fairbanks, R.P. (2012) On Theory and Method: Critical Ethnographic Approaches to Urban Regulatory Restructuring. *Urban Geography* 33, 545–65.

Färber, A. (2014) Low-Budget Berlin: Towards an Understanding of Low-Budget Urbanity as Assemblage. *Cambridge Journal of Regions, Economy and Society* 7.1, 119–36.

Ferguson, J. (2015) *Give a Man a Fish: Reflections on the New Politics of Distribution.* Duke University Press, Durham and London.

Ferguson, J. and A. Gupta (2002) Spatializing States: Toward an Ethnography of Neoliberal Governmentality. *American Ethnologist* 29.4, 981–1002.

Ferreri, M., G. Dawson, and A. Vasudevan (2016) Living Precariously: Property Guardianship and the Flexible City. *Transactions of the Institute of British Geographers* 42.2, 246–59.

Fields, D. (2018) Constructing a New Asset Class: Property-led Financial Accumulation after the Crisis. *Economic Geography* 94.2, 118–40.

Förste, D. and M. Bernt (2016) Black Box Verdrängung: Bleiben im Kiez oder Wegzug an Den Rand. In I. Helbrecht (ed.), *Gentrifizierung in Berlin: Verdrängungsprozesse und Bleibestrategien*, Urban Studies, Transcript, Bielefeld, 45–67.

Fourchard, L. (2011) Lagos, Koolhaas and Partisan Politics in Nigeria. *International Journal of Urban and Regional Research* 35, 40–56.

Friedrich, A. (2007) Vom Feldhäusschen zum Bungalow: Die Laube im Heutigen Kleingarten. In Landesverband Berlin der Gartenfreunde e.V. (ed.), *Kleine Gärten einer großen Stadt: Die Kleingartenbewegung Berlins in nationaler und internationaler Sicht*, Wächter, Berlin, 100–5.

Gerodetti, N. and S. Foster (2016) "Growing Foods from Home": Food Production, Migrants and the Changing Cultural Landscapes of Gardens and Allotments. *Landscape Research* 41.7, 808–19.

Gesetz zur Ergänzung der Kleingarten- und Kleinpachtlandordnung (1935): RGBl. I S. 809; BGB1 III 235-2.

Ghertner, D.A. (2010) Calculating Without Numbers: Aesthetic Governmentality in Delhi's Slums. *Economy and Society* 39, 185–217.

Ghertner, D.A. (2018) Hindu Extrastatecraft? Coding the Future Hindu, or the Infrastructural Inertia of Indian Urbanism. In T. Bunnell and D.P.S. Goh (eds.), *Urban Asias: Essays on Futurity Past and Present*, Jovis, Berlin, 97–107.

Goldman, M. (2011) Speculative Urbanism and the Making of the Next World City. *International Journal of Urban and Regional Research* 35.3, 555–81.

Granados, F. and D. Knoke (2005) Organized Interest Groups and Policy Networks. In T. Janoski, R. Alford, A. Hicks, and M.A. Schwartz (eds.), *The Handbook of Political Sociology: States, Civil Societies and Globalization*, Cambridge University Press, New York.

Grashoff, U. (2011) *Schwarzwohnen: Die Unterwanderung der staatlichen Wohnraumlenkung in der DDR*, Berichte und Studien/Hannah-Arendt-Institut für Totalitarismusforschung. Vol. 59, V & R Unipress, Göttingen.

Grashoff, U. (2016) Schwarzwohnen als subversive und zugleich systemstabilisierende Praxis [WWW Document]. URL www.bpb.de/222535 (accessed 3 April 2019).

Grashoff, U. (2019) Cautious Occupiers and Restrained Bureaucrats: Schwarzwohnen in the German Democratic Republic. Somewhat Different from Squatting. *Urban Studies* 56.3, 548–60.

Greenop, K. (2017) Understanding Housing Precarity: More than Access to a Shelter, Housing Is Essential for a Decent Life. *Global Discourse* 7.4, 489–95.

Groening, G. (2000) Aspects of Allotment Gardening Politics in Berlin, Germany, Between 1985 and 1995. *Acta Horticulturae* 523, 167–82.

Groth, J. and E. Corijn (2005) Reclaiming Urbanity: Indeterminate Spaces, Informal Actors and Urban Agenda Setting. *Urban Studies* 42, 503–26.

Grünbedarf (2017) Grünbedarf Faktencheck: Wie viel kostet ein Kleingarten? [WWW Document]. URL https://www.gruenbedarf.de/wp-blog/gruenbedarf-faktencheck-wie-viel-kostet-ein-kleingarten (accessed 27 June 2020).

Guggenheim, M. (2010) Mutable Immobiles: Change of Use of Buildings as a Problem of Quasi-Technologies. In I. Farias and T. Bender (eds.), *Urban Assemblages: How Actor-Network Theory Changes Urban Studies*, Routledge, London and New York.

Gupta, A. (1995) Blurred Boundaries: The Discourse of Corruption, the Culture of Politics, and the Imagined State. *American Ethnologist* 22.2, 375–402.

Hackenbroch, K. (2011) Urban Informality and Negotiated Space. *disP – The Planning Review* 47.187, 59–69.

Hackenbroch, K. and S. Hossain (2012) "The Organised Encroachment of the powerful": Everyday Practices of Public Space and Water Supply in Dhaka, Bangladesh. *Planning Theory & Practice* 13, 397–420.

Haeussermann, H. and A. Kapphan (2004) Berlin: From Divided into Fragmented City. *The Greek Review of Social Research* 113, 25–61.

Haid, C.G. and H. Hilbrandt (2019) Urban Informality and the State: Geographical Translations and Conceptual Alliances. *International Journal of Urban and Regional Research* 1.1, 551–62.

Hann, C. and K. Hart (2011) *Economic Anthropology: History, Ethnography, Critique*, Polity Press, Cambridge.

Harrison, P. (2007) The Space Between Us: Opening Remarks on the Concept of Dwelling. *Environment and Planning D: Society and Space* 25.4, 625–47.

Hart, K. (1973) Informal Income Opportunities and Urban Employment in Ghana. *Journal of Modern African Studies* 11.1, 61–89.

Hartman, C. and D. Robinson (2003) Evictions: The Hidden Housing Problem. *Housing Policy Debate* 14.4, 461–501.

Häußermann, H., A. Holm, and D. Zunzer (2002) *Stadterneuerung in der Berliner Republik: Modernisierung in Berlin-Prenzlauer Berg*, Stadt, Raum und Gesellschaft. Leske + Budrich, Opladen.

Häußermann, H. and A. Kapphan (2002) *Berlin: Von der geteilten zur gespaltenen Stadt? Sozialräumlicher Wandel seit 1990*, Leske + Budrich, Opladen.

Häußermann, H. and A. Kapphan (2013) Berlin: From Divided to Fragmented City: Socio-Spatial Changes since 1990. In M. Bernt, B. Grell, and A. Holm (eds.), *The Berlin Reader: A Compendium on Urban Change and Activism*, Transcript, Bielefeld, 77–95.

Hawley, J.C. and R. Krishnaswamy (2008) *The Postcolonial and the Global*, University of Minnesota Press, Minneapolis.

Hehl, R. (2012) Introduction. In M. Angélil and R. Hehl (eds.), *Informalize! Essays on the Political Economy of Urban Form*, Ruby Press, Berlin, 7–19.

Heinz, U. and W. Kiehle (2000) Wohnungspolitik. In U. Andersen (ed.), *Handwörterbuch des politischen Systems der Bundesrepublik Deutschland*, Springer, 675–80

Heinz, W. and B. Belina (2019) Die kommunale Bodenfrage: Hintergrund und Lösungsstrategien [WWW Document]. URL https://www.rosalux.de/publikation/id/40013/die-kommunale-bodenfrage (accessed 3 July 2020).

Helbrecht, I. (ed.) (2016) *Gentrifizierung in Berlin: Verdrängungsprozesse und Bleibestrategien*, Urban Studies, Transcript, Bielefeld.

Hentschel, C. (2015) Postcolonializing Berlin and the Fabrication of the Urban: Postcolonializing Berlin and the Fabrication of the Urban. *International Journal of Urban and Regional Research* 39, 79–91.

Hernádi, S. (2015) Eine Favela in Berlin? Informelle Siedlungen werden auch bei uns Realität. *MieterEcho* 372, 10.

Hesse, M. (2018) In Grund und Boden: Wie die Finanzialisierung von Bodenmärkten und Flächennutzung Städte unter Druck setzt. *ARCH+* 231, 78–83.

Hilbrandt, H. (2015) Housing Constellations: Three Fault Lines of Informality Research. In S. Quadflieg and G. Theune (eds.), *Nadogradnje: Urban Self-Regulation in Post-Yugoslav Cities*, M Books, Weimar, 110–25.

Hilbrandt, H. (2019) Everyday Urbanism and the Everyday State: Negotiating Habitat in Allotment Gardens in Berlin. *Urban Studies* 56.2, 352–67.

Hilbrandt, H., S. Neves Alves, and T. Tuvikene (2017) Writing Across Contexts: Urban Informality and the State in Tallinn, Bafatá and Berlin. *International Journal of Urban and Regional Research* 41.6, 946–61.

Hobbs, M. (2012) "Farmers on Notice": The Threat Faced by Weimar Berlin's Garden Colonies in the Face of the City's Neues Bauen Housing Programme. *Urban History* 39.2, 263–84.

Hodkinson, S. (2012) The Return of the Housing Question. *Ephemera* 12.4, 423–44.

Hodkinson, S. and C. Essen (2015) Grounding Accumulation by Dispossession in Everyday Life. *International Journal of Law in the Built Environment* 7, 72–91.

Hoggett, P. (2001) Agency, Rationality and Social Policy. *Journal of Social Policy* 30, 37–56.

Holm, A. (2005) Hartz IV und die Konturen einer neoliberalen Wohnungspolitik: Berlin. In V. Eick and J. Sambale (eds.), *Erweiterte Dokumentation der Arbeitstagung „Public Housing and Work (Re)Integration – Lessons from Germany and North America,"* Working paper der Abteilung Politik, John-F.-Kennedy-Institut, Freie Universität Berlin, 135–47.

Holm, A. (2008) Privatisierung des kommunalen Wohnungsbestandes. In N. Gestring, H. Glasauer, C. Hannemann, W. Petrowsky, and J. Pohlan (eds.), *Jahrbuch StadtRegion 2007/2008: Schwerpunkt: Arme reiche Stadt*, Barbara Budrich, Opladen and Farmington Hills, 101–8.

Holm, A. (2010) *Wir bleiben alle! Gentrifizierung – städtische Konflikte um Aufwertung und Verdrängung*. Unrast Verlag, Münster.

Holm, A. (2011) Wohnungspolitik der rot-roten Regierungskoalition in Berlin. In A. Holm, K. Lederer, and M. Naumann (eds.), *Linke Metropolenpolitik: Erfahrungen und Perspektiven am Beispiel Berlin*, Raumproduktionen, Westfälisches Dampfboot, Münster.

Holm, A. (2014) Zeitschleife Kreuzberg: Gentrification im langen Schatten der "Behutsamen Stadterneuerung." *Zeithistorische Forschungen/Studies in Contemporary History* 11.2, 300–11.

Holm, A. (2017) Eine Politische Ökonomie der Ferienwohnungen. Berlin: Wie Verändert Airbnb den Wohnungsmarkt? [WWW Document]. URL https://www.untergrund-blättle.ch/politik/deutschland/berlin_airbnb_wohnungs markt_3927.html (accessed 30 July 2020).

Holm, A. and A. Kuhn (2011) Squatting and Urban Renewal: The Interaction of Squatter Movements and Strategies of Urban Restructuring in Berlin. *International Journal of Urban and Regional Research* 35, 644–58.

Holm, A. and G. Schulz (2016) GentriMap: Ein Messmodell für Gentrification und Verdrängung. In I. Helbrecht (ed.), *Gentrifizierung in Berlin: Verdrängungsprozesse und Bleibestrategien*, Urban Studies, Transcript, Bielefeld, 287–318.

Holm, A., S. Junker, H. Lebuhn, and K. Neitzel (2017) Wohnverhältnisse in Deutschland – Eine Analyse der sozialen Lage in 77 Großstädten: Bericht aus dem Forschungsprojekt „sozialer Wohnversorgungsbedarf" (Berlin, Düsseldorf) [WWW Document]. URL https://www.boeckler.de/pdf_fof/99313.pdf (accessed 5 July 2020).

Hommels, A. (2005) Studying Obduracy in the City: Toward a Productive Fusion Between Technology Studies and Urban Studies. *Science, Technology & Human Values* 30, 323–51.

Hommels, A. (2008) *Unbuilding Cities: Obduracy in Urban Sociotechnical Change*, MIT Press, Cambridge MA.

Hommels, A. (2010) Changing Obdurate Urban Objects: The Attempts to Reconstruct the Highways Through Maastricht. In I. Farias and T. Bender (eds.), *Urban Assemblages: How Actor-Network Theory Changes Urban Studies*, Routledge, London and New York, 135–59.

Honert, M. (2018) "Dass Berlin mal fertig ist, können Sie vergessen": Interview mit Andreas Becher. Der Tagesspiegel, 24 September [WWW document]. URL https://www.tagesspiegel.de/gesellschaft/interview-mit-andreas-becher-dass-berlin-mal-fertig-ist-koennen-sie-vergessen/23065550.html (accessed 27 June 2020).

Hönicke, C. and R. Schönball (2019) Berlin plant 7000 Wohnungen auf Kleingarten-Flächen. Der Tagesspiegel, 22 February [WWW document]. URL https://www.tagesspiegel.de/berlin/stadtentwicklung-berlin-plant-7000-wohnungen-auf-kleingarten-flaechen/24025116.html (accessed 17 April 2020).

Hou, J. (2010) *Insurgent Public Space: Guerrilla Urbanism and the Remaking of Contemporary Cities*, Routledge, Abington, New York.

Huchzermeyer, M. (2011) *Tenement Cities: From 19th Century Berlin to 21st Century Nairobi*, Africa World Press, Trenton and NJ.

Huning, S. and N. Schuster (2015) "Social Mixing" or "Gentrification"? Contradictory Perspectives on Urban Change in the Berlin District of Neukölln. *International Journal of Urban and Regional Research* 39.4, 738–55.

Hunter, S. (2008) Living Documents: A Feminist Psychosocial Approach to the Relational Politics of Policy Documentation. *Critical Social Policy* 28.4, 506–28.

Hunter, S. (2015) *Power, Politics and the Emotions: Impossible Governance?* Routledge, New York.

ILO (1972) *Employment, Incomes and Equality: A Strategy for Increasing Productive Employment in Kenya.* Geneva.

Investitionsbank Berlin (2002) *Der Berliner Wohnungsmarkt: Entwicklung und Strukturen 1991–2000*, Berlin wohnen, Regioverlag, Berlin.

Investitionsbank Berlin (2007) IBB Wohnungsmarktbericht 2007: „Weiterentwicklung der Wohnungsbestände" (Berlin) [WWW Document]. URL https://www.ibb.de/media/dokumente/publikationen/berliner-wohnungsmarkt/wohnungsmarktbericht/ibb_wohnungsmarktbericht_2007.pdf (accessed 01 August 2020).

Investitionsbank Berlin (2012) IBB Wohnungsmarktbericht 2011 (Berlin) [WWW Document]. URL https://www.stadtentwicklung.berlin.de/wohnen/wohnungsmarktbericht/pdf/wohnungsmarktbericht_2011.pdf (accessed 01 August 2020).

Investitionsbank Berlin (2017) IBB Wohnungsmarktbericht 2016: Inklusive Schwerpunktthema: Wanderungen Berlin.

Iveson, K., C. Lyons, S. Clark, and S. Weir (2019) The Informal Australian City. *Australian Geographer* 50.1, 11–27.

Jackson, E. (2015) *Young Homeless People and Urban Space: Fixed in Mobility.* Routledge, New York.

Jacobs, J. (1993 [1961]) *The Death and Life of Great American Cities*, Random House, New York.

Jaffe, R. (2013) The Hybrid State: Crime and Citizenship in Urban Jamaica. *American Ethnologist* 40.4, 734–48.

Jayne, M. and S.M. Hall (2019) Urban Assemblages, (In)formality, and Housing in the Global North. *Annals of the American Association of Geographers* 109.3, 685–704.

Jeffrey, A.S. (2013) *The Improvised State: Sovereignty, Performance and Agency in Dayton Bosnia*, RGS-IBG Book Series, Wiley Blackwell.

Jenkis, H. (1985) *Die gemeinnützige Wohnungswirtschaft zwischen Markt und Sozialbindung*, Duncker und Humblot, Berlin.

Jensen, U. (2005) Der Kleingarten. In A. Geisthövel and H. Knoch (eds.), *Orte der Moderne: Erfahrungswelten des 19. und 20. Jahrhunderts*, Campus Verlag, 316–25.

Jessop, B. (2016) *The State: Past, Present, Future*, Polity Press, Malden.

Jones, H. (2011) Uncomfortable Positions: How Policy Practitioners Negotiate Difficult Subjects. Unpublished PhD thesis, University of London.

Joronen, M. (2019) Negotiating Colonial Violence: Spaces of Precarisation in Palestine. *Antipode* 51.3, 838–57.

Joronen, M. and M. Griffiths (2019) The Affective Politics of Precarity: Home Demolitions in Occupied Palestine. *Environment and Planning D: Society and Space* 37.3, 561–76.

Kantor, P., H.V. Savitch, and S.V. Haddock (1997) The Political Economy of Urban Regimes: A Comparative Perspective. *Urban Affairs Review* 32.3, 348–77.

Katsch, G. and J.B. Walz (2008) Deutschlands Kleingärtner im Dritten Reich. *Schriftenreihe des deutschen Kleingärtnermuseums* 5, Leipzig.

Kemp, P.A. (2015) Private Renting After the Global Financial Crisis. *Housing Studies* 30.4, 601–20.

Kemp, P.A. and S. Kofner (2010) Contrasting Varieties of Private Renting: England and Germany. *International Journal of Housing Policy* 10.4, 379–98.

Klaufus, C. (2010) The Two ABCs of Aided Self-Help Housing in Ecuador. *Habitat International* 34.3, 351–58.

Kleinlosen, M. and J. Milchert (1989) *Berliner Kleingärten*, Berlin Verlag, Berlin.

Kneist, S. and T. Röttger (2016) Kleingartenanlage will keine weiteren Migranten, 30 June [WWW document]. URL https://www.tagesspiegel.de/berlin/diskrim inierung-in-berliner-laubenkolonie-kleingartenanlage-will-keine-weiteren-mi granten/13807558.html (accessed 4 June 2020).

Knorr-Siedow, T. (2005) Gegenwertige Trends im Sozialen Wohnungsbau und in der Arbeitsmarktpolitik. In V. Eick and J. Sambale (eds.) *Erweiterte Dokumentation der Arbeitstagung „Public Housing and Work (Re)integration – Lessons from Germany and North America*, Working paper der Abteilung Politik, John-F.-Kennedy-Institut, Freie Universität Berlin, 32–50.

Kraftl, P. and P. Adey (2008) Architecture/Affect/Inhabitation: Geographies of Being-in Buildings. *Annals of the Association of American Geographers* 98.1, 213–31.

Krätke, S. (2001) Berlin: Towards a Global City? *Urban Studies* 38.10, 1777–99.

Krätke, S. (2004a) City of Talents? Berlin's Regional Economy, Socio-spatial Fabric and "Worst Practice" Urban Governance. *International Journal of Urban and Regional Research* 28, 511–29.

Krätke, S. (2004b) Economic Restructuring and the Making of a Financial Crisis. *disP – The Planning Review* 40.156, 58–63.

Krätke, S. and R. Borst (2000) *Berlin: Metropole zwischen Boom und Krise*, Leske + Budrich, Opladen.

Krishnaswamy, R. (2005) Globalization and Its Postcolonial (Dis)contents. *Journal of Postcolonial Writing* 41.1, 69–82.

Kuhn, G. (2006) „Wildes" Siedeln und „stille" Suburbanisierung. Von den Wohnlauben zu den privaten Stadtrandsiedlungen. In A. Janatková (ed.), *Wohnen in der Großstadt: 1900–1939; Wohnsituation und Modernisierung im europäischen Vergleich; interdisziplinäre Tagung am Geisteswissenschaftlichen Zentrum Geschichte und Kultur Ostmitteleuropas e.V. an der Universität Leipzig im Februar 2001*, Forschungen zur Geschichte und Kultur des östlichen Mitteleuropa, Steiner, Stuttgart, 111–32.

Künkel, J. (2018) Die städtische Produktion von „Armutsmigration." *PROKLA. Zeitschrift für kritische Sozialwissenschaft* 48.191, 283–98.

Kusenbach, M. (2009) Salvaging Decency: Mobile Home Residents' Strategies of Managing the Stigma of "Trailer" Living. *Qualitative Sociology* 32.4, 399–428.

Laguerre, M.S. (1994) *The Informal City*, Macmillan, Houndmills, Basingstoke, Hampshire.

Lamont, M. and V. Molnár (2002) The Study of Boundaries in the Social Sciences. *Annual Review of Sociology* 28.1, 167–95.

Lamotte, M. (2017) The Ñeta Law, the Ñeta World: Ethics and Imaginaries in Circulation Between the South Bronx, Barcelona and Guayaquil. *Current Sociology* 65.2, 302–14.

Lancione, M. (2016a) The Assemblage of Life at the Margins. In M. Lancione (ed.), *Rethinking Life at the Margins: The Assemblage of Contexts, Subjects and Politics*, Cultural Geographies, Routledge Taylor & Francis Group, London and New York, 3–26.

Lancione, M. (ed.) (2016b) *Rethinking Life at the Margins: The Assemblage of Contexts, Subjects and Politics*, Cultural Geographies, Routledge Taylor & Francis Group, London and New York

Lancione, M. (2019a) The Politics of Embodied Urban Precarity: Roma People and the Fight for Housing in Bucharest, Romania. *Geoforum* 101, 182–91.

Lancione, M. (2019b) Weird Exoskeletons: Propositional Politics and the Making of Home in Underground Bucharest. *International Journal of Urban and Regional Research* 43, 535–50.

Lancione, M. and C. McFarlane (2016) Life at the Urban Margins: Sanitation Infra-making and the Potential of Experimental Comparison. *Environment and Planning A* 48.12, 2402–21.

Land Berlin. (2009) Verwaltungsvorschriften über Dauerkleingärten und Kleingärten auf landeseigenen Grundstücken vom 15.Dezember 2009. *Amtsblatt Berlin (ABl)* 58, 2835–30.

Landesverband Berlin der Gartenfreunde e.V. (2001) *Ein starkes Stück Berlin 1901–2001: 100 Jahre organisiertes Berliner Kleingartenwesen*, Wächter, Berlin.

Landesverband Berlin der Gartenfreunde e.V. (ed.) (2007) *Kleine Gärten einer großen Stadt: Die Kleingartenbewegung Berlins in nationaler und internationaler Sicht*, Wächter, Berlin.

Landesverband Berlin der Gartenfreunde e.V. (2018) Zahlen und Fakten [WWW Document]. URL https://www.gartenfreunde-berlin.de/ueber-uns/zahlen-und-fakten (accessed 6 July 2020).

Landgraf, G. and H. Kraetsch (2008) Rechtlich ist die Sache so! Rechtsverhältnisse an Garten- und Erholungsflächen seit Oktober 1990 (II. Teil). *Der Gartenfreund* 11, 22–23.

Landman, K. and M. Napier (2010) Waiting for a House or Building Your Own? Reconsidering State Provision, Aided and Unaided Self-Help in South Africa. *Habitat International* 34.3, 299–305.

Lange, A. (1984) *Berlin zur Zeit Bebels und Bismarcks: Zwischen Reichsgründung und Jahrhundertwende*, Dietz, Berlin/Ost.

Lange, B. (2011) Re-scaling Governance in Berlin's Creative Economy. *Culture Unbound: Journal of Current Cultural Research* 3, 187.

Larson, J.E. (2002) Informality, Illegality, and Inequality. *Yale Law & Policy Review* 20.1, 137–82.

Lawhon, M. and Y. Truelove (2019) Disambiguating the Southern Urban Critique: Propositions, Pathways and Possibilities for a More Global Urban Studies. *Urban Studies*, OnlineFirst.

Lea, T. (2008) *Bureaucrats and Bleeding Hearts: Indigenous Health in Northern Australia*, University of New South Wales Press, Sydney.

Lebuhn, H., A. Holm, S. Junker, and K. Neitzel (2017) Wohnverhältnisse in Deutschland: eine Analyse der sozialen Lage in 77 Großstädten (Berlin, Düsseldorf). [WWW Document]. URL https://www.boeckler.de/pdf_fof/99313.pdf (accessed 6 July 2020).

Lederer, K. and M. Naumann (2011) Linke Metropolenpolitik und öffentliche Unternehmen: Eine Bestandsaufnahme am Beispiel Berlins. In A. Holm, K. Lederer, and M. Naumann (eds.), *Linke Metropolenpolitik: Erfahrungen und Perspektiven am Beispiel Berlin*, Raumproduktionen, Westfälisches Dampfboot, Münster, 128–45.

Lee, J. and T. Ingold (2006) Fieldwork on Foot: Perceiving, Routing, Socializing. In S. Coleman and P.J. Collins (eds.), *Locating the Field: Space, Place and Context in Anthropology*, A.S.A. monographs, Berg, Oxford and New York, 67–86.

Lemanski, C. (2009) Augmented Informality: South Africa's Backyard Dwellings as a By-Product of Formal Housing Policies. *Habitat International* 33.4, 472–84.

Levi, R. and M. Valverde (2008) Studying Law by Association: Bruno Latour Goes to the Conseil d'état. *Law & Social Inquiry* 33, 805–25.

Linde, C. (2015) Von der Wohnung zur Unterkunft: Politik der Provisorien hebelt Recht auf angemessenen Wohnraum immer mehr aus. *MieterEcho* 372, 6–8.

Lindell, I. (2008) The Multiple Sites of Urban Governance: Insights from an African City. *Urban Studies* 45, 1879–901.

Lindell, I., C. Ampaire, and A. Byerley (2019) Governing Urban Informality: Reworking Spaces and Subjects in Kampala, Uganda. *International Development Planning Review* 41.1, 63–84.

Lipsky, M. (2010 [1980]) *Street-Level Bureaucracy: Dilemmas of the Individual in Public Services*, Russell Sage Foundation, New York.

Loesdau, A. (2007) *Kleine Gärten in einer grossen Stadt*. Wächter, Berlin.

Lombard, M. (2019) Informality as Structure or Agency? Exploring Shed Housing in the UK as Informal Practice. *International Journal of Urban and Regional Research* 43.3, 569–75.

Lorbek, M. and M. Martinsen (2015) Allotment Garden Dwellings: Exploring Tradition and Legal Framework. *Urbani Izziv* 26, 98–113.

Loy, T. (2018) Lieber Wohnungen als Kleingärten – Investor Fordert Tabubruch: Offener Brief an Senatorin Lompscher. Der Tagesspiegel, 22 April [WWW document]. URL https://www.tagesspiegel.de/berlin/offener-brief-an-senatorin-lompscher-lieber-wohnungen-als-kleingaerten-investor-fordert-tabubruch/21200112.html (accessed 27 June 2020).

Mack, J. and J.S. Parscher (2017) The Right to the Garden: Allotments and the Politics of Urban Green Space in Sweden. In P. Clark, M. Niemi, and C. Nolin (eds.), *Green Landscapes in the European City, 1750–2010*, Routledge Studies in Modern European History, Routledge Taylor & Francis Group, London and New York, 87–104.

Madden, D. and P. Marcuse (2016) *In Defense of Housing: The Politics of Crisis*, Verso, London and New York.

Maeckelbergh, M. (2012) Mobilizing to Stay Put: Housing Struggles in New York City. *International Journal of Urban and Regional Research* 36.4, 655–73.

Mainczyk, L. (2005) Baulichkeiten in Kleingartenanlagen. *Neue Justiz* 59.6, 241–46.

Marcuse, P. (1985) Gentrification, Abandonment and Displacement: Connections, Causes and Policy Responses in New York City. *Journal of Urban and Contemporary Law* 28, 195–240.

Marquardt, N. (2013) Räume der Fürsorge: Regieren der Wohnungslosigkeit im betreuten Wohnen. *Geographische Zeitschrift* 101.3+4, 148–65.

Marquardt, N., H. Füller, G. Glasze, and R. Pütz (2013) Shaping the Urban Renaissance: New-build Luxury Developments in Berlin. *Urban Studies* 50.8, 1540–56.

Marx, C. and E. Kelling (2019) Knowing Urban Informalities. *Urban Studies* 56.3, 494–509.

Mattern, P. (2015) Kommen die Billigunterkünfte? Was der Markt im „preisgünstigen" Segment anbieten kann. *MieterEcho* 372, 4–6.

Mattern, P. (2018) Droht ein neuer Substandard? *PROKLA. Zeitschrift für kritische Sozialwissenschaft* 48.191, 334–45.

Matthiessen, H. (2005) 10 Jahre Schuldrechtsanpassung: Ein gelungenes Beispiel sozialverträglicher deutsch-deutscher Rechtsangleichung? *Neue Justiz* 59.1, 1–6.

Mayer, M. (2009) Combating Social Exclusion with Activating Policies: Lessons from Recent German Policy Reforms. *The Urban Reinventors [Online]* 3, 1–36.

McCann, E., A. Roy, and K. Ward (2013) Assembling/Worlding Cities. *Urban Geography* 34, 581–89.

McDermont, M. and J. Clarke (2017) Introduction: Working the Boundaries of Law. *Oñati Socio-Legal Series* 7.7, 1383–96.

McFarlane, C. (2010) The Comparative City: Knowledge, Learning, Urbanism. *International Journal of Urban and Regional Research* 34.4, 725–42.

McFarlane, C. (2011a) Assemblage and Critical Urbanism. *City* 15.2, 204–24.

McFarlane, C. (2011b) Encountering, Describing and Transforming Urbanism. *City* 15, 731–39.

McFarlane, C. (2011c) The City as Assemblage: Dwelling and Urban Space. *Environment and Planning D: Society and Space* 29, 649–71.

McFarlane, C. (2012) Rethinking Informality: Politics, Crisis, and the City. *Planning Theory & Practice* 13, 89–108.

McFarlane, C. (2018) Fragment Urbanism: Politics at the Margins of the City. *Environment and Planning D: Society and Space* 36.6, 1007–25.

McFarlane, C. (2019) Thinking with and Beyond the Informal–formal Relation in Urban Thought. *Urban Studies* 56.3, 620–23.

McFarlane, C. and J. Robinson (2012) Introduction: Experiments in Comparative Urbanism. *Urban Geography* 33.6, 765–73.

McFarlane, C. and J. Rutherford (2008) Political Infrastructures: Governing and Experiencing the Fabric of the City. *International Journal of Urban and Regional Research* 32.2, 363–74.

McKinsey (2010) Berlin 2020: Unsere Stadt. Wirtschaftliche Perspektiven durch neue Wachstumskerne [WWW Document]. URL https://docplayer.org/12331529-Berlin-2020-unsere-stadt-wirtschaftliche-perspektiven-durch-neue-wachstum skerne.html (accessed 18 September 2020).

Melissaris, E. (2004) The More the Merrier? A New Take on Legal Pluralism. *Social & Legal Studies* 13.1, 57–79.

Mendez, P. and N. Quastel (2015) Subterranean Commodification: Informal Housing and the Legalization of Basement Suites in Vancouver from 1928 to 2009. *International Journal of Urban and Regional Research* 39.6, 1155–71.

Merrill, S. and S. Jasper (2014) Was ist so Berlin? Eine kritische Rezension aktueller Linien und Fragestellungen der Stadtforschung in der deutschen Hauptstadt. *Sub\urban. zeitschrift für kritische stadtforschung* 2, 143–54.

Merry, S.E. (1988) Legal Pluralism. *Law & Society Review* 22.5, 869–96.

Meth, P. (2010) Unsettling Insurgency: Reflections on Women's Insurgent Practices in South Africa. *Planning Theory & Practice* 11, 241–63.

Mihai, S. (2013) Rumänen in Berlin Neukölln: Der Slum von nebenan. Berliner Zeitung, 11 August [WWW document]. URL https://www.berliner-zeitung.de/berlin/rumaenen-in-berlin-neukoelln-der-slum-von-nebenan-4465104 (accessed 6 July 2020).

Miraftab, F. (2009) Insurgent Planning: Situating Radical Planning in the Global South. *Planning Theory* 8, 32–50.

Misztal, B. (2002) *Informality: Social Theory and Contemporary Practice*, Routledge.

Mitchell, D. (1995) *The End of Public Space? People's Park, Definitions of the Public, and Democracy*, Annals of the Association of American Geographers.

Mitchell, P.A. (2017) Socialism's Empty Promise: Housing Vacancy and Squatting in the German Democratic Republic. In J. Fürst and J. McLellan (eds.), *Dropping out of Socialism: The Creation of Alternative Spheres in the Soviet Bloc*, Lexington Books, Lanham and Boulder, 277–302.

Mitchell, T. (1999) Society, Economy, and the State Effect. In G. Steinmetz (ed.), *State/Culture: State-Formation After the Cultural Turn*, The Wilder House Series in Politics, History, and Culture, Cornell University Press, Ithaca, NY, 76–97.

Mohanty, C.T. (2003) "Under Western Eyes" Revisited: Feminist Solidarity Through Anticapitalist Struggles. *Signs: Journal of Women in Culture and Society* 28.2, 499–535.

Moss, T. (2014) Socio-Technical Change and the Politics of Urban Infrastructure: Managing Energy in Berlin Between Dictatorship and Democracy. *Urban Studies* 51, 1432–48.

Mufti, A.R. (2005) Global Comparativism. *Critical Inquiry* 31.2, 472–89.

Mukhija, V. (2014) Outlaw In-Laws: Informal Second Units and the Stealth Reinvention of Single-Family Housing. In V. Mukhija and A. Loukaitou-Sideris (eds.), *The Informal American City: From Taco Trucks to Day Labor*, Urban and Industrial Environments, MIT Press, Cambridge, MA, 39–59.

Muñoz, S. (2017) A Look Inside the Struggle for Housing in Buenos Aires, Argentina. *Urban Geography* 38.8, 1252–69.

Muñoz, S. (2018) Urban Precarity and Home: There Is No "Right to the City." *Annals of the American Association of Geographers* 108.2, 370–79.

Myers, G. (2014) From Expected to Unexpected Comparisons: Changing the Flows of Ideas About Cities in a Postcolonial Urban World. *Singapore Journal of Tropical Geography* 35, 104–18.

Neupert, P. (2016) Leben im Wohnwagen – ein Phänomen der Verdrängung? In I. Helbrecht (ed.), *Gentrifizierung in Berlin: Verdrängungsprozesse und Bleibestrategien*, Urban Studies, Transcript, Bielefeld.

Newman, J. (2012) *Working the Spaces of Power: Activism, Neoliberalism and Gendered Labour*, Bloomsbury Academic, London.

Nijman, J. (2007) Introduction: Comparative Urbanism. *Urban Geography* 28.1, 1–6.

Nikolaidou, S., T. Klöti, S. Tappert, and M. Drilling (2016) Urban Gardening and Green Space Governance: Towards New Collaborative Planning Practices. *Urban Planning* 1.1, 5–19.

Nilsen, M. (2014) *The Working Man's Green Space: Allotment Gardens in England, France, and Germany, 1870–1919*, University of Virginia Press.

Novy, J. (2013) Berlin Does Not Love You: Notes on Berlin's "Tourism Controversy" and Its Discontents. In M. Bernt, B. Grell, and A. Holm (eds.), *The Berlin Reader: A Compendium on Urban Change and Activism*, Transcript, Bielefeld, 223–39.

Nowakowski, G. (2018) Abschied vom Reich der Gartenkolonien: Wohnungsbau in Berlin. Der Tagesspiegel, 27 April [WWW document]. URL https://www.tagesspiegel.de/berlin/wohnungsbau-in-berlin-abschied-vom-reich-der-garten kolonien/21220136.html (accessed 27 June 2020).

O'Donnell, G.A. (2001) Democracy, Law, and Comparative Politics. *Studies in Comparative International Development* 36, 7–36.

Painter, J. (2007) Stateness in Action. *Geoforum* 38.4, 605–07.

Pasquetti, S. and G. Picker (2017) Urban Informality and Confinement: Toward a Relational Framework. *International Sociology* 32.4, 532–44.

Peck, J. (2012) Austerity Urbanism. *City* 16.6, 626–55.

Peck, J. (2015) Cities Beyond Compare? *Regional Studies* 49, 160–82.

Philippopoulos-Mihalopoulos, A. (2010) Law's Spatial Turn: Geography, Justice and a Certain Fear of Space. *Law, Culture and the Humanities* 7, 187–202.

Picker, G. (2019) Sovereignty Beyond the State: Exception and Informality in a Western European City. *International Journal of Urban and Regional Research* 43.3, 576–81.

Picker, G. and S. Pasquetti (2015) Durable Camps: The State, the Urban, the Everyday: Introduction. *City* 19, 681–88.

Piepgras, A. (n.d.) Gartenstädte statt Gartenzwerge! Warum die Verlängerung der Kleingartenpachtverträge eine Katastrophe für Berlin wäre! [WWW Document]. URL https://bezahlbarer-wohnraum-berlin.de/#brief (accessed 27 June 2020).

Piepgras, A. (2018) Weg mit den Kleingärten: Gartenstädte statt Gartenzwerge! Wohnungsnot in Berlin. Der Tagesspiegel, 10 November [WWW document]. URL https://www.tagesspiegel.de/politik/wohnungsnot-in-berlin-weg-mit-den-kleingaerten-gartenstaedte-statt-gartenzwerge/23601056.html (accessed 27 June 2020).

Poling, K. (2014) Shantytowns and Pioneers Beyond the City Wall: Berlin's Urban Frontier in the Nineteenth Century. *Central European History* 47.02, 245–74.

Porter, L., M. Lombard, M. Huxley, A.K. Ingin, T. Islam, J. Briggs, D. Rukmana, R.T. Devlin, and V. Watson (2011) Informality, the Commons and the Paradoxes for Planning. *Planning Theory & Practice* 12, 115–53.

Portes, A. (1983) The Informal Sector: Definition, Controversy, and Relation to National Development. *Review (Fernand Braudel Center)* 7, 151–74.

Povinelli, E.A. (2011) *Economies of Abandonment: Social Belonging and Endurance in Late Liberalism*, Duke University Press, Durham, NC.

PROKLA (2018) Zur (neuen) Wohnungsfrage. 48.2.

Purser, G. (2016) The Circle of Dispossession: Evicting the Urban Poor in Baltimore. *Critical Sociology* 42.3, 393–415.

Rada, U. (1997) *Hauptstadt der Verdrängung: Berliner Zukunft zwischen Kiez und Metropole*, Verlag Schwarze Risse – Rote Straße Libertäre Assoziation, Berlin.

Rada, U. (2000) Der barbarische Osten. In A. Scharenberg (ed.), *Berlin, Global City oder Konkursmasse?: Eine Zwischenbilanz zehn Jahre nach dem Mauerfall*, Dietz, 129–33.

Radnitz, S. (2011) Informal Politics and the State. *Comparative Politics* 43.3, 351–71.

Rakowski, C.A. (ed.) (1994) *Contrapunto: The Informal Sector Debate in Latin America*, SUNY Series in Power and Political Economy, State University of New York Press, Albany.

Rao, V., F.D. Boeck, and A. Simone (2007) Invisible Urbanism in Africa. *Perspecta* 39, 78–91.

Rau, C. (2012) Grenzen und Spielräume in der „Fürsorgediktatur." Staatliche Wohnungspolitik und städtische Wohnraumlenkung in Leipzig in den 1970er und 1980er Jahren. *Informationen zur modernen Stadtgeschichte* 2, 132–63.

Reeves, M. (2009) Materialising State Space: "Creeping Migration" and Territorial Integrity in Southern Kyrgyzstan. *Europe–Asia Studies* 61.7, 1277–313.

Reeves, M. (2011) Fixing the Border: On the Affective Life of the State in Southern Kyrgyzstan. *Environment and Planning D: Society and Space* 29, 905–23.

Richie, A. (1998) *Faust's Metropolis: A History of Berlin*, Carroll & Graf, New York.

Richter, E. (1930) Das Kleingartenwesen in wirtschaftlicher und rechtlicher Hinsicht dargestellt an der Entwicklung von Gross-Berlin. Dissertation, Berlin.

Robinson, J. (2002) Global and World Cities: A View from off the Map. *International Journal of Urban and Regional Research* 26.3, 531–54.

Robinson, J. (2006) *Ordinary Cities Between Modernity and Development*, Routledge, London and New York.

Robinson, J. (2011) Cities in a World of Cities: The Comparative Gesture. *International Journal of Urban and Regional Research* 35.1, 1–23.

Robinson, J. (2013) The Urban Now: Theorising Cities Beyond the New. *European Journal of Cultural Studies* 16.6, 659–77.

Rollka, B. and V. Spiess (1987) *Berliner Laubenpieper*, Haude u. Spener, Berlin.

Rolnik, R. (2019) *Urban Warfare: Housing Under the Empire of Finance*, Verso, London.

Rose, M. (2012) Dwelling as Marking and Claiming. *Environment and Planning D: Society and Space* 30.5, 757–71.

Rosol, M., V. Béal, and S. Mössner (2017) Greenest Cities? The (Post-)Politics of New Urban Environmental Regimes. *Environment and Planning A* 49.8, 1710–18.

Routhier, G. (2019) Beyond Worst Case Needs: Measuring the Breadth and Severity of Housing Insecurity Among Urban Renters. *Housing Policy Debate* 29.2, 235–49.

Roy, A. (2005) Urban Informality: Toward an Epistemology of Planning. *Journal of the American Planning Association* 71, 147–58.

Roy, A. (2009a) Strangely Familiar: Planning and the Worlds of Insurgence and Informality. *Planning Theory* 8, 7–11.

Roy, A. (2009b) Why India Cannot Plan Its Cities: Informality, Insurgence and the Idiom of Urbanization. *Planning Theory* 8, 76–87.

Roy, A. (2009c) Civic Governmentality: The Politics of Inclusion in Beirut and Mumbai. *Antipode* 41, 159–79.

Roy, A. (2009d) The 21st-Century Metropolis: New Geographies of Theory. *Regional Studies* 43.6, 819–30.

Roy, A. (2011) Slumdog Cities: Rethinking Subaltern Urbanism. *International Journal of Urban and Regional Research* 35, 223–38.

Roy, A. (2015) Who's Afraid of Postcolonial Theory? *International Journal of Urban and Regional Research* 40.1, 200–09.

Roy, A. (2018) The Potency of the State: Logics of Informality and Subalternity. *The Journal of Development Studies* 54.12, 2243–46.

Roy, A. and A. Ong (2012) *Worlding Cities: Asian Experiments and the Art of Being Global*, Wiley Blackwell, Chichester and West Sussex.

Roy, A. and N.A. Sayyad (eds.) (2004) *Urban Informality: Transnational Perspectives from the Middle East, Latin America, and South Asia*, Lexington Books, Lanham, Oxford.

Rusanov, A. (2019) Dacha Dwellers and Gardeners: Garden Plots and Second Houses in Europe and Russia. *Population and Economics* 3.1, 107–24.

Schenk, K. (2011) Das historisch gewachsene Problem des Dauerwohnens in Kleingartenkolonien [WWW Document]. URL http://www.kleingaertner-weissensee.de/Dokumente/Dokumente/heft_19.pdf (accessed 2 April 2020).

Schilling, H., T. Blokland, and A. Simone (2019) Working Precarity: Urban Youth Tactics to Make Livelihoods in Instable Conditions in Abidjan, Athens, Berlin and Jakarta. *The Sociological Review* 67.6, 1333–49.

Schindler, S. (2014a) Understanding Urban Processes in Flint, Michigan: Approaching "Subaltern Urbanism" Inductively: "Subaltern Urbanism" in Flint, Michigan. *International Journal of Urban and Regional Research* 38, 791–804.

Schindler, S. (2014b) A New Delhi Every Day: Multiplicities of Governance Regimes in a Transforming Metropolis. *Urban Geography* 35.3, 402–19.

Schindler, S. (2015) Governing the Twenty-First Century Metropolis and Transforming Territory. *Territory, Politics, Governance* 3.1, 7–26.

Schipper, S. (2018) Zur politischen Ökonomie der Gentrifizierung: Warum kommt es zu Verdrängungsprozessen und wie lassen sich diese verhindern? In B. Emunds, C. Czingon, and M. Wolff (eds.), *Stadtluft macht reich/arm: Stadtentwicklung, soziale Ungleichheit und Raumgerechtigkeit*, Die Wirtschaft der Gesellschaft Jahrbuch, Metropolis-Verlag, Marburg.

Schmidt-Räntsch, J. (2005) 10 Jahre Sachenrechtsbereinigung. *Neue Justiz* 59.2, 49–54.

Schönig, B. and L. Vollmer (2018) Wohnungsnot gestern und heute. *Informationen zur Raumentwicklung* 4, 6–19.

Schönig, B., J. Kadi, and S. Schipper (eds.) (2017) *Wohnraum für alle?! Perspektiven auf Planung, Politik und Architektur*. Urban Studies Transcript, Bielefeld.

Schulz, G. (2017) Aufwertung und Verdrängung in Berlin: Räumliche Analysen zur Messung von Gentrifizierung. *WISTA* 4, 61–71.

Scott, J.C. (1990) *Domination and the Arts of Resistance: Hidden Transcripts*, Yale University Press, New Haven.

Scott, J.C. (1998) *Seeing Like a State: How Certain Schemes to Improve the Human Condition Have Failed*, Yale University Press, New Haven.

Senatskanzlei Berlin (2016) Berlin gemeinsam gestalten. Solidarisch. Nachhaltig. Weltoffen. Koalitionsvereinbarung 2016-2021 [WWW Document]. URL https://www.berlin.de/rbmskzl/regierender-buergermeister/senat/koalitionsvereinbarung (accessed 2 August 2020).

Sennett, R. (1977) *The Fall of Public Man: On the Social Psychology of Capitalism*, Vintage Books, New York, NY.

SenStadt (Senatsverwaltung für Stadtentwicklung) (2004) Kleingartenentwicklungsplan (KEP) [WWW Document]. URL http://www.villakunterbunt.info/wp-content/uploads/2016/02/Kleingartenentwicklungsplan-Textteil-Stand-2004.pdf (accessed 01 August 2020).

SenSU (Senatsverwaltung für Stadtentwicklung und Umwelt Berlin) (2015) Monitoring Soziale Stadtentwicklung Berlin 2015 [WWW Document]. URL https://www.stadtentwicklung.berlin.de/planen/basisdaten_stadtentwicklung/monitoring/download/2015/MonitoringSozialeStadtentwicklung2015.pdf (accessed 27 June 2019).

SenSW (Senatsverwaltung für Stadtentwicklung und Wohnen) (2017) Monitoring Soziale Stadtentwicklung [WWW Document]. URL https://www.stadtent

wicklung.berlin.de/planen/basisdaten_stadtentwicklung/monitoring/down
load/2017/Monitoring_Soziale_Stadtentwicklung_2017-Bericht.pdf   (accessed
13 May 2020).

SenSW (Senatsverwaltung für Stadtentwicklung und Wohnen) (2018) Beantwortung
der Fragen aus der Online-Beteiligung zum Projekt „stadt behutsam Weiterbauen
im Blankenburger Süden [WWW Document]. URL https://www.stadtentwick
lung.berlin.de/wohnen/wohnungsbau/blankenburger-sueden/download/Blan
kenburger_Sueden_Fragen_und_Antworten_Online-Beteiligung_Maerz_2018.
pdf (accessed 2 August 2020).

SenSW (Senatsverwaltung für Stadtentwicklung und Wohnen) (2019) Stadtent-
wicklungsplan Wohnen 2030 [WWW Document]. URL https://www.stadtent
wicklung.berlin.de/planen/stadtentwicklungsplanung/de/wohnen/download/
StEPWohnen2030-Kurzfassung.pdf (accessed 27 June 2020).

SenUVK (Senatsverwaltung für Umwelt, Verkehr und Klimaschutz) (2018) Kleingärten: Daten und Fakten, Stand Mai 2018 [WWW Document]. URL https://
www.berlin.de/senuvk/umwelt/stadtgruen/kleingaerten/de/daten_fakten/index.
shtml (accessed 15 June 2020).

SenUVK (Senatsverwaltung für Umwelt, Verkehr und Klimaschutz) (2019) Kleingärten in Berlin: Kleingartenentwicklungsplan Berlin 2030 - Entwurf [WWW
Document]. URL https://www.berlin.de/senuvk/umwelt/stadtgruen/kleingaerten/
downloads/kep/Broschuere_KEP.pdf (accessed 10 April 2019).

SenWEB (Senatsverwaltung für Wirtschaft, Energie und Betriebe) (2018)
Wirtschafts- und Innovationsbericht: Berlin 2017/2018 [WWW Document].
URL https://www.berlin.de/sen/web/presse/pressemitteilungen/2018/pressemit-
teilung.733130.php (accessed 3 March 2019).

Shaw, K. (2005) The Place of Alternative Culture and the Politics of Its Protection in
Berlin, Amsterdam and Melbourne. *Planning Theory & Practice* 6, 149–69.

Sheppard, E., H. Leitner, and A. Maringanti (2013) Provincializing Global Urbanism: A Manifesto. *Urban Geography* 34, 893–900.

Shlomo, O. (2017) Sub-Formality in the Formalization of Public Transport in East
Jerusalem. *Current Sociology* 65.2, 260–75.

Sidaway, J.D., C.Y. Woon, and J.M. Jacobs (2014) Planetary Postcolonialism. *Singapore Journal of Tropical Geography* 35, 4–21.

Silver, J. (2014) Incremental Infrastructures: Material Improvisation and Social Collaboration Across Post-Colonial Accra. *Urban Geography* 35.6, 788–804.

Simmel, G. (2006 [1903]) *Die Großstädte und das Geistesleben*, Suhrkamp Verlag,
Frankfurt am Main.

Simone, A. (2001) Straddling the Divides: Remaking Associational Life in the Informal African City. *International Journal of Urban and Regional Research* 25,
102–17.

Simone, A. (2010) *City Life from Jakarta to Dakar: Movements at the Crossroads*,
Global Realities, Routledge, New York, NY.

Smart, A. (2018) Ethnographic Perspectives on the Mediation of Informality Between People and Plans in Urbanising China. *Urban Studies* 55.7, 1477–83.

Smart, A. and T. Aguilera (2017) Squatting, North, South and Turnabout: A Dialogue Comparing Illegal Housing Research. In F. Anders and A. Sedlmaier (eds.), *Public Goods Versus Economic Interests: Global Perspectives on the History of Squatting*, Routledge Studies in Modern History, Routledge Taylor & Francis Group, New York and London, 29–55.

Smith, D.E. (1990) *Texts, Facts, and Femininity: Exploring the Relations of Ruling*, Routledge, London u.a.

Smith, D.E. (1999) *Writing the Social: Critique, Theory, and Investigations*, University of Toronto Press, Toronto.

Smith, D.E. (2005) *Institutional Ethnography: A Sociology for People*, The Gender Lens Series, AltaMira Press, Lanham, MD.

Soederberg, S. (2015) Subprime Housing Goes South: Constructing Securitized Mortgages for the Poor in Mexico. *Antipode* 47.2, 481–99.

Soederberg, S. (2017) Governing Stigmatised Space: The Case of the "Slums" of Berlin-Neukölln. *New Political Economy* 22.5, 478–95.

Soederberg, S. (2018) The Rental Housing Question: Exploitation, Eviction and Erasures. *Geoforum*, 89, 114–23.

Sparke, M. (2007) Everywhere but Always Somewhere: Critical Geographies of the Global South. *The Global South* 1.1–2, 117–26.

Statistisches Bundesamt (2018) Bevölkerung und Erwerbstätigkeit: Bevölkerung mit Migrationshintergrund – Ergebnisse des Mikrozensus 2017 – [WWW Document]. URL https://www.destatis.de/DE/Themen/Gesellschaft-Umwelt/Bevoelkerung/Migration-Integration/Publikationen/Downloads-Migration/migrationshintergrund-2010220177004.pdf?__blob=publicationFile&v=4 (accessed 22 June 2020).

Statistisches Jahrbuch für das Deutsche Reich (1943) Die bei den Arbeitsämtern gemeldeten Arbeitslosen im Jahr 1932, 291–318.

Statistisches Landesamt Berlin (1999) Statistisches Jahrbuch 1999 (Berlin) [WWW Document]. URL https://www.destatis.de/DE/Startseite.html (accessed 14 January 2015).

Steenberg, R. (2016) The Art of Not Seeing Like a State. On the Ideology of "Informality." *Journal of Contemporary Central and Eastern Europe* 24.3, 293–306.

Stein, H. (2000) *Inseln im Häusermeer: Eine Kulturgeschichte des deutschen Kleingartenwesens bis zum Ende des Zweiten Weltkriegs Reichsweite Tendenzen und Gross-Hamburger Entwicklung*, Peter Lang, Frankfurt am Main and New York.

Stone, C.N. (1993) Urban Regimes and the Capacity to Govern: A Political Economy Approach. *Journal of Urban Affairs* 15.1, 1–28.

Stoner, J. (2012) *Toward a Minor Architecture*, MIT Press, Cambridge, MA.

Straughn, J.B. (2005) "Taking the State at Its Word": The Arts of Consentful Contention in the German Democratic Republic. *American Journal of Sociology* 110.6, 1598–650.

Streule, M. (2018) *Ethnografie urbaner Territorien: Metropolitane Urbanisierungsprozesse von Mexiko-Stadt*, Raumproduktionen. Band 32, Westfälisches Dampfboot, Münster.

Streule, M. (2019) Doing Mobile Ethnography: Grounded, Situated and Comparative. *Urban Studies* 39.1, online first.

Sullivan, E. (2017) Displaced in Place. *American Sociological Review* 82.2, 243–69.

Sullivan, E. (2018) *Manufactured Insecurity: Mobile Home Parks and Americans' Tenuous Right to Place*, University of California Press, Oakland, CA.

Swyngedouw, E. (2005) Governance Innovation and the Citizen: The Janus Face of Governance-Beyond-the-State. *Urban Studies* 42, 1991–2006.

Tanasescu, A., E.C. Wing-tak, and A. Smart (2010) Tops and Bottoms: State Tolerance of Illegal Housing in Hong Kong and Calgary. *Habitat International* 34, 478–84.

Thieme, T., M. Lancione, and E. Rosa (2017) The City and Its Margins. *City* 21.2, 127–34.

Tilly, C. (1999) Survey Article: Power – Top down and Bottom Up. *Journal of Political Philosophy* 7, 330–52.

Tilly, C. (2009) Grudging Consent. *American Interest* 3.1, 1–7.

Tissot, V. (1989) *Reportagen aus Bismarcks Reich: Berichte eines Reisenden Franzosen, 18741976*, Verlag Neues Leben Berlin, Berlin.

Tonkiss, F. (2012) Informality and Its Discontents. In M. Angélil and R. Hehl (eds.), *Informalize! Essays on the Political Economy of Urban Form*, Ruby Press, Berlin, 55–70.

Tschacher, S. (2009) Berlin ist Hauptstadt der Laubenpieper. MieterMagazin 6 [WWW Document]. URL https://www.berliner-mieterverein.de/magazin/online/mm0609/060914.htm (accessed 25 September 2020).

Tucker, J.L. and R.T. Devlin (2019) Uncertainty and the Governance of Street Vending: A Critical Comparison Across the North/South Divide. *International Journal of Urban and Regional Research* 43.3, 460–75.

Turner, J.F.C. (1972) Housing as a Verb. In J.F.C. Turner and R. Fichter (eds.), *Freedom to Build: Dweller Control of the Housing Process*, Macmillan, New York, 148–75.

Tuvikene, T., S. Neves Alves, and H. Hilbrandt (2016) Strategies for Relating Diverse Cities: A Multi-sited Individualising Comparison of Informality in Bafatá, Berlin and Tallinn. *Current Sociology* 65.2, 276–88.

Uffer, S. (2013) Wohnungsprivatisierung in Berlin. Investitionsstrategien und ihre Konsequenzen für die Stadt und ihre Bewohner. In A. Holm (ed.), *Reclaim Berlin: Soziale Kämpfe in der neoliberalen Stadt*, Assoziation A, Berlin/Hamburg, 64–83.

Uffer, S. (2014) The Uneven Development of Berlin's Housing Provision Institutional Investment and Its Consequences on the City and Its Tenants. In M. Bernt, B. Grell, and A. Holm (eds.), *The Berlin Reader: A Compendium on Urban Change and Activism*, Transcript, Bielefeld, 155–70.

Unger, K. (2017) Financialization of Mass Rental Housing in Germany: Understanding the Transaction Cycles in the Mass Rental Housing Sector 1999–2015. In B. Schönig, J. Kadi, and S. Schipper (eds.), *Wohnraum für alle?! Perspektiven auf Planung, Politik und Architektur*, Urban Studies, Transcript, Bielefeld, 176–90.

Unger, K. (2018) Mieterhöhungsmaschinen: Zur Finanzialisierung und Industrialisierung der unternehmerischen Wohnungswirtschaft. *PROKLA* 48.2, 205–226.

Urban, F. (2013) The Hut on the Garden Plot: Informal Architecture in Twentieth-Century Berlin. *Journal of the Society of Architectural Historians* 72, 221–49.

Valverde, M. (2009) Jurisdiction and Scale: Legal "Technicalities" as Resources for Theory. *Social & Legal Studies* 18, 139–57.

Valverde, M. (2011) Seeing like a City: The Dialectic of Modern and Premodern Ways of Seeing in Urban Governance. *Law & Society Review* 45, 277–312.

Valverde, M. (2012) *Everyday Law on the Street: City Governance in an Age of Diversity*, University of Chicago Press, Chicago.

van Schipstal, I.L.M. and W.J. Nicholls (2014) Rights to the Neoliberal City: The Case of Urban Land Squatting in "Creative" Berlin. *Territory, Politics, Governance* 2.2, 173–93.

Varley, A. (2013) Feminist Perspectives on Urban Poverty: De-essentialising Difference. In M. Rieker (ed.), *Rethinking Feminist Interventions into the Urban*, Routledge, London, 125–41.

Vasudevan, A. (2011) Dramaturgies of Dissent: The Spatial Politics of Squatting in Berlin, 1968–. *Social & Cultural Geography* 12, 283–303.

Vasudevan, A. (2015a) *Metropolitan Preoccupations: The Spatial Politics of Squatting in Berlin*, RGS-IBG Book Series, Wiley Blackwell, Chichester.

Vasudevan, A. (2015b) The Makeshift City. *Progress in Human Geography* 39.3, 338–59.

Veith, D. and J. Sambale (1998) Berliner Wagenburgen: Transformation peripherer Räume, Stigmatisierung sozialer Gruppen und die Abwehr von Marginalisierung. *PROKLA* 28.1, 67–95.

Voll, D. (1983) *Von der Wohnlaube zum Hochhaus: Eine geographische Untersuchung über die Entstehung und die Struktur des Märkischen Viertels in Berlin (West) bis 1976*, Abhandlungen des Geographischen Instituts, Anthropogeographie. Vol. 34, Reimer, Berlin.

Vollmer, L. (2018) Mieter_innenproteste von den 1960er bis in die 1980er Jahre in der BRD. *Sub\urban. zeitschrift für kritische stadtforschung* 6.2/3, 137–48.

Wachsmuth, D. and H. Angelo (2018) Green and Gray: New Ideologies of Nature in Urban Sustainability Policy. *Annals of the American Association of Geographers* 108.4, 1038–56.

Wacquant, L.J.D. (1993) Urban Outcasts: Stigma and Division in the Black American Ghetto and the French Urban Periphery. *International Journal of Urban and Regional Research* 17, 366–83.

Waite, L. (2009) A Place and Space for a Critical Geography of Precarity? *Geography Compass* 3.1, 412–33.

Waite, L., G. Craig, H. Lewis, and K. Skrivankova (eds.) (2015) *Vulnerability, Exploitation and Migrants: Insecure Work in a Globalised Economy*, Migration, Diasporas and Citizenship, Palgrave Macmillan, Basingstoke.

Ward, C. (2002) *Cotters and Squatters: Housing's Hidden History*, Five Leaves, Nottingham.

Ward, P.M., F.D. Souza, and C. Giusti (2004) "Colonia" Land and Housing Market Performance and the Impact of Lot Title Regularisation in Texas. *Urban Studies* 41, 2621–46.

Watson, V. (2009) Seeing from the South: Refocusing Urban Planning on the Globe's Central Urban Issues. *Urban Studies* 46.11, 2259–75.

Weinstein, L. (2014) *The Durable Slum: Dharavi and the Right to Stay Put in Globalizing Mumbai*, University of Minnesota Press, Minneapolis.

Weinstein, L. (2017) Insecurity as Confinement: The Entrenched Politics of Staying Put in Delhi and Mumbai. *International Sociology* 32.4, 512–31.

Wigle, J. (2014) The "Graying" of "Green" Zones: Spatial Governance and Irregular Settlement in Xochimilco, Mexico City. *International Journal of Urban and Regional Research* 38.2, 573–89.

Wijburg, G. and M.B. Aalbers (2017a) The Alternative Financialization of the German Housing Market. *Housing Studies* 32.7, 968–89.

Wijburg, G. and M.B. Aalbers (2017b) The Internationalization of Commercial Real Estate Markets in France and Germany. *Competition & Change* 21.4, 301–20.

Wischermann, C. (1997) Mythen, Macht und Mängel: Der deutsche Wohnungsmarkt im Urbanisierungsprozeß. In J. Reulecke (ed.), *Geschichte des Wohnens. 3: 1800–1918 Das bürgerliche Zeitalter*, Deutsche Verlags-Anstalt, Stuttgart, 333–502.

Wisler, D. and I.D. Onwudiwe (2008) Community Policing in Comparison. *Police Quarterly* 11, 427–46.

Yiftachel, O. (2009a) Theoretical Notes on "Gray Cities": The Coming of Urban Apartheid? *Planning Theory* 8, 88–100.

Yiftachel, O. (2009b) Critical Theory and "Gray Space": Mobilization of the Colonized. *City* 13, 246–63.

Index

Note: Page numbers referring to figures are indicated with *italics* 'f' and those referring endnotes are indicated as 'n' with the notes' number.

Housing in the Margins: Negotiating Urban Formalities in Berlin's Allotment Gardens, First Edition. Hanna Hilbrandt.
© 2021 John Wiley & Sons, Ltd. Published 2021 by John Wiley & Sons, Ltd.

.